P9-CPY-818

The Experts Praise
Public Relations: The Complete Guide

"I spent all of my adult life in what most people considered to be a highly successful career in public relations.

"Had I read Joe Marconi's book, it would have been even more so.

"There is not a single facet of the huge area covered by the term *public relations*, which he has not examined and succinctly commented upon. It is a tour de force, a true PR bible and absolute must reading for anyone contemplating a public relations career as well as for executives in any field. Bravo!"

Marj Abrams
Marj Abrams Public Relations

"Informative, spin-free, and right on target. Required reading for anyone who wants to design and implement a winning program."

Tom Asacker
Author, *Sandbox Wisdom: Revolutionize Your Brand with the Genius of Childhood*

"I am not sure that a more comprehensive and more comprehensible book about public relations has ever been written. If a person is simply curious about the PR business, this is the first book he or she should read. And for PR practitioners, it should be the foundation of their professional resource libraries. This is the new 'Bible' of public relations."

Joe Cappo
Former Publisher of *Advertising Age*
Author of *The Future of Advertising*

"In this step-by-step guide, Joe Marconi delineates how and why Public Relations is an integral ingredient in successful marketing campaigns. His comprehensive insights serve as invaluable information to the PR beginner and timely reminders to the seasoned professional. I wish I'd had this book when I started my career over two decades ago."

Terry J. Erdmann, Motion Picture Publicist
Author, *Star Trek: The Deep Space Nine Companion*

"It's all here. Joe Marconi's guide is an all-in-one book crammed with information on the what, why and how of public relations. It is an invaluable resource for everyone who practices PR from corporate managers to volunteers who want to bring positive attention to their organizations. The most comprehensive guide to PR ever written includes as a special added attraction a portfolio section, packed with real world samples of successful programs, words and pictures."

Thomas L. Harris
Former president of Golin/Harris International
Author, *The Marketer's Guide to Public Relations*

"Joe Marconi knows PR and provides great insight into how it can be used most effectively in almost any environment. He gives practical advice for developing PR plans and then provides all the "how to" for putting the plans into action and achieving great results. From the "importance of staying on message" to "creating a plan for an uneven playing field," the useful concepts in *Public Relations: The Complete Guide* make it a great tool for seasoned PR professionals who want to double-check their strategies as well as marketing pros and others who want to integrate public relations into their existing communications toolbox."

Patricia T. Whalen, Ph.D., APR
Medill Integrated Marketing Communications
Northwestern University

Public
Relations
The Complete Guide

JOE MARCONI

RĀCOM
COMMUNICATIONS

AMERICAN
MARKETING
ASSOCIATION

THOMSON
™

Australia • Canada • Mexico • Singapore • Spain • United Kingdom • United States

THOMSON
™

Public Relations: The Complete Guide
By Joe Marconi

Vice President/
Editorial Director
Jack Calhoun

Vice President/
Editor-in-Chief
Dave Shaut

Acquisition Editor
Steve Momper

Consulting Editor in
Marketing
Richard Hagle

Channel Manager, Retail
Chris McNamee

Channel Manager,
Professional
Mark Linton

Production Manager
Tricia Matthews Boies

Production Editor
Todd McCoy

Manufacturing Coordinator
Charlene Taylor

Compositor
Sans Serif Inc.

Printer
Phoenix Book Technology
Hagerstown, MD

ISBN: 0-324-20304-7
Printed in the United States of America

2 3 4 5 6 7 08 09 07 06 05

For more information, contact South-Western Educational Publishing, 5191 Natorp Boulevard,
Mason, Ohio 45040; or find us on the World Wide Web at www.swlearning.com

INTERNATIONAL DIVISION LIST

ASIA (Including India):
Thomson Learning
60 Albert Street, #15-01
Albert Complex
Singapore 189969
Tel 65 336-6411
Fax 65 336-7411

LATIN AMERICA:
Thomson Learning
Seneca 53
Colonia Polanco
11560 Mexico, D.F. Mexico
Tel (525) 281-2906
Fax (525) 281-2656

UK/EUROPE/MIDDLE EAST/ AFRICA:
Thomson Learning
Berkshire House
168-173 High Holborn
London WC1V 7AA
United Kingdom
Tel 44 (0)20 497-1422
Fax 44 (0)20 497-1426

AUSTRALIA/NEW ZEALAND:
Nelson
102 Dodds Street
South Melbourne
Victoria 3205
Australia
Tel 61 (0)3 9685-4111
Fax 61 (0)3 9685-4199

CANADA:
Nelson
1120 Birchmount Road
Toronto, Ontario
Canada M1K 5G4
Tel (416) 752-9100
Fax (416) 752-8102

SPAIN (includes Portugal):
Paraninfo
Calle Magallanes 25
28015 Madrid
España
Tel 34 (0)91 446-3350
Fax 34 (0)91 445-6218

For Todd and Kristin and Emily
And for Karin

Contents

Contents 9

Introduction

This is a book on public relations, not sociology, psychology, or anthropology. Yet, to truly understand public relations and to use it effectively, it is important to understand that people respond to suggestion and stimuli, and to appreciate why people behave as they do in a community, social, business, and cultural context.

Public relations is a powerful force on its own. When it is part of a marketing mix—a combination of other disciplines and techniques—its impact can be *tremendous* (a term often associated with the practice of public relations). But for all its popular identification with *hype*, PR is serious business, effective and highly cost efficient when compared to other marketing functions.

An expression used for many years in sales training programs was *nothing happens until somebody sells something*. Certainly the sales process sets things in motion, but a great deal of activity precedes that process. It starts with an idea that leads to a plan that requires a sharing of information, generating awareness and interest, packaging and producing the results of that idea, and developing a delivery system. These are only a few of the components of marketing, of which public relations is a key element at virtually every stage.

Anyone looking for an example of the power of marketing need look no further than a day in June 2003. The world was uneasy, with conflicts that ranged from pockets of hostility to full-scale war,

13

financial crises around the globe, high unemployment, political strife, outbreaks of mysterious diseases, threats of revolution, and a seemingly daily dose of scandals of every variety involving corporate titans, military leaders, newspaper editors and high-profile reporters, church officials, baseball players . . .

Yet, all over this unsettled globe, at the stroke of midnight (and not a moment sooner, under a threat of legal action), lines would form as people—many in elaborate costumes—stepped forward to purchase the first 8.5 million copies of a new *children's book* that was an unprecedented length of nearly 900 pages. Its suggested list price was $29.99, and it was expected to sell out of its first printing within a few days of its release. The book's author, an unemployed, broke single mother a decade earlier, was now reported to be wealthier than the Queen of England.

And for those who would wave a dismissive magic wand and call J. K. Rowling's "Harry Potter" books—with their spin-off array of films, toys, computer games, clothes, candy, and other merchandise— a phenomenon that would hardly be testimony to marketing as a power source, consider the bleak backdrop painted above and note that, in the United States alone, people paid nearly $300 million dollars in the six weeks prior to June 21 to watch a special-effects martial arts movie that most film critics told them wasn't very good. Additionally, more than 20 million people paid a single company $25 each for a month of Internet access, and the June issue of *Power & Motor Yacht* magazine carried 198.5 pages of paid advertising. Marketing can indeed move people around the world in numbers large and small.

This book is intended for anyone who needs to make public relations work for them, whether they work in the public relations business now, or in any of the other marketing disciplines—particularly advertising and marketing research. For virtually all levels of almost any business, public relations is an aspect of a great deal of what people do, whether they realize it or not. Even those who are *not* in business might find this material helpful when their objectives include winning friends and influencing people. Because public relations is, by its very definition, about influencing how the public relates to a subject, from superficial interest to passionate commitment, greater knowledge and skill about its operations, operating concepts, and mindset are invaluable to almost anyone involved in a group endeavor.

The practice is nearly always identified (and confused with) *publicizing* a subject, and that, while it is an extremely important aspect, is only a part of the process.

Among the people who could benefit most from the information in this book are those in executive or senior management positions. It is they, after all, who are charged with the responsibility of creating, building, maintaining and, in some cases, *changing* an organization's public image or reputation. In such instances public relations can be both a means and an end in that company's relationship with its various constituent groups. It is an ongoing process always requiring attention and reflection on sudden changes in the market climate.

While Edward Bernays is commonly referred to as "the father of public relations" (a title he might very well have conferred upon himself, in the finest traditions of a great PR man) for his groundbreaking campaigns to promote cigarette smoking in the 1930s, much about the business and the process has obviously changed—and much has not.

In Mr. Bernays's time, public relations professionals were considered promoters. In the 21st century the business has taken on both a broader and more formal quality. Though promotion is still often a core element of most PR efforts, the practitioner must understand that public relations is just as much about influencing the opinions and attitudes of a targeted group. A PR person today may hold a doctorate or a law degree and is often a senior advisor and strategist.

In earlier days a public relations professional was called "a flack"—much the way psychiatrists are called "shrinks." A more popular contemporary label is "spin doctor," a term with perhaps a more upscale ring, but it is usually intended to be no less derogatory. Much like lawyers, many people in business and media regard public relations professionals as necessary evils and even sometimes harbor feelings of contempt.

A PR person's role is to present a person, company, or subject in the best possible light, a function which is often regarded with suspicion, as if that objective could only be achieved by lying or misrepresentation. The sentiment is not surprising, however, given that once—

in Mr. Bernays's time—a fact was a fact, but today virtually everything appears to be subject to interpretation and the old rules of civility don't seem to apply. "Attack" strategies aimed at competitors are regarded as perfectly acceptable, aggressive tactics and barely an eyebrow is raised.

So while this book is not social commentary, the cultural climate at a given time is a key element in determining the parameters and standards under which a program can be employed. The limitations—or the *lack of limitations*—imposed by society, social mores, and the economic and political environment can allow a great deal of latitude in defining, addressing, and responding to a brand or message "positioning."

The intensely competitive business environment—marked by corporate scandals and the collapse of some once hard-driving and glamorous segments of the market—has elevated public relations to an even greater level of importance in virtually every business plan. Indeed, it is a factor in *selling* the plan itself. The collapse of the U.S. savings and loan industry around 1990 sent out shock waves that reverberated around the world. A financial industry so strong was not supposed to be able to fall apart. It left a residual cynicism among much of the public. When the technology industry, which had so much strength and promise, collapsed little more than a decade later, public consciousness was again shaken. In public relations and marketing, context is important. In cynical times, the proliferation of media and a heightened level of consumer sophistication pose new and greater challenges.

Creating, sustaining, or changing a public image, generating and shaping awareness, influencing opinions and decisions is the role of public relations today. Though some would say that has always been the case, the tools and methods employed in the 21st century are far more diversified, and the stakes have never been higher. For example, the local "Mom and Pop" business now reaches a global market.

References in this book to "companies and organizations" anticipate that readers may represent a variety of entities, from corporations to trade associations, nonprofit organizations, professional committees, campaigns, and institutions.

Critics' attacks on companies and products (and on individuals in the public eye) routinely reach a level of harshness that would have been unthinkable in polite society not so long ago.

What was called "the generation gap" when baby boomers were coming of age, is now characterized as "generation *wars*" as boomers, seniors, and members of Generation X maneuver for greater power and influence in social, political, and business matters. Ethnic considerations that were a relatively minor concern as recently as the 1980s are now mainstream issues to marketers, agencies, and their consultants.

It is against such a backdrop that this book offers public relations professionals—and others—a variety of options on what to do and how to do it regarding the ways and means of communicating and influencing decisions and public opinion. The public has been promised that modern technology—vast stores of information and highly sophisticated systems, capabilities, and methods—can deliver more of just about everything. This book is offered as a guide to help deliver on that promise.

Rather than only use fictional examples of the programs and campaigns of the ubiquitous "XYZ Corporation" in this book, in Part Two I have included the actual work of a number of organizations, marketing and consulting firms, and public relations agencies that were generous in contributing material that reflects actual public relations efforts for which they were responsible or in which they played a major role. Many thanks to Bill Novelli, Executive Director and CEO of AARP; Ginny LaVone and Christopher Janson of DiMeo & Company; Ken Price, Director of Public Relations for the Palmer House Hilton; Bob Matha of Matha MacDonald LLC; Ron Cohn at Firestar Communications; Jerry Murray of the Murray Communications Group; Judi Schindler of Schindler Communications; Patricia Whalen, Medill/IMC, Northwestern University; and Gary Slack, Dana Kessler, and Kyra Kyles at Slack Barshinger.

For support and assistance, thanks also to Lonny Bernardi, Richard Girod, Guy Kendler, to Joe Cappo, Tom Harris, Rich Hagle, and as always to Karin Gottschalk Marconi.

PART I

The Theory and Practice of Public Relations

1

Public Relations: Art or Science?

Public relations seems like a self-explanatory term, yet after more than a century as a profession, a business, and a process, controversy and confusion might be greater than ever about what public relations is and what it does. Most people would probably agree that PR is an information function, but that would likely be the point at which agreement ended.

One Term, Many Meanings, Lots of Misunderstanding

When a scandal becomes the big news of the day, it is not uncommon for someone to describe those at the center of the scandal as "having a PR problem." Well, if they are good people and have been caught up in the scandal unjustly, then public relations might indeed be the best way to clarify the situation, resolve the issues, and preserve and restore good reputations—perhaps ultimately leaving the people in even *better* standing for having overcome an ordeal. On the other hand, if those involved in a scandal or charged with wrongdoing are *not* good people, then theirs is *not a PR problem*, but rather a problem with the fact that they are not good people.

Contrary to a belief held by many, public relations is not a system designed to make bad people and bad things seem like something else. This is not to suggest that unethical practitioners in PR or any other profession can't pull off a sleight of hand and confuse people for a time, but such tactics are, like patches on a bad tire, only temporary and ultimately there's the price to be paid for the deed itself, as well as for the deception.

Perhaps one of the greatest areas of misunderstanding is that public relations is the same as *publicity*—that PR people are publicists or press agents and that their only reason to exist is to generate attention in the media. Public relations is an umbrella term that covers a variety of areas and functions, including *communications, community relations, customer relations, consumer affairs, employee relations, industry relations international relations, investor relations, issues management, media relations, member relations, press agentry, promotions, publicity, public affairs, shareholder relations, speechwriting,* and *visitor relations.*

Clearly some of these functions overlap and many are virtually indistinguishable from others. They become distinctive in the ways that individuals, companies, and organizations regard a particular function relative to their own needs and objectives. Promotion, for example, has evolved into a large area of practice that may or may not be revenue generating, but raises the subject to a higher level of visibility. Many of the functions listed include the creation, production, and publication of literature, research reports, surveys, audio and video materials, online programs, newsletters, posters, seminars, or workshops.

Agencies may specialize in particular areas, such as financial relations, event management, or crisis communications, and a company's PR department will not necessarily require or desire the full range of capabilities or services listed above. It is important, however, to understand that not all experts in one discipline are experts in every other aspect of public relations.

Another misunderstanding about PR gained momentum in the 1990s when the term *spin* came into common usage and eventually became extremely popular in some media circles. The term was applied to a practice by public relations people that was similar to the efforts of propagandists of another era who focused solely on promoting a particular doctrine or point of view, almost at any cost. *Spin* is in fact just putting information in either a positive or negative light, depending on the side of the issue the presenter is representing. There is nothing devious or sinister about it, though "the spinmeisters" and "spin doctors" were often referred to as if they were engaged in practicing a form of black magic.

Yet another area of confusion has to do with lobbyists, who are in many instances lawyers or experts on a particular subject, engaged in efforts to persuade regulators and legislators to support or oppose the creation, expansion, or elimination of certain rules or laws. Typically, lobbyists refer to what they do as a form of public relations, which it is. Unfortunately, the only time the general public hears the term *lobbyist* used is when one is rumored to be exerting unreasonable pressure or alleged to have bribed public officials with bags of money or a junket to an island resort.

The typical lobbyist tries to persuade bureaucrats by showing why a particular education subsidy or airport runway will be good for local constituents. Lobbyists are involved on both sides of most major issues, urging or recommending consideration of changes regarding health care, agriculture, transportation, energy, communications, environmental matters, and most of the lesser issues as well. It's not all about the heavy-handed wielding of extraordinary power and huge campaign contributions in small, unmarked bills.

A Potent Persuader and Problem-Solver

Veteran public relations specialist Robert L. Dilenschneider calls PR "the art of influence." In *Power and Influence: Mastering the Art of Persuasion,* he notes, "Power comes from remembering and using the linkage of communication, recognition and influence. . . . The art of influence is defining, realizing, and gradually strengthening your personal agenda."

Public relations means, in the vernacular of creative advertising people, giving the public "permission to believe." If a message resonates, people want to accept it; they just need a reason. So PR experts give them that reason. They tell the public that the product was "ranked number one by J.D. Power and Associates!" Or that the subject recently won a prestigious Snerkle Award for Excellence in its class!

Who are J.D. Power and Snerkle?

It doesn't matter. The overwhelming number of people don't actually care. They are just pleased to be reassured that their product has been favorably recognized by some type of accrediting authority or some impressive-sounding organization.

Despite being head of one of the largest PR agencies in the world, William D. Novelli never actually considered himself a public relations man. The co-founder and President of Porter Novelli, who later served as the Executive Vice President of CARE and as Executive Director and CEO of AARP, believes in integrated marketing solutions. "At CARE we distributed t-shirts to everyone with the words 'integrate or die,' " he says. "It's necessary to step back and look at the whole picture. Look at what needs to be accomplished and use whatever tactics and tools in the marketing mix will get it done." PR's wide range of functions can be tapped and merged to create a plan and strategy to address the specific requirements of a project, from responding to requests for statistics or producing the company's annual report to writing seminar presentations and building archives. Not all PR people are publicists, lobbyists, or *spinmeisters*. And not everything a PR person devises is a "publicity stunt."

The Role of the PR Professional

That not all practitioners adhere to a common standard of ethics or are supremely competent is another issue PR people confront. In a later chapter this subject will be explored more fully, but certainly the issue of ethical conduct has become more subjective than it was in earlier times.

The late Philip Lesly, a leading figure in the profession for nearly fifty years, held that public relations "involves complete analysis and understanding of all the factors that influence people's attitudes toward an organization." Such analysis and understanding must certainly extend beyond generating media interest.

In some of the most visible situations, a PR person is often an organization's liaison to the outside world. A press secretary for a candidate for public office or a spokesperson for a department of government, for example, is usually the senior public relations person. Such high visibility and the potential impact that might result from remarks delivered—whether carefully crafted or offered spontaneously—underscore the importance of the "complete analysis and understanding" requirement of Mr. Lesly's position. It also calls for a certain degree of diplomacy and good presentation skills.

The PR person in many situations is second only to the CEO as the "face" or "voice" of an organization to its most important constituent groups. Additionally, as a front line contact person, fielding questions and receiving comments from people outside of the organization, the PR person is a critical source of information about what members of the public are thinking or saying about the organization. He or she has an open line to those that management seeks to influence, and it is a line that must be managed with care.

Art or Science? Even the Professionals Don't Agree

Members of the profession continue to debate whether public relations is best described as an *art* or *science*, while a pragmatic third view is simply that it's a job and a function and PR people should not take themselves too seriously, conferring exaggerated importance on their tasks and devising new reasons to give themselves awards. Since the 1970s, PR specialists, realizing how much a client or company receiving an award can be used to enhance its reputation and status in its industry, have increasingly lavished honors on themselves.

It is certainly true that, after more than a hundred years, many management-level people still don't have a clear appreciation for PR or an understanding of its importance to both the company's reputation and the marketing mix. Too many executives still regard PR largely as the entity set up to release earnings statements and handle questions from pesky reporters.

But such executives hold to this attitude at their peril. Influencing how the public views a company is hardly an incidental function. In the days of instant messaging, instant access, and 24/7 news cycles, strong, professionally run public relations operations have been critical to the success of the most successful organizations.

Writing and presenting information that properly describes a subject, an issue, or a company in the best possible light obviously requires a certain degree of creative ability, and a job that demands the crafting of "message points" calls for organizational as well as presentation skills. It clearly is an art. And PR's reliance on demographic and psychographic research, lifestyle studies, census data, and opinion surveys reflects a scientific approach to most key PR processes.

Public Relations and the Media

Public relations professionals are expected (and required) to have an expert understanding of the workings of various media and at least some knowledge of emerging technology and research, as well as legal, cultural, political, and behavioral considerations that might be factors in addressing the concerns of particular constituent groups.

A PR person who writes or disseminates a press release for an event on the community calendar is performing a function that will benefit an organization. While we know that writing is not something anyone or everyone can do with great skill, writing is only one of the basic skills of PR professionals. But expect the billing rate to be even higher for the unique and special capabilities of an experienced crisis management expert. From a business perspective, fees for expertise in crisis management, reputation management, investor relations, and mergers and acquisitions services are comparable to those of many top lawyers, financial advisors, and management consultants.

So, public relations is an art *and* a science and for all that it can contribute to a company's reputation, market position, and bottom line, it is surely a serious factor in marketing and business as well.

SUMMARY

- Public relations means giving the public "permission to believe" your message is true and has value. If a message resonates, people want to accept it; they just need a reason.
- One of the greatest areas of misunderstanding is the perception that public relations is the same as publicity.
- Public relations is an umbrella term for communications, community relations, customer relations, consumer affairs, employee relations, industry relations, international relations, investor relations, issues management, media relations, member relations, press agentry, promotions, publicity, public affairs, shareholder relations, and speechwriting.
- The term *spin* is commonly thought to have a negative connotation, but in fact it is simply putting information in either a positive or negative light, depending on the side of the issue the presenter is representing.
- PR people are often the "face" or "voice" of an organization to its public, fielding questions and receiving comments from important constituent groups.

References

Robert Dilenschneider, *Power and Influence* (New York: Prentice-Hall, 1990).

Philip Lesly, ed., *Lesly's Handbook of Public Relations and Communications,* Fifth Edition (Chicago: McGraw-Hill/Contemporary, 1998).

William D. Novelli, Executive Director and CEO of AARP, quoted in a 2003 interview with the author.

2

The Public Relations Plan

Few successes—especially in business—are accidents. Successful ventures begin with well-crafted plans and follow those plans through to their completion, which usually means when their objectives have been achieved.

A public relations plan defines the targeted audience for the effort, sets goals, and establishes priorities. While public relations goals are usually publicity related, the specific objectives of most plans will be very distinct. Sometimes the goal is strictly awareness and name recognition, which can be exploited at a later time. Usually, it's more.

For example, a PR plan for a political candidate will have numerous objectives besides the obvious high visibility. While ultimately the candidate wants votes, he or she also hopes public relations activities will generate enthusiastic crowds, visible support, financial contributions, campaign volunteers, broad media coverage, endorsements and word-of-mouth referrals. A corporate campaign, on the other hand, might be aimed at simply differentiating a product from those of the competition or pumping interest into a languishing stock. Both candidate and company want publicity, but a PR plan goes beyond aiming for good press coverage.

Key Elements of the Plan

The cultural, economic and political environment in which a PR program might be carried out is constantly changing. With each change comes the prospect of new and exciting opportunities, sometimes necessitating a reworking of the plan or a reassessment of objectives. Public relations is typically—though not always—a part of a company or organization's marketing effort, and the marketing plan is the essential roadmap, checklist, and overall guide.

In some cases, the PR plan is a section or subsection of the marketing plan and may involve little more than creating a consumer hotline to receive and respond to comments and complaints or issuing press releases on major initiatives or changes. In other situations the PR plan will totally focus on generating a change in the public's perceptions of a subject or establishing and maintaining a positive relationship with the media.

The essential elements of the marketing plan are the *situation analysis; objectives; strategy; tactics; time line;* and *budget* for the total marketing effort. Marketing plans can be as unique as the people who write them, being thick and detailed or summarized in bullet points on a single page. The company, its size, needs, goals, capital and management style are the guiding factors in developing the plan.

If the PR plan is modest in terms of its objectives and budget, it may be little more than a few lines on the overall marketing plan. If, however, PR is going to be a uniquely or singularly large component of the company or organization's overall marketing effort, it might very well benefit from having a more detailed plan of its own that, while supporting the general objectives of the marketing department, focuses needed attention on specific public relations activities that might include a range of actions from publicity and speechwriting to the preparation of specialty publications, audience-specific web sites, or the management of a governmental relations program.

In organizations where the public relations effort is built around educational programs, fundraising, directing a community outreach effort utilizing the experience and talent of both staff members and volunteers, the plan can be long-term, multi-faceted and highly specialized.

Entire books are devoted to preparing marketing plans and PR plans. It is important to note, however, that there is no one absolute form the plan must follow. Again, it is appropriate that the style and form of the plan reflect and be consistent with the management style of the organization or it is unlikely the plan will be read, much less followed.

The Situation Analysis

Following the same format as a typical marketing plan, the Situation Analysis briefly summarizes the prevailing situation as it affects the company or organization relative to its position in the market and to its various constituent groups—customers, clients or members, investors, regulators, prospects, competitors and the media. Also, it notes the positive attributes of the subject, as well as the negatives and challenges that contribute to the need for public relations. An example would be:

> As Internet usage increases, traffic is declining at retail branches. Competitors with more varied lines and products— and a much larger advertising budget—are countering this trend by aggressively advertising and offering deep discounts on some items, then cross-selling other products once the consumer is on the premises. As the Internet market continues to grow and competitors draw a larger market share with ads, discounts, and a broader selection of products, the prospects for sustaining and expanding current business levels is severely threatened.

Obviously, each company or organization's "situation" will be different and other factors might be incorporated. Note if the organization has historically been successful defining its value proposition, communicating its message, and delivering on its promises, as well as building value into its products and services . . . or if the opposite is the case.

Rely on research. Be objective, and be honest. Defining a situation so it appears favorable to members of a management team reading the plan might score some short-term points, but it defeats the very purpose of constructing a serious program.

There is no substitute for knowing the market, but it is especially important to know what the market thinks of the company or organization—alone and relative to competition or alternative entities. This is why current market research is essential.

Consider any changes that might have taken place in the market, the economy or other such conditions, as well as changes in the organization's structure or management and what impact that might have had on its mission or relative to goals and objectives set down in the marketing plan. To accurately gauge the current environment, it is sometimes useful to compare current data with historic information, such as from a year or two (or longer) ago and identify both changes in the market environment and changes in the organization that might explain the differences.

Market research—particularly attitude and awareness research—can provide an unbiased overview and perspective that can help guide the plan. If such research confirms what is already believed to be true, the validation is worthwhile. But it is when research provides information that was not known, or even suspected, that it is invaluable. The point is to emphasize to all who will be involved in implementing the plan *why* it is necessary to do what the plan outlines.

Additionally, a PR audit can be useful. Such an audit should include:

- Interviews with management and specific other constituents, such as shareholders and members of the media.
- Review and analysis of current issues, problems, and opportunities.
- A reexamination to determine whether or not the target

market and the makeup of other constituent groups have changed since the previous plan was adopted.

- An assessment of attitudes and concerns of a cross-section of customers, as well as employees, vendors, persons of influence within the community, and other target audiences.
- A review to determine whether or not media outlets and contacts on the current list are adequate to reach the desired target market segments.
- A critical review of web site content and all other marketing and communications materials, such as literature, press kits (with bios and photographs), advertising, reprints, and other components to determine if they are adequate under current conditions.

Specifying Objectives

The objectives of the PR plan will help identify the particular types of public relations activities the company or organization requires. That is, most public relations programs aim to create greater awareness and visibility, yet a PR effort that emphasizes investor relations or governmental relations, for example, would logically focus on identifying, reaching, and making a specific connection with a particular constituency and in fact may not require or prefer publicity. Similarly, if the PR program involves crisis management, the degree of visibility and public awareness would be closely managed.

The process of defining objectives should take into account any specific concerns of the targeted audience or market segments and make certain no conflict exists between what the company or organization wants and what the public wants. Matters of commonality or conflict might be addressed in what message or messages are to be conveyed through the PR effort. For example, objectives might include:

1. Bring back lost customers.
2. Increase traffic to retail outlets by 25% this year.
3. Hold revenue steady in this quarter; increase revenue by at least 5% next quarter.

Again, one organization might want to increase its public awareness by a specific percent in a specific period of time, while another might seek to do damage control following a period of negative news. But it is important to be specific. This is goal setting and goals cannot be so general as to permit random interpretations of their meaning.

Consider whether or not the same message is appropriate for employees, volunteers, customers, vendors, trade media, national and regional media, community leaders and members, and others who may be part of the target market or public to be reached by the program. Be clear about what the program is to accomplish among which constituent group or groups.

Strategy

Consider what methods will be most effective in sending the right message to the target market. Not everyone responds to the same words in the same way, particularly when the message is intended for members of more than one generation or other demographic targets. This is an area where, again, research indicating what is most important to members of the target market should be useful.

Consider too the kind of *image* of the company or organization the strategy is to project, making certain it is consistent with the subject's history and mission, as well as with the overall image as represented in the marketing plan. Strategy and tactics are often referenced in the same breath as if they represented the same idea. They don't. While the strategy presents the *approach* and the *focus* of the effort, the tactics describe *how* the strategy will be executed. For example, a strategy would be:

> Convince the public there is greater benefit to dealing directly with a representative of the organization onsite than to connecting with an impersonal, indifferent and perhaps unreliable computer program driving a web site.

> Or

> Exploit the long history and reputation for quality and dependability as compared to a perhaps "hot"—though untested—new competitor or rival.

Implementing Tactics

There are numerous methods for influencing the opinions and behavior of target audiences. For example, tactics and ideas to influence *employees* include:

- Ceremonies (such as annual dinners) that publicly recognize outstanding performance and achievements with awards and bonuses in the form of cash, redeemable certificates or perhaps a trip that has special significance to both the employee and the organization. Target Stores, for example, awards employees trips to Memphis, Tennessee where the employees are given tours of Target House, a facility that provides support and assistance to families of children undergoing treatment at St. Jude Children's Hospital. The company helps fund the facility and employees return with a greater understanding and appreciation for the scope of Target's good work in the community, which translates into goodwill on several levels.
- Encouraging employees to contribute to organization magazines, newsletters and other communications vehicles that expand the organization's message and promotes a sense of commitment, loyalty and team spirit.

Among the means typically employed to influence *customers, clients* or *consumers* are:

- Brochures, booklets, informational guides and other types of promotional literature, both general and specifically-oriented to particular market segments and distributed by mail or onsite.
- Catalogs, magalogs and newsletters.
- Web site testimonials.
- DVDs, CD-ROMs, videos and audio cassettes.
- Seminars and workshops.
- Interactive programs on diskettes or the organization's web site.

- Event sponsorships.
- Co-sponsorship of events with local or national radio and television stations and cable systems.
- Participation in charity and cause-related community and national events.
- Promotional programs such as auctions, contests, sweepstakes or other competitions.
- Creative use of premiums.
- Advertising.

Tactics aimed at influencing *vendors* and *suppliers* include:

- Co-branding of premium items with vendors and suppliers.
- Co-sponsorships.
- Co-op advertising.
- Links to participating vendor and supplier web sites.

Approaches used to reach the general public or a specific targeted audience segment using *the media*:

- Press releases (via e-mail, messenger, fax or postal service).
- Presentation of studies, surveys, white papers, comparative analysis and position papers.
- Personal contact through interviews, luncheons, receptions, press conferences and briefings.

Tactics and promotions aimed at influencing *the trade, national, regional media,* and *online media:*

- Integrate new features and benefits available through the company or organization web site.
- Develop a monthly industry- or product-related advertorial or infomercial.
- Include key executives or spokespersons in trade association programs.
- Participate in online forums and newsgroups.

- Co-sponsor informational articles presented as paid ads in trade publications.

Creating a Time Line

Whether the tactics employed to implement the strategy and achieve the objectives are scheduled to occur within a narrow calendar period or over several stages or phases over months or years, prepare a time line to determine if the efforts aimed at reaching the objectives are progressing on schedule or if they are stalled or appear to have peaked. Be realistic about what can be accomplished in specific periods of time. Be flexible and allow for modifications to the plan to reflect changes in the economy or business climate.

Developing the Budget

Public relations is an extremely cost-effective form of marketing and communications, particularly when compared with media advertising. Nonetheless, "cost effective" is a relative term, depending on the budget, and it does not mean there is no cost at all. Maintaining an information center, printing, travel and entertainment, sponsorships, staging events and a myriad of other production services and fee-related activities come at a price. Budget realistically for the tactics to be implemented to reach the objectives within the allotted time frame. If they cannot be achieved realistically within the budget or time frame, modify the objectives, alter the time frame for completion or change the budget.

The Plan

Obviously not all companies' profiles or objectives are comparable and such distinctions will dictate the scope and focus for the various PR plans unique to each of them. This particular plan was developed to help establish the U.S. presence of a British technology firm.

Exhibit 2.1: Outline of the Public Relations Plan and Strategy

September 30–December 31

I. Objectives
   a. raise awareness
   b. establish credibility
   c. promote differentiation

II. Identify target
   a. media
   b. industry analysts
   c. others of influence

III. Develop media lists
   a. primary (a-list) media targets
   b. secondary (b-list)
   c. newswires

IV. Develop media kit
   a. fact sheets/backgrounders
   b. management and team profiles
   c. press releases
   d. case studies
   e. (optional educational) white papers
   f. (optional) photos, brochures, CD-ROM
   g. other, as required by event or subject

V. Develop schedule for contacts/ disseminating material/events
   a. product introductions
   b. trade shows
   c. hospitality suites
   d. seminars
   e. speaking engagements

    f. media tours

    g. promotions/sponsorships

    h. follow-up calls

    i. clipping/taping services to monitor media
     coverage

  VI. Media maintenance program

    a. schedule calls, meetings, meals to promote
     relationships.

Objectives of the Public Relations Plan

Public relations does not sell the product, the sales team sells the product. What PR can be expected to achieve are higher levels of (1) *awareness,* (2) *credibility,* and (3) *differentiation of the company from its competitors.*

  Points two and three cannot be accomplished until point one has been initiated. Awareness is the primary objective of our effort over the short term (30 to 60 days) and is the achievement upon which we will establish credibility over the longer term.

Media Kit

The media kit is the basic tool of the public relations effort, serving to introduce the company, the product, the brand, the management team and other principals, and to define the subject and focus of the program. Essential elements of the press kit are a two-pocket folder that establishes a corporate look and image, a corporate fact sheet or backgrounder, a product fact sheet or backgrounder, a profile of the members of the management team (on individual sheets or grouped and summarized on a single sheet), press releases and/or case studies that help position the company and product. Optional items that may be included are photographs of management principals, charts or illustrations relating to the product, research white papers, brochures if applicable to the event or subject being promoted, copies of favorable articles about the company, a demo disk or CD-ROM.

Web Site

The corporate web site is a marketing tool, a vehicle for information and education and serves as an electronic version of the media kit. It provides the company with a showcase for consumer information, recruiting and promotional material, as well as opportunities to promote seminars, features, specific and general content, programs and events.

Media List

In media, as with direct mail, the list is the key to the success of the PR effort. The main list should include the names, titles, addresses, phone numbers, fax numbers and e-mail addresses of the members of the media who cover technology (specifically our sector of technology, if possible) and media (publishing and the entertainment industry), as well as media analysts, editors and reporters covering business, technology, and known freelance writers, columnists and producers who are qualified targets for receiving our information. A secondary (or B) list can include general financial or business, education, graphic design, and business-to-business media. Media lists require continuous updating as reporters, editors and sometimes producers change jobs or rotate assignments, often without notice. It is important to know your audience and determine the manner in which members of the media prefer to receive information, by phone, fax, e-mail, surface mail, FedEx/messenger service.

Lists can be purchased or constructed. The PR Newswire provides a variety of lists and services. The PR Newswire's "US1" list includes more than 2,400 media entries; the technology media list has several hundred additional names and, upon request (and for an additional charge), a list of several thousand members of the media who have specifically asked to receive information on technology.

Clipping Service

A clipping and taping service is essential in that a press release, media alert, bulletin or other announcement disseminated to several thousand media outlets is likely to result in coverage that will go unnoticed in the routine scanning of daily, weekly, monthly and trade publications and programs. It is advised that a clipping service monitor media (including Internet media) for coverage of the company and/or references to the company and its products, as well as articles and coverage of major competitors.

Advertising

Advertising and public relations can each achieve specific objectives separately, but together the combination provides a synergy that goes beyond what either could do alone. Advertising, however, can be expensive compared to other media and careful target marketing is critical. A recommendation for a modest trade advertising program to achieve brand awareness, credibility and differentiation will be offered in a marketing communications plan to be presented separately.

Budget

Fees, travel and expenses, business meals with media representatives, out-of-pocket expenses; production and dissemination of press releases, newswire, and clipping/taping service costs; development and production of informational and educational brochures, white papers, folders, photography and graphics will be presented in a detailed budget summary.

Additional Comments

When the actual completed plan is submitted to the client or company management, specifics regarding costs and media will be more detailed. Note that the example shown was created for a technology company. A PR plan focusing on shareholder or governmental relations would include details specific to those areas, perhaps targeting regulators or legislators and their staff members, rather than securities analysts or media. The process is essentially standard, but each industry has constituent groups and areas of interest and influence that are usually in some way unique.

SUMMARY

- The public relations plan defines the targeted audience, sets goals, and establishes priorities. PR goals are usually publicity related, but the specific objectives of most plans will be very distinct.
- The cultural, economic and political environment for a PR program is constantly changing, at times requiring reworking the plan or reassessing objectives.
- As with a marketing plan, the essential elements of the PR plan should include a *situation analysis; objectives; strategy; tactics; time line;* and *budget.*
- Be aware of the subject's position relative to various constituent groups, such as customers, clients or members, investors, regulators, prospects, competitors and the media, noting both the positive attributes as well as its negatives.
- Be realistic. If the objective cannot be reached in the designated time frame for the funds allocated, modify the objectives, alter the time frame for completion, or change the budget.

3

The Public(s)

Almost everyone refers to "the media" as if it were a singular entity and not a term that encompasses many diverse entities in print, broadcast and cable TV, radio, and the Internet—a group with a focus and perspective that is a long way from unified. Similarly when one refers to "the public" (or, more commonly, to "the general public"), it is to suggest a similar type of singular body and again, of course, that is anything but the case.

The Many Faces and Places of "The Public"

Research professionals have come a long way in providing both demographic and psychographic breakouts of women, men, students, widows, married couples, working mothers, veterans, homeowners, transients, and others that are age-specific, ethnic-specific, multilingual, bi-coastal, and the myriad of other subcategories that constitute "the public" and validate its diversity.

What PR professionals have known for decades is that in marketing terms "public" is a very plural term indeed and, since roughly the 1970s, target marketing has described the variety of constituent groups that make up many different *publics*.

Addressing the Needs and Concerns of Each "Public"

The in-house PR specialist or agency account team might prepare a press release to be directed to science writers; a letter to the company's stockholders; a report to the market analysts who cover the company's particular sector; an announcement to employees; an e-mail to partners; a mailer to sales prospects; a notice to regulators. And even if the message is essentially the same to everyone, it is in this example alone being directed to seven different *publics*, each of which is likely to have its own set of concerns that need to be addressed.

In other situations, *regional bias* must be considered. While that term might at first seem as if it should be unconstitutional, it is actually only a recognition that a particular piece of information is likely to be received and considered differently in areas that may have a heightened (or lesser) interest in it for their own unique reasons.

For example, an announcement that an automaker is closing four plants will be far more (or less) important to people in different regions, depending on whether or not the plant is located there and what related industries or businesses might be affected. In areas around each of the plants, how many jobs will be lost? What might it mean to the local economy? How might it alter the balance of competition—which in turn creates interest in competitors' market centers? What related regional businesses are likely to feel the impact of the closings? What percentage of the company's investors is located in the four areas and how might they be touched by this action? How will it affect the company's other investments?

What local vendors could be damaged? What about the areas where the plant closings are not local issues? How might attitudes toward the company be altered by people whose lives are both directly and indirectly touched by the decision?

Different publics react differently to the same news. The impact is in the eye of the beholder. How individuals in different regions, situations, and demographic segments react to a particular piece of news, and whether or not those reactions will be great enough to be considered significant, is a concern that needs to be factored into planning.

Now, consider the reverse of the announcement—news that the company will soon *expand* into several new markets regionally as a step toward expanding globally. Again, such news will be received differently in different markets.

Will a large company creating a physical presence in the region create new job opportunities, infuse local construction, help boost tourism, and have an impact on local real estate? Will it be good or bad for smaller local companies in the same industry?

Perhaps the company's expansion is into a totally different product area, such as if the automaker also publishes a magazine about automobiles that is very popular with people who really like cars, such as race fans and owners of customized or vintage cars. Now it wants to launch a cable TV channel under the magazine's name. It will need people, programs, features, advertisers, a production support staff, and a presence in the marketplace—letting the public and suppliers of programming information know it is ready for business.

Certainly a press release sent to wire services will get the word out to some degree and would be standard operating procedure in such a situation. There is also not only a justification for a more dramatic general announcement, but a particular reason to address unique audiences that would have greater interest in the subject than might be true of most of the general public.

To take only a shotgun approach to reach the masses misses opportunities to potentially enhance a company's image and reputation among certain specific prime target constituent groups. Public relations professionals need to identify opportunities in as many areas as possible and carefully analyze the characteristics of each new and potential market.

Marketers who say their target audience is *everyone*—as makers of products such as soap, toothpaste, shampoo, or fingernail clippers might insist—may be right in theory in that their products might be correct for all people in all market segments. But trying to *reach* and *influence* everyone in every segment with a single message, and do it effectively, would likely use a message and a media plan that would be a case of extreme overkill and fail to appeal to key market targets—the people who actually make the purchase decisions.

The "public" not only has many faces with many pairs of eyes and ears, but it resides in many different places and responds to different signals. The challenge is to find where the target public lives and be both seen and heard.

Keeping a "Forgotten Public" Informed

A primary "public" is sometimes assumed to be supportive of an effort so it is overlooked in the list of marketing targets. That public is the management of the client or company on whose behalf the program has been developed and that assumption of approval can be a significant mistake.

One of the most painful phrases a public relations professional can hear from a client (besides "I need you to explain your invoice") is "Tell me again why we are doing this."

After so many high-profile success stories have been credited to good public relations efforts—from new product launches to successful brand extensions and spin-offs to acquisitions and merges—that result in career-making cover stories in *Forbes* and *Fortune*, it is astounding how many CEOs and other corporate heads still do not understand what PR can do (and does) or what it represents to a company's bottom line. The short explanation, whether the subject of the public relations effort is a person, a company, a product or brand, or an issue, is that PR provides a systematic process that utilizes a variety of techniques and disciplines to assure:

1. *That* a specific target audience (a public) is aware of a subject and
2. *How* the public ultimately regards the subject.

It comes down to awareness and influence. From there, the rest of the marketing effort can do its job.

While it is important that practitioners reach the target market with their message, it is also important to remember the many different publics that must be served and that senior management—one of those publics—must understand and support the program or it will move forward as if attached to a chain and an anchor. When the chain reaches the point where the anchor pulls it to a stop, the program comes to an abrupt halt. Trying to secure additional funding and support for a program that was not understood or recognized as important from the start is a losing proposition. Keeping management informed as to a program's progress will pre-empt questions regarding "why we are doing this."

Using PR to Deflect Bad Publicity

The most common goal of the public relations effort is to generate awareness for a subject. Research indicates that a better-*known* company or brand is perceived to be a *better* company or brand. But generating awareness is not where the effort ends. It is *not* true that in the quest for greater recognition, "*any* publicity is *good* publicity." That famous phrase and its cousin, "I don't care what they say about me as long as they spell my name right," it can safely be concluded, were not uttered by PR people.

In fact, the opposite is true.

A company, organization, or client should be *very* concerned about bad publicity and the damage to the brand that comes with it. Normally, on the day negative publicity hits the news media, if the company is a publicly traded company, its stock price can be expected to drop. If the company is privately held, the likely result will be a significant decline in business, from which some companies never recover.

The degree of damage bad publicity does is in part a function of where the company was positioned *before* the bad publicity hit. If the public already had a low opinion of the company—or *no opinion* of the company—the bad publicity will likely not inflict major damage, although that reflects other problem issues that should be addressed.

Most companies that adopt a PR plan or program have a goal of not only becoming better known, but of building brand equity and brand loyalty, increasing the value of the stock, enhancing recruiting capabilities, and increasing market share, not necessarily in that order. These are reasonable goals that will typically produce a positive impact on a company's market position, both short-term and long-term.

Negative publicity generally results in negative impact on a company or brand. The public tends to choose products or brands they have heard good things about or even brands they know nothing about before brands about which they have heard something bad.

The reaction to bad publicity can be particularly damaging if the company begins from a position of relatively low name recognition. If the first time the public becomes aware of a company is by associating it with bad news—fraud, scandal, charges of discrimination, sanctions for health or safety violations, etc.—it is highly unlikely the public will seek out the company or find it desirable to enter into a business relationship.

Bad news can arrive in a variety of forms, none of them ever advantageous to a company seeking to improve its position in the marketplace. For example:

- A disgruntled former (or current) employee may charge a company with some form of discrimination or harassment, often hoping to get a quick financial settlement, but more importantly, perhaps, to gain some satisfaction by publicly embarrassing an organization he or she believes committed an injustice.
- Another company in the same business can run into trouble, causing some members of the news media to paint the industry with a broad brush and suggest problems might be wide-ranging.
- A government agency can announce it is studying health or safety concerns associated with a product the company manufactures or distributes.

The potential problems almost any company can experience, often through no fault of its own, are virtually open-ended. The point is that bad news—while it may get a company's name in a headline— is not necessarily a good thing. Preparing the public in advance with material that generates a positive image of a company can have a pre-emptive value at times when negative news might break.

Certainly the purchase of large amounts of advertising time and space in targeted media will usually (but not always) provide a shortcut to greater awareness and recognition with the audience that media serves. Well-crafted ads, well positioned and repeated with enough frequency will likely create an increased level of awareness, but such an approach can be costly and must be sustained and reinforced on a regular basis. Additionally, the public today has become more sophisticated regarding ad content and can usually distinguish between true testimonials and paid commercial endorsements, understanding that ads present only the company's not unbiased perspective.

Public relations, on the other hand, employs a variety of techniques to influence opinions and decision-making through the use of *unpaid* media and other means. Credibility is comparatively higher in that the subject is immediately perceived—by an impartial entity such as a newspaper columnist or reporter, magazine writer, radio or TV personality— as being newsworthy enough to be singled out from among competitors and others vying for attention. People who are aware of how the process works know that even when publicists are bringing information to the attention of members of the media, that a story chosen for presentation was in fact one of hundreds submitted on any given day, again underscoring its importance among other news and features.

Identifying favorable opportunities to present a company, organization, or cause message to the appropriate public is a function of public relations. Merchandising the results of such endeavors increases awareness even further as well as helping to influence how the subject is perceived.

Advertising and PR: Two Ways to Reach a Common Goal

In an effort to reach the right public, a number of alternative avenues of awareness are open to experimentation. Advertising is arguably the most expensive and manageable and is unquestionably a very powerful tool.

Advertising and PR professionals have been debating the comparative value and effectiveness of the two disciplines—*advertising versus public relations*—for decades and the fact is, the better and more viable alternative depends on the size of the budget, the particular objectives of the campaign, the level of previous awareness or visibility of the subject, and the amount of time allotted for achieving the objectives. As in most every situation, one size rarely fits all and different goals and circumstances require different approaches.

Agency clients or corporate management executives usually don't understand advertising any more than they understand public relations, or the public would likely not be emphasizing its dislike of advertising quite so much. Too often, ads reflect the personal tastes of the advertiser without consideration of what will be informative, interesting, and entertaining (and therefore *acceptable*) to the public. Yet, advertisers *do* understand that because they are paying for the time or space to present their message, rightly or wrongly, they can insist on doing it their way. Not so with public relations, where the actual final presentation to the public is typically edited and reinterpreted with far less direct influence or control by the subject company, organization, or individual.

Overcoming Management Objections

While the forms are not especially complicated, the actual reasons clients and management don't seem to understand how the system works can probably be attributed to a *desire* not to understand it. Often that desire is linked to money.

In the decision-maker's mind, when setting priorities, approving content, and ultimately allocating funds for advertising and PR, agencies report a historic hesitancy to give that final *thumbs up*. Despite the impressive amount of research that exists to support arguments that either or both advertising and public relations are extremely effective in influencing the public, these two line items are usually the last to be approved and the first to be cut from the budget when times are hard. People who are not great *believers* in advertising and PR seem to be the ones who are routinely hesitant in approving and funding a program. They seem to find comfort in insisting they "don't understand it" and need to be reassured again and again as to why it is a good idea.

As with anyone who needs constant reassurance, these executives need to be reminded *that* PR will work for them, *how* it will achieve its objectives, and *why* it remains a worthwhile allocation of funds. PR people too often find a good campaign cancelled in its early stages because they assumed management support that was not there.

Rather than trying to justify parts of a program out of context, a good approach might be that which salespeople have used in pitching their products and messages for decades: *Tell them what you're going to tell them, tell them, then tell them what you just told them.*

Recognizing that management is one of the publics to be served, address the rationale for the effort in the initial planning document and issue interim status reports frequently. The plan can be as detailed as the decision-maker requires it to be, but the basic structure follows that of the standard marketing plan:

1. Prepare a situational analysis.
2. Define the program's objectives.
3. Develop a strategy to reach the objectives.
4. List the tactics that will be employed to implement the strategy.
5. Set a deadline for reaching the objective.
6. Prepare a realistic budget to fund the program.

The last five of the six steps really need to be in sync. That is, if it is concluded that the objective cannot be reached in the allotted time with the budget allocated, then either the deadline, the budget, or the objective needs to be reconsidered.

Remember, the issue is how to best reach the public with the correct message. Again, while most PR programs cost less to implement than advertising, PR is not free. Presentation materials, production and distribution costs, photography, travel, shipping charges, and fees are only some of the predictable expenses.

A good PR agency, like a good law firm or a fine hotel, will cost more than the cheapest alternative available and the difference in cost is usually visible in experience, the quality of service, and the results.

To return to that client or CEO looking for the big story in *The Wall Street Journal* or the cover of *Forbes*, the answer might well be that the best plan didn't call for such placements at a particular time because, apart from being unrealistic under normal circumstances, the objective was to reach a specific public for a specific reason in the time frame and within the budget allowed.

Even the best known companies or organizations—McDonald's, Microsoft, Starbucks, General Motors, etc.—do not get the lead story for every announcement they issue. Companies that are less well-known need to be realistic and appreciate that a well-conceived and properly orchestrated plan will reach objectives that make sense and create value. Fireworks fill the skies with light and excitement, but fade within seconds and are quickly forgotten, while a candle can burn and create light for a long time. As exciting as the fireworks can be, choose the candle.

SUMMARY

- The "public" is commonly referred to as if the term described a unified group, when, in fact, it is a highly diverse collection of many groups.
- Different publics react differently to the same news, influenced by region, lifestyle, ethnicity, and a host of other considerations.
- The role of the public relations professional is to identify opportunities in as many areas as possible and carefully analyze the characteristics of each new and potential market.

- Marketers who insist their target audience is *everyone* might be right in theory, but trying to effectively *reach* and *influence* everyone in every segment with a single message would be overkill and would likely fail to appeal to people who actually make the decisions.
- Keeping management informed of a program's progress will maintain a level of support and pre-empt the question "Why are we doing this?"
- Whether to emphasize advertising or PR depends on the size of the budget, the particular objectives of the campaign, the level of awareness of the subject, and the time allotted for achieving the objectives.

4

Public Relations and the Marketing Mix

With a public relations plan outlined so that it includes a clear and objective *situation analysis,* a defined set of *objectives, strategy, tactics, time line, and budget,* company management must now consider the best approach to achieve the specific goals within the budget. While the focus of this book is on public relations, an aspect of "relating" is understanding that no process exists in a vacuum and that executing the PR plan in combination with other disciplines can often extend and enhance its range, depth, and cost-efficiency.

PR and Other Marketing Functions

Marketing is the *packaging, positioning, pricing, promotion, distribution,* and *selling* of a product, service, or elements associated with a particular cause or point of view. Public relations is, in some respects, a part of each of these processes. Advertising, PR, promotion, research, and education are the basic avenues of marketing. This explanation is offered because, to many clients, advertising, marketing, and PR are interchangeable terms for the same thing.

They're not.

In a perfect world, PR and advertising professionals would control the marketing budget and determine how much will be allotted for each campaign. Alas, the system does not operate that way. The practitioners in the various discipline fight for, and are very protective of, their respective budgets and areas of responsibility, and, historically, they are extremely sensitive about what department or agency is credited (or blamed) for a program's outcome.

When functions overlap and interact, cooperation and coordination is necessary, but competitive considerations remain very real and usually the client or senior management does little to alter that situation. As with conglomerates, management demands and expects each unit and division to support and assist every other unit and division, but as each is considered an individual profit center, competition is intense and incentives for selflessly promoting another division's interests can come with a high price—most commonly, being left out in the cold when credit and recognition is awarded.

Typically in organizations with PR, advertising, and research departments or agencies, it is the organization's senior marketing executive who oversees these areas. It is that person who is responsible for making certain all parts come together with as little friction as possible (a sometimes difficult task in companies and organizations where such rivalries are encouraged at the top).

As the PR plan is executed, if advertising is also a factor in the overall effort, it is important that the two programs' message points are consistent and not working at cross-purposes. This seems like such an obvious necessity for success, and yet in many companies the PR and ad agencies operate independently, and their account representatives have virtually no contact. The result of this is that the program accomplishes less than it might have if all the professional communicators would have been able to communicate with one another. This is not as much a criticism of ad or PR executives as much as it is a fact of life.

Advertising is a very effective means of driving a company's message to its various publics in that the advertiser has total control over the ad's content, the choice of media in which it will appear, the number of times it will be seen (within limits of the budget), and even has a reasonable degree of influence as to what other ads appear near it. Obviously the reality of the marketplace is a factor here as well. Smaller advertisers get courtesy and respect, while the larger advertisers get pretty much whatever they want.

There is a level of immediacy in advertising in that the advertiser can usually make changes up to literally the last minute, which is something that cannot be said about the media. Ads can also be developed and placed in a wide range of media—newspapers, magazines, radio, television, outdoor and out-of-home placements, direct mail, telemarketing, the Internet, point-of-sale displays, product placements, and an assortment of sponsorships and events.

The cartoon that shows a man's bald head stamped with the words "your ad here" is not far from reality. Ads are on the roofs and insides of taxicabs, on shopping carts, on bus stop benches, ATM receipts, claim checks, and public restroom walls, and are regarded by the public more as clutter than innovative placement. But despite the complaints from what would seem to be all demographics of the public that ads are overwhelming and a nuisance, the adverting community delights in opening still more venues.

It is, of course, a great irony that research indicates the public hates being bombarded with advertising, yet sits glued to TV screens for infomercials, as well as HSN (the Home Shopping Network) and its rival QVC, for 24 hours a day of solid sales pitches. New brides-to-be buy thousands of copies of women's magazines just for the ads and fashion magazines learned long ago that fashion trends are much more influenced by fashion advertising than designers' runway shows.

Despite the complaints, advertising obviously continues to be

immensely effective. Overall, companies that advertise sell more products then companies that do not advertise. Yet of greater concern to
many businesses is not the public outcry, but the soaring cost of advertising at the very same time that segmented audience numbers are declining and media becomes more fractionalized. The audience that was
once measured as a single mass is now divided among the proliferation
of media alternatives. Even as the credibility of much advertising
comes under fire, the public still responds to it and rates keep going up.

Tailored PR Solutions for Every Program

Public relations has also become more specialized. Companies and
organizations can choose the person or firm with the type of expertise and approach most appropriate to a program's specific objectives,
budget constraints, and time line, as well as what seems to be the
best fit with an individual company's reputation, image, and the audience it wants to reach.

Some companies find newsletters a good fit for their particular
image and constituent group, while others find press briefings, business
breakfasts, town meetings, teleconferencing, or white papers more effective in getting their message across in the manner that appears most
fitting. And, after decades of innovation, thousands of companies still
do little more than post a press release on the PR newswire and accept
whatever coverage it generates—and sometimes that is enough.

Proponents of advertising point out a limitation of PR: Once a
press release or a media interview has been given, the company has little or no control over *how* its message will ultimately be presented (or
if it will be presented at all), what other information will appear within
or adjacent to the story (such as the inclusion of strongly negative comments from competitors or critics), and how much of the most valuable information provided will actually make it into the story.

Executives or other individuals who are the subjects of media attention are often frustrated when a day spent with a reporter in interviews or large amounts invested in filling a press kit with useful infor-

mation, is edited or compressed or paraphrased into a few sentences or paragraphs. Even more frustrating is when a reporter finds a contrary opinion or view of a subject to be—in his or her opinion—more persuasive or interesting and a story that started out being favorable to a company takes a very different or even a negative slant.

On the other hand, a writer might be so impressed with the subject that the story becomes larger than expected and includes comments from more sources that even end up being tributes or endorsements. There are no guarantees, but there are reasons why certain PR specialists are so well regarded for what they do. Years spent developing relationships with members of the media, knowing what they want, how they want it presented, and what is reasonable to expect in the final story, is why they are successful.

Public relations professionals, whether working on behalf of large companies, small companies, an entertainer, a medical or legal practice, a political candidate, a cause or an issue, understand how to distinguish between what a subject is doing that qualifies as "news" and what is a potential feature story or "filler" piece. He or she must be able to evaluate the possible risks in certain situations, such as avoiding talking—and/or only communicating in writing—with members of the media who invariably tend to overplay a story or make it seem needlessly controversial, or, in a few words, screw things up.

At the same time, the expert knows to encourage meetings with media people known for being consistently fair and accurate. Getting interviews and generating press releases is only a part of the process. PR professionals must also understand the importance of aggressively *merchandising* coverage and *leveraging* the results of each media encounter into something more.

The Importance of "Buzz"

Having emphasized that PR must be regarded as more than publicity, for some organizations it is nonetheless important to "generate buzz"—to be recognized as a player in places where it matters most, such as in the client or company's own industry or profession. In some professions that is considered more valuable than a magazine cover or a front-page story.

As an example, a company or organization's CEO or other individual might be slated to be the keynote speaker at an important industry function (though a lesser slot than keynote speaker would also be noteworthy). Copies of the speech could be distributed (with additional material on the speaker) and a summary or highlights posted on the speaker's own company web site as well as that of the host organization. Audio and video highlights could be made available.

The speech should have a powerful title, a strong lead, and be replete with sound bites—concise, colorful quotes worth repeating out of context—which itself should justify its being showcased in a conference-related publication that typically covers subjects important to the attendees. An added punch would be to have the speaker then host (or be featured or the honored guest) at a sponsored cocktail party or hospitality suite following an afternoon conference session. The speaker's own company or someone other than the host organization should pick up the tab for this.

The cumulative effect is that people should leave the conference with a sense that the speaker is a respected leader in the industry or profession. Such status typically leads to being invited to chair (or at least serve on) high-profile industry task forces or committees or to sit on panels or advisory groups, which in turn provides even higher visibility and influence in directing the course of business—and all without utilizing the press.

Professional colleagues and industry leaders constitute another "public." A high degree of recognition among one's professional circle can be an important factor in generating more buzz, business, referrals, capital, and attracting a high level of talent to the company.

Staying "On Message" in the Most Effective Way

Public relations specialist Judith Rich points out that "Professionals know that most of the creative work is only effective if it is on line with the organization's strategy. Bright ideas that don't communicate a company's message to the proper target audience are best left on the conference room floor."

Whether choosing advertising, public relations, or both in combination, the plan must require staying "on message" and never losing sight of the objectives. Certainly a combination of advertising and PR covers more bases and, if managed correctly, can go a long way to enhance a company or organization's image and reputation. If budget constraints, inadequate staff, corporate politics, or other considerations limit the program to only one function, the choice should be based on which approach best serves the objectives of the plan, not which is the cheapest.

PR Budgeting

Invariably, someone in management will ask, *"What percentage of the marketing budget should be allotted for public relations and should it come at the expense of advertising?"* (Note: If no one asks, anticipate the question anyway and be prepared to address it.)

It will not, of course, surprise PR or marketing professionals to discover there is no stock answer to that question.

While it is true that PR budgets—like advertising budgets— normally appear on the accountant's page, usually as an item under "Marketing," that department is most often not (nor should it be) PR's sole source of funding. Depending on the particular PR needs a company or organization has listed in the plan, funding may come from a variety of sources.

Various programs and projects that are public relations efforts have links to several areas other than marketing, as well as possible co-op programs and dollars outside of the organization. A company's annual report, for example, like other shareholder communications, would likely be prepared by the PR department or agency, but would not be considered a marketing program. Governmental relations (the area in which the company or organization's lobbyists operate) might be in the budget of the legal department, research, administration, or perhaps business development.

Some organizations continue to follow a rather antiquated rule-of-thumb that puts a specific percentage of sales on general revenue into the budget for advertising and PR. Such allocation reflects a lack of understanding of both functions, as well as a lack of knowledge of what things cost in a free market.

PR and ad budgets must be determined based on plans and goals—on what management hopes to accomplish—and realistic funding for the plan should be allocated accordingly. If such funds are not available then the plan's objectives, strategy, tactics, and time line need to be reviewed and reconsidered, and one or more of those elements needs to change.

Advertising and public relations are not commodities that are bought and sold by the pound. Certainly in a business organization, budgets need to be prepared and some fixed costs obviously can be estimated, but in actuality there are only two ways to deal with the issue of finances:

1. Prepare the strategy outline, estimate the cost of implementing it, and budget that amount, or
2. Set a fixed budget for public relations, determine how much the plan can be financed within the limits of the budget, and modify the plan accordingly.

And be realistic. While PR can be extremely cost effective (particularly when compared to the cost of media advertising), a $200,000 plan can not be implemented for $20,000 simply because "that's the budget."

The answer to the question of what percentage of the marketing budget should go to PR is *no percentage.* Public relations budgets should not be calculated based on revenues from unrelated activities, but on the basis of what it costs the company to achieve the plan's objectives.

Again, PR executive Judith Rich emphasizes, "Public relations must be one of the management's frequently considered choices. Too often, it's a leftover, when it should be a main course. Continuing the metaphor, effective marketing is like a healthy diet. It needs all the basic groups. And public relations is a basic component of successful marketing."

The *budget* section of the PR plan allocates funding based on the elements of the proposed program—the cost of implementing its tactics. This is the only sensible approach to the budget issue, based on what the program will cost, not on accepting a predetermined budget and going out to see what it will buy. A realistic public relations budget, in addition to staff salaries and/or agency fees, should anticipate costs for printing and production of a range of projects and collaterals, such as:

- Press kits (printed pocket folders and folder contents, which can include printed material and current and/or archival photos, promotional pieces, executive bios, reprints of articles, transcripts, photos, CDs or CD-ROMs).
- Research materials, studies, surveys, executive summaries.
- Photography—current photos of members of the management team, products, facilities.
- Fulfillment material to be sent to people who request information through web site, phone and mail contacts (anticipate printing, production, shipping and handling).
- Literature (brochures, reprints, books and booklets, speech transcripts, educational documents).
- Press releases—the number of which might be estimated and budgeted on an annual basis, though it is conservative to allow for four to six unscheduled press releases or media alerts over a year.
- Costs relating to press conferences and/or media briefings (cost of appropriate conference room, hall or other facility, travel, sound system).
- Hospitality suites and entertainment relating to media tours and conference or trade show participation.
- Video recording and reproduction of tapes of important presentations and meetings.
- Development of appropriate PR-related content for web site;
- Travel and entertainment.

Printing and mailing budgets are frequently underestimated because it is difficult to anticipate needs annually. Opportunities arise; responses are required. Postage is often overlooked but (with messenger and FEDEX or UPS expenses) can amount to many thousands of dollars a year.

How much should these items typically cost? Obviously there is o one answer. Some organizations will issue press releases quarterly or even annually, while others disseminate such releases 20 to 30 times during the year, announcing new staff appointments, facility enhancements, new product features, notice of meetings or comments on industry issues, or a myriad of other subjects. While some organizations prefer to keep a lower profile and relate to specific groups such as stock analysts or shareholders, other organizations make their annual meetings media events—complete with multi-city press tours and "road shows."

Some companies or organizations can take advantage of "co-op" opportunities, such as participating in a conference or program where expenses are paid fully or partially by a host organization, trade group or sponsor. Other organizations have no such options available to them. Any and all such actual or potential opportunities should be studied and included in the PR budget.

Marketing Public Relations

The respected veteran public relations expert Thomas L. Harris has made a specialty of *marketing public relations*, which studies have shown was perceived as being effective in a variety of areas that are traditionally the responsibility of advertising. He notes some 43 uses of marketing public relations, from positioning companies as leaders and experts and building customer trust to reinforcing weak markets and cultivating new markets—hardly something to be treated as an afterthought. Clearly the function of PR in the marketing mix is mature and versatile. In addition to event sponsorships and affinity programs aimed at specific target groups, marketing public relations opportunities can be developed with:

- Seminars
- Workshops
- Contests

- Support for socially responsible causes
- Community relations activities, from organizing parades to collecting food for local shelters or coordinating volunteers for park beautification or other environmental projects
- Education programs, such as teaching computer literacy, mentoring or tutoring.

Marketing public relations offer a variety of alternative approaches available under the marketing umbrella.

Cause Marketing Programs

Companies are routinely solicited to sponsor or otherwise lend their names and financial support to a variety of good causes. From the most extreme issues, such as world hunger or research to find cures and treatments for AIDS, cancer, other deadly diseases, as well as worldwide efforts to save and protect forests and waterways, to helping a local school buy a bus, meal-on-wheels programs for the elderly, or programs for kids with special needs, there are a multitude of causes that provide both help to people and things in need and give organizations an opportunity to identify themselves as caring forces for good.

While the theory is that something is better than nothing, the process is so involved and demanding that it makes better sense to commit to a program and make it outgoing, rather than a program that is day or date specific—when the day after finds that, despite a long and successful effort, much of the program is, as the computer folks like to say, "sent to the recycling bin."

A community outreach program is an excellent non-media public relations program. It is an example of cause marketing, often described as doing well by doing good.

A business puts together a plan, either independently or in partnership with an established nonprofit operation, to provide assistance and support for a good cause. Apart from the obvious payback that often results from performing acts of kindness for their own sake, companies have found they can generate solid returns on their investments in building socially responsible programs by increasing the levels of awareness, customer loyalty, referrals, and goodwill from a variety of segments and publics.

Opposition to Cause Marketing

Among the available marketing options, it would seem that "doing good" should be a relatively uncontroversial business tactic. Yet, cause marketing is not embraced by everyone. One point of view holds that a business has an obligation to deliver a product or service at a fair price, as determined by the market, and to provide a return on investment to shareholders. People who subscribe to this belief regard the concept of "giving something back to the community" as quaint, and greatly overrated.

The companies, this position emphasizes, have no justification for using company (and investors) money to become "do-gooders" and should instead be focusing on just taking care of business. This point of view—as much an *attitude*, really—would not so long ago have been met with a chorus of "boos" and derided by comparisons to Dickens's cold-hearted character Ebenezer Scrooge.

But times change.

As the social, economic, and political climate becomes more polarized, such positions gain support. *Political correctness* is mocked, ridiculed, and becomes itself politically incorrect—a seemingly minority view held by radical liberals. And isn't marketing supposed to be about "listening to the voice of the market and being responsive to what the public says it wants?"

Yes, it is. But experienced marketers can recognize manipulation of statistics and emotions. A broadcaster who quotes a statistic that "95 percent of people who write to this program . . . " is not mentioning that virtually *everyone* choosing to listen to that program shares the host's particular ideology or point of view on many subjects, but they are a relatively small percentage of the general public in total numbers.

The "everybody knows" type of research is favored by many politicians and preachers who presume to be speaking for the total population, suggesting they are all of one mind. What the person is actually saying is "everybody who has chosen to tell me they agree with me knows" and that comes in at quite a different number than might have first been suggested.

Causes and cause marketing have long been "hot button" issues. When opponents of cause marketing suggest research shows opposition to social responsibility programs is growing, they are failing to reveal that when such opposition grows from 9 percent of people surveyed to 10 percent, it hardly represents a massive shift in public sentiment.

Beyond "Doing Good"

Statistically the do-gooders have a pretty strong case, backed up by definitive research. For example, a 1996 study conducted by Research International indicated that 86 percent of consumers were more likely to buy a product associated with a cause or social issue. The same study also concluded that 86 percent of consumers have a more positive image of a company they believe is doing something to make the world a better place.

The same organization reported in a separate study in 1998 that 75 percent of the companies surveyed believed cause-marketing programs can enhance corporate or brand management.

Such enhanced reputation and improved corporate image can be reflected in a variety of ways, including less volatile stock prices, lower recruiting costs, less employee turnover, less absenteeism, fewer on-the-job accidents, and more loyal customers.

A company or organization's programs should indeed be in sync with the mood of the market. When a public relations professional presents a client or company's message—whether it is in agreement with a majority point of view *or takes an opposing view*—the unique selling proposition or the value statement should nonetheless provide a solid argument that makes a compelling case for the company's position.

It is necessary for a cause marketing program to be a good fit with the company. The public must believe that the company is really interested in helping the cause achieve its objectives. An overtly self-serving campaign that simply seeks to exploit a company's association with a good or popular issue will not only most likely be unsuccessful, but can also *backfire*, leaving the company's reputation or image in worse shape than if it had done nothing at all.

Also, the program must be more than an afterthought on management's part. If the people who speak for the company or organization do not appear to be convincingly committed to the cause, the public will likely see that early on, and assume it cannot trust the company's purported commitments to other issues or concerns.

A PR professional should review and update the public relations plan at regular intervals (most pros suggest quarterly) and be open to some "fine tuning" or modifications if needed. While a plan should be allowed sufficient time to work, and few produce instant long-term results, market conditions are constantly changing. Revising does not mean *scrapping* a plan, but in most situations, a three-month period is long enough to determine if a program is working—whether it is *on track* or not.

It is also necessary to be sensitive to shifting concerns among major constituent groups (customers, stockholders, employees, regulators, community and civic leaders, and the media) and to create bonds with them. A major news event or economic change can dramatically affect how the public will react or relate to a subject.

Remembering the Human Factor

PR is not only about influencing how people view a particular subject, it is about maintaining a sensitivity to factors that influence people's feelings. Even in these technology-driven times, most business decision-makers prefer to do business with *people* they believe share their values and priorities. This does not mean a PR person must compromise his or her values to land a job or a client. It *does*, however, suggest that when such values are *not* shared, a strong sense of professionalism must prevail in order to provide services a client has a right to expect. Not all doctors share the values of their patients, but all doctors are required to provide services to those who need them to the best of their ability. In a perfect world, creating bonds with one another would be easy. Relating well to a public creates a bond that is good for business.

That clients and executives understand both *what* PR efforts are being undertaken and *why* is important and cannot be taken for granted. Public relations expert Kenneth G. Trantowski notes:

> A real challenge that public relations people have is trying to explain to lay audiences—let alone the management public relations professionals serve—what is it that we do and how we can help management address and solve business problems. . . .
>
> No matter what the priority, in order to become a valuable and actively involved member of the organization's team, a public relations professional must be able to understand and address senior management's concerns, embrace change, and deal with the public relations ramifications of their decisions. One major—and constantly growing—concern is management's need to justify everything from the organization's existence to its procedures.

It is true that, despite the widely covered apparent increase in corporate malfeasance—or at least the perception of it—in the early years of the 21st century, managers are buried in forms (both electronic and paper) that are supposed to address the accountability of every department, what it does and why, as well as the relationship of vendors to the corporation.

Companies commissioning services from other divisions of the company or from companies owned by the parent organization—long a procedure that was encouraged by management—was coming under scrutiny. The cover-your-rear-end document is more important than ever, especially in publicly owned companies.

Executives acknowledge that it becomes increasingly difficult to be bold or dramatic while having to continually justify all previously approved activities and phases of a program, yet it is a fact of life.

A CEO or corporate leader who does not understand how public relations fits in the marketing mix, much less its value, will be hard pressed to explain or justify the program to a board of directors or at a shareholders meeting. For this reason, it is important that PR professionals stay current and keep not only their colleagues informed, but those who lack understanding of the process and could therefore unwittingly undermine its success.

The marketing mix takes advertising and PR in their many forms— events, publications, mail, posters, online, and civic or cause-related networking, and whatever other vehicles help to achieve the objectives of the plan. While business has become increasingly technology-dominated, proven methods that continue to deliver should not be dismissed. Most people who *relate* through personal communication rarely find the system down.

SUMMARY

- The PR plan in combination with other disciplines can often extend and enhance the program's range, depth, and cost-efficiency.
- Public relations professionals understand how to distinguish between what a subject is doing that qualifies as "news" and what is a potential feature story or "filler."
- PR people must evaluate possible risks, such as avoiding talking with the press, and/or only communicating in writing with members of the media who invariably overplay stories or promote controversy.
- PR professionals must aggressively *merchandise* coverage and *leverage* the results of each media encounter into something more.
- Make certain the CEO and other corporate leaders understand public relations and the marketing mix or they will not be supportive of the program when dealing with a board of directors or shareholders.
- It is important that PR professionals keep everyone informed.
- The marketing mix includes advertising and PR in many forms—events, publications, mail, posters, online, and civic or cause-related networking, and other vehicles to achieve its objectives.

References

Thomas L. Harris, *Marketer's Guide to Public Relations* (New York: John Wiley & Son, 1991).

Judith Rich, "Public Relations and Marketing," in Philip Lesly, Ed., *Lesly's Handbook of Public Relations and Communications*, Fifth Edition (Chicago: McGraw-Hill/Contemporary, 1998).

Kenneth G. Trantowski, "Positioning Public Relations with Management," Robert L. Dilenschneider, ed., *Dartnell's Public Relations Handbook*, Fourth Edition (Chicago: The Dartnell Corporation, 1996).

5

Focusing on the Message

What is the message to be conveyed to the public?

How will it be conveyed in a marketplace crowded with media alternatives and methods?

And with so much being said in so many places, *why* should people care?

Concentrating on the Real Market

In the excitement over producing a dazzling print ad or a high-powered commercial with celebrities and special effects or staging an event that will be remembered after its purpose is long forgotten, many marketers forget that the point of the program is to create awareness of and support for a particular product, service or subject. The message (if it makes it into the effort at all) gets lost or is presented in an environment unnoticed by the target audience.

Columnist and author Joe Cappo noted in his book *The Future of Advertising*:

> Public relations will become more common, if for no other reason than there are more media at PR practitioners' disposal, and it will be easier to obtain exposure for clients than it is to get time on the networks and space in national magazines. Just imagine what the proliferation of regional business publications has done to expand the opportunities for public relations efforts. There are probably more than two hundred of these journals in the United States, compared with only a handful of national business publications.

Yet, because so often clients and organizations do not grasp the importance of focusing on their core massage, building a solid base, and merchandising it to their lasting advantage, they would gladly forego major stories in *Crain's Detroit Business*, *San Diego*, and *Philadelphia* for a half-column reference in prestigious, high-profile publications such as *Fortune* or *Business Week*.

Unrealistic Expectations

Every day, public relations agencies solicit clients and promise to get these clients a story in *The Wall Street Journal* or a spot on *The Today Show*. While a discussion on the ethics of such promises will come later, suffice to say these highly coveted story placements rarely come to pass.

For their part, clients and executives regularly pressure their agencies to secure unrealistic placements in such premier national media with little more ammunition in their arsenals than the fact that their company exists. CEOs and others in senior management must, at least theoretically, be intelligent people to attain the positions they hold.

Yet, amazingly, an otherwise bright person has an exaggerated sense of importance about what he or she is doing when it comes down to what warrants media attention. Some of this can be attributed to the Andy Warhol belief that everyone will get their fifteen minutes of fame at some point, regardless of what they do. It's happened enough times to be closer to reality than just the glib remark everyone assumed it was at the time.

A person or a company's success is generally assumed to be a good thing, but *it is not news*. Nor is being the largest family-owned wallpaper manufacturer in North America the kind of news that routinely bumps profiles of Cameron Diaz, Mary Higgins Clark, or the Secretary General of the United Nations from their spot on the myriad of morning TV news programs.

Agencies and their clients, who should have done their homework enough to know better, too often have an odd sense of what producers and editors consider to be stories that will catch and hold audience interest. It is true that the range of media choices continues to expand. However, just because media have time and space to fill does not mean they will take anything that is directed to them—or that the public will give the subject its attention—unless a "value message" is clearly in evidence. This is especially the case if the medium and the message are not an appropriate fit.

The developer of a useful new software program or a person who makes guitars or someone who believes the public deserves to know more about the importance of seat belts in baby carriages all have stories that *segments* of the public would be interested in knowing, but those segments do not include the readers of the front page of *The Wall Street Journal*.

In place of the Unique Selling Proposition that is supposed to define the value of a subject, writers of ad copy and press releases presume to catch the interest of editors and audiences with descriptions of products that use words like "exciting" or "explosive" or simply "hot." The presumption is that if something is declared "hot," a producer, editor, or writer will have no choice but to initiate a showcase story around it.

Wrong.

The "What" and the "How" of the Message

The revered communications theorist Marshall McLuhan believed "The medium is the message," meaning that the methods of communicating (particularly television) have a greater influence on the public than the messages themselves. But that does not constitute proof that the message is irrelevant. It is simply another way of phrasing an earlier theory: it's not *what* you say, but *how you say it* that matters. In marketing terms, however, it cannot be an "either/or" issue.

How something is said reflects creative effort and reasoned presentation choices concluded to be most likely to get and hold attention.

What is said is the promise upon which companies, products, or issues often succeed or fail. The Unique Selling Proposition—the value statement—is as important in modern marketing, advertising, and public relations as it was a half century ago when marketers and business leaders began reviewing such issues in scientific terms.

Add to that the matter of *why* people should respond to the message amid the myriad of choices being offered to them.

Perhaps the McLuhan theory held greater currency when electronic media was in its infancy and was a novelty that held the public's fascination because it was something new and different. A more sophisticated public is considerably more discriminating in part because of the proliferation of media. In many homes, offices, and businesses, television is a waiting room diversion or an alternative to background music.

In much the same way many clients ask the unanswerable question about what PR should cost, some clients also ask what the company or organization's message should be. This seems as if it should be perhaps the one statement that members of senior management might want to know before calling in someone to communicate it. Management is, after all, the final authority on what the company stands for and how it should be positioned in the marketplace.

Maybe.

Self-Interest

Very often, senior management will have a surprisingly narrow or limited view of its own operation and can rarely see what it is—or has—in an objective way. Further, while management is the best source regarding what's in the best interests of the company, each segment of the public is collectively asking the company the same question: What's in it for me? The answer will not necessarily be the same for everyone who asks the question.

With all the available alternatives, why should the public decide in favor of a particular entity over all the others? Whether the subject is a company, a product, a brand, organization, or cause, why *that* one?

There can be a long list of reasons, each more noble than the one before, but the term "self-interest" did not invent itself. Ultimately, privately, the public wants some *payback* for the decisions it makes in favor of a brand, an issue, a candidate, an investment, a product . . . or whatever.

That is what the company or organization's message needs to address and public relations professionals should be able to help guide their clients through this process, mindful of what is in the clients' best interests and, just as important, *what will resonate with the public.*

Clarity

Consider the success of the book *Think and Grow Rich* that millions of people purchased more than a half-century ago, but most never read. Its message was right on the cover, in the book's title: Positive thinking will bring a person what he or she wants if they believe in it strongly enough. With a message that clear, people felt they didn't actually *need* to read the book once they grasped its point. Some other examples of message clarity:

- An ad, targeted to people with money problems, begins with the words: *Change your life in 4 minutes.*
- The popular diet promised to lower cholesterol in eight weeks.
- Another plan guaranteed just "10 days to a slimmer you!"

What research told the marketers of these and other programs is that people are looking for something that will *bring impressive results quickly and easily—even effortlessly.* And if it helps improve general health and well being as well, that's added value.

While this might seem a cynical and simplistic approach to serious matters, it must be remembered—and what companies tend to keep forgetting—is what people care about most is not what is best for a product or company, but how or what the product or company offers is relevant to *them.* This can be applied to anything (or anyone) that is the subject of the public relations message, from an urge to be more socially responsible to the purchase of a time-share condominium. The message must be concise and carry a promise of *value to the consumer*—the person to whom the message is targeted.

Making the Message Compelling

Public relations relies on a variety of techniques to influence the attitudes, decisions, and behavior of its target audience or market segment. But the process cannot be undertaken effectively on behalf of a company or organization until the practitioner has defined its message. In short, when attempting to relate to the public, a company should first be clear as to what it stands for and what it wants to say.

In fiercely competitive times, with cable TV channels and Internet sites suggesting an insatiable hunger for content, not everything submitted makes it into print or onto the screen. Producers and editors still require that subjects ideally have *unique* elements, but at the very least have something of interest or value for their readers, viewers, and other consumers—and that it be offered in a way that attempts to suggest something the audience has not seen or heard before.

They still want what's new and newsworthy. PR professionals must aggressively represent the interests of their clients and companies in presenting and interpreting their message in ways that will interest the end user—the public, offering both style and substance, the sizzle and the steak. Being the *best* or the *oldest* or the *largest* producers of English muffins that are "still made the old-fashioned way" is not enough to land a prize media placement.

There are manufacturers of products that diagnose life-threatening diseases and, if more people knew about them, lives might be saved. But even these products and people are rarely seen on news magazine programs or in national magazines because, quite simply, their story was not presented to editors and producers as being interesting enough to hold audience attention. *A story with life-and-death implications was not interesting enough.* It is a good bet that the story was not presented to editors at all or was presented in language so technical that editors and producers believed audiences would not be able to follow it, much less grasp its true importance to them.

Consider an example such as that against the pitch for the one-person company that developed the new software or the woman who wants to be on the news to tell people TV commercials are lowering the intelligence levels of children or the guy who invented a better popcorn popper.

Which story is likely to be scheduled for presentation?

That will depend on which PR spokesperson presents the story best. It's all in the packaging.

Finding the Right Media to Reach Your Public

A company's message needs to be succinct, persuasive, and convincing. To generate media interest in an arena where perhaps hundreds of others are vying for the same space in any given week or month, the message must be particularly interesting.

The perception that publicity is everything is just that—a perception. PR professionals must understand and underscore that publicity is only one avenue of awareness, albeit certainly an important one. A public relations effort to influence a target audience might be accomplished in ways other than publicizing a subject through traditional media.

In any discussion of media, it is worth noting that for nearly a half-century the term *media* meant newspapers, magazines, TV, and radio. Times change. Some people contend that before long the

Internet will be *the* dominant information medium, as well as the primary form of communication. That has already become the case for millions of people, though others insist that when the dust settles and the Internet is fully matured, it will be only one means of informing and communicating, but very likely not *the* means of doing so.

Some 21st-century theorists maintain that every form of communication should be considered *media*. They insist *people talking to each other* must be considered media, as it is indeed a form of communication. Such a position would have been absurd as late as the 1990s, but less than a decade later, people sitting at home, equipped with personal computers and modems were claiming to be journalists or publishers.

The entire media landscape was redefining itself. Many of the world's most respected newspapers and television networks cite online newsletters as their sources—alongside *Time* magazine, *Newsweek*, *The Journal of the American Medical Association*, and the *Harvard Business Review*, conferring equal credibility to all. Researchers measure "hits" as if measuring circulation.

In that context, someone imparting a message to a roomful of people, they say, should regard it as a media venue. Certainly there have always been those who have considered the regular luncheon meetings of members of the National Press Club as about as much a media event as one could stage—communicating with a roomful of reporters, editors, publishers, and broadcasters.

It all becomes relative, as well as eclectic, the form and the forum, fragmented and nearly impossible to measure for effectiveness in every case. It has only recently been given a formal name: word-of-mouth.

Word-of-mouth has long been regarded as a highly effective form of public relations and advertising, and it could be argued that a minister addressing a congregation can be a communication far more influential than a six-column story in the morning paper.

Such examples certainly support the Marshall McLuhan position. Clearly the playing field that communicators once sought to level has become more vast and sprawling with more than a few potentially treacherous turns along the way.

Public relations specialists no longer just pitch stories to editors and producers or develop strategic plans to fit the standards of once predictable media. But no one hires a PR firm to talk to nine people in someone's living room. Big media—with big numbers generating big results—is the only media that matters.

While it's true that has been how the system worked almost from the beginning, the winds have clearly shifted. For example:

- Consider how Starbucks evolved over little more than a decade to create a new category—gourmet coffee for the masses—sold and served in places that are not the traditional restaurant or coffee house or grocery store bakery or gallery.
- Avon products, Amway, Shaklee, Mary Kay Cosmetics, and other successful multi-level marketers, built companies that rival the giants of any industry for size and profitability.
- The Christian Coalition grew in less than a decade to be one of the most powerful and influential forces in fundraising, social issues, and mobilizing support and voters in huge numbers.
- *The Onion* became a successful web site, newspaper, and publisher of several best-selling books.

All of these entities achieved their objectives *without advertising* and with only a moderate and very carefully controlled degree of media exposure, usually radio and direct mail.

What each of these companies or organizations had was a message that resonated with a particular segment of the public. As people in small numbers spread the message, its impact was felt exponentially.

The challenge of influencing a mass audience might be greater and more complex as the public becomes more sophisticated, cynical, or discriminating in an age of innovation and technology. But above all else, a message that makes a promise, provides a value statement, suggests uniqueness is key. Even the wizards who admit they work their magic with mirrors need the right something to reflect.

SUMMARY

- The *message* is the value statement that gives the public a reason to care about the subject of the public relations program.
- Many clients and organizations fail to focus on their core massage, build a solid base, and merchandise it, preferring instead to produce a flashy ad or event and aim for a large audience, even if it's the *wrong* audience.
- CEOs, clients and other executives regularly pressure their agencies to secure placements that are unrealistic relative to the importance of the subject.
- "The medium is the message" means the methods of communicating have a greater influence on the public than the messages themselves.
- *How* something is said, *what* is said, and *why* people should respond to the message are essential elements to a successful PR program.
- A company's message must be succinct, persuasive, and convincing to generate media interest and, in turn, resonate with the public.
- Despite the wide array of media options available, hundreds of subjects are vying for the same time and space in any given week or month. The message must be particularly interesting to connect with editors, producers and the public.

References

Joe Cappo, *The Future of Advertising* (Chicago: McGraw-Hill, 2003).

6

Crafting an Image

The *message* is the definitive statement of what the subject of the public relations program stands for—the literal reason why the public should want to connect with the subject and use it as a starting point from which to pursue a dialog or learn more. It is a "value statement" in that it describes or infers the value in the subject to the members of public.

The *image* is what the majority of the public presumably *perceives* the subject to stand for, based on what the company, organization, or public relations counsel might have learned from discussion, commentary, advertising, direct mail, point-of-sale displays, word-of-mouth endorsements (or criticism), or virtually any other source.

With that noted, public relations is a major factor in how that image comes into focus—and the degree of detail, color, and brilliance of that focus, like beauty, is very much in the eye of the beholder.

Image, Perception, and Reputation

Filmmaker Linda Obst spoke volumes about images and perceptions with just the title of her memoir of Hollywood and the motion picture industry, *Hello, He Lied*. It makes the point that things are not always as they appear to be or are represented to be.

Public relations practitioners are often described as "image makers," and their clients and employers hire them because of a concern for their images—about looking right to the public. Image is synonymous with perceptions, and in the opinion of many, the gap between perception and reality usually exists and can be significant. It is here that public relations specialists have fallen short of excellence.

To assume that perception is not reality is to suggest that a subject's image is a lie. Obviously, that is not always the case and, as a rule, it is hopefully *rarely* the case. It is incumbent upon the PR people to establish and reiterate this point. Not only should the task of creating a positive image be a top priority, but with such a task should go the responsibility of validating the fact that the image is not based on smoke and mirrors, sleight-of-hand, or any of the other clichés that suggest trickery.

Image is also synonymous with *reputation*, a term that implies a level of truth, whereas *image* carries a more superficial connotation, perhaps even illusion. These distinctions are not important. Yet, national public relations agencies have created "reputation management" practices to underscore the perceived seriousness of the issue. No one as yet has created an "image management" practice with the expectation of being taken seriously. Where a company or organization is concerned, as with an individual, it is true that *actions speak louder than words,* but words *do* matter in creating and maintaining a reputation.

The Importance of Consistency

A single event or appearance can project an image, but a reputation is time-tested, usually suggesting a history, a consistency, and a certain degree of predictability in performance or behavior.

Robert L. Dilenschneider, CEO of the public relations firm The

Dilenschneider Group, notes that "unpredictable people undermine their own influence. . . . Leaders derive great strength from their consistency . . . they present a continuous style in everything they do and in all the places they are heard: books, public appearances, personal conversations, press releases, and all other channels."

The Gap, the retail clothing chain, produced a series of television commercials and print ads that conveyed a very contemporary, upbeat image. The ads promoted a certain look and a youthful sense of style that was represented by the latest fashions. But consumers told researchers that upon visiting The Gap stores, the merchandise—and the fashion look presented in the ads—was not to be found—and that what *was* available in the stores conveyed a wholly different (and less stylish) look. In another era, retailers called this the "bait and switch"—an advertising tactic in which a retailer lures people into a store with a virtually irresistible offer of a particularly desirable item, claims it is not available at the present time, and then attempts to sell something else that is considerably less desirable, but is at least in stock and since the customer is already in the store. . . .

But maybe The Gap ads were not intentionally deceptive. Maybe the people who make such decisions for The Gap stores really believed (without benefit of research) that the items were stylish.

Maybe the ads began running before the stores had time to order the merchandise they showed.

Maybe.

It doesn't matter. What matters is that The Gap quickly developed a reputation among younger customers—its core market—that it did not carry the merchandise it showed in its ads.

For marketers, this was actually *two* problems:

1. The reputation for having very fashionable merchandise in ads, but *less* fashionable merchandise in stores.
2. A reputation for running misleading ads.

Overcoming Negativity

Once such perceptions are created, they *can* be changed, but such changes take time and cost a great deal of money that would be better allocated for new marketing programs, not for correcting old mistakes.

Meanwhile, the damage to the company's image over the short-term and to its reputation over the longer term has already been done.

Unfortunately, sometimes such problems can take on a life of their own. For example, when negative reviews appear in the media and are posted on web sites, they become part of an archive that can be revisited whenever someone enters the company or organization's name in an Internet search engine. And that, in turn, creates yet a third problem which, in the words of everyone's first grade teacher, "becomes part of your permanent record and will follow you all through life."

The Power of Images and Brands

A consumer's choice of a popular brand name product over a nor-mally lower priced generic or "house brand" version of the same product is a reflection of the power of marketing and how the con-sumer responds to the popular brand's image.

Another example of the power of a brand is when the name that is the central identifier of the brand has little or nothing to do with the actual design, development, manufacture, marketing, or distri-bution of that brand, as in products that are off-shoots of the fashion industry where designers of clothing license their names as brands for fragrances, jewelry, bedding, home furnishings and the colors of paint. Calvin Klein and Tommy Hilfiger, for example, may truly be renaissance men, but does the public assume these men actually cre-ate jeans, underwear, furniture, fragrances, and all the other prod-ucts that bear their names? More than products they created *brands* and that brand power is certainly evident in the designers' clothing—where labels, which for years were always sewn discreetly *inside* the clothes, are now more often the key to sales success than the designs themselves.

As brand images become more the driver of sales and a "trade-mark look" of a well-known designer is no longer enough—in part because of the many lower-priced copies and knock-offs—legendary designers, top retailers, and virtual unknowns incorporate their logos and often their names not only on the *outside* of their clothes and spin-off products and accessories, but position them without the slightest suggestion of subtlety, wherever it would be most obvious. Anyone who might be wondering if a particular article of clothing might be the work of DKNY, Ralph Lauren, Calvin Klein, Tommy Hilfiger, Burberry, Brooks Brothers, or Abercrombie & Fitch need look no further than the most visible expanse of cloth.

By embracing this trend so willingly, consumers are actually taking a short-cut to achieving a sense of style by wrapping themselves in whatever image the prominent designer or retailer has created and established. As much as buying clothes, consumers are unashamedly buying image.

Commuters waiting on a train platform, while holding a copy of *The Wall Street Journal* in one hand and a take-out, branded Starbucks coffee cup in the other, are making a statement of brand preferences and, at the same time, making a statement about their status and image to their fellow commuters: They choose a newspaper that is not for everyone, but known to be the choice of upscale, literate, more successful people with an interest in business and they can also afford to buy a cup of coffee that costs approximately two-to-three times the price of an "ordinary" cup of coffee. They are buying the *image*.

Corporate Image and Market Research in the New World of Business

Some members of senior management are uncomfortable even discussing corporate image issues, dismissing the subject as superficial and irrelevant to the actual business of business. This suggests a huge lack of understanding of how business has changed through the decades, not uncommon in situations where the same management guides the organization and continues to operate with a comfortable profit margin. They believe that if their public needs what they manufacture and sell and if they continue to meet that need, *image* is not a factor.

But substitute the word *reputation* in place of *image*, and the superficial becomes a serious matter. To many creative, innovative, ambitious, or simply *younger* people in business this seems like an exercise in corporate silliness, but it remains one of the great mysteries of business life and an example of the power—and the *imagery*—associated with a single word.

Research has confirmed for decades that a significant number of people make their final purchase decisions in virtually every product category, from their daily newspapers and the restaurants they choose for lunch to their homes, cars, vacation destinations, and children's schools, based on considerations of image and reputation.

Price, quality, service, warranty, value, and a myriad of other considerations can often be matched point-by-point by major competitors—Coke and Pepsi; Ford and Chevrolet; Budweiser and Miller; United Airlines and American Airlines; Tiffany and Cartier; Wendy's and Burger King. . . . Finally, it is each product's, brand's, or company's image that sets it apart for the consumer.

For so pivotal a consideration, it remains a mystery why the leaders of so many companies and organizations with so much at risk in terms of support and market share, move ahead in the way they do business without the benefit of current market research. Attitudes change. Needs change. A company that is not attuned to those changes and chooses not to ask questions is riding a train on a dangerous track.

Market research is a critically important component in a public relations plan, particularly with regard to creating a corporate image. Unfortunately, many PR planners often skip this step, counting on research developed by the marketing department, outside consultants, or advertising agencies to be available and adequate to their needs. Sometimes that is the case, but when it is not so, to pursue the implementation of a program without first taking the pulse of the market seems a potentially hazardous and expensive course. It is a lot like arriving alone at an event and expecting to see friends there. Instead, many faces are familiar, but you can't remember why. Only, in business, the stakes can be a great deal higher than sitting alone.

Many executives are reluctant to commission research, usually characterizing it as spending money to learn things they already know. Certainly many of these people hold this opinion because they are indeed knowledgeable and expert in their fields, but very often their reluctance is because they believe people assume that they know pretty much all there is to know about a particular market or industry and to request research might suggest that they are out of touch.

In other instances there is a fear that research might very well tell them things they did not know or plan for . . . but *should have.*

To worry about such a situation would be understandable if the executive were ten years old, but competent professionals at the executive level clearly cannot be expected to know all things at all times, which is why so many market research firms exist and prosper. Avoidance of taking a measurement of the market for reasons relating to ego is a very dangerous position to be in. Much of what makes marketing and public relations interesting and challenging is that, even for the best and the brightest, the learning never stops.

If research provides new insights or changes in attitudes or levels of awareness, this could indicate that some modifications to a plan would improve it. If what is learned confirms or validates what had been assumed, that information should make members, stockholders, employees, media, and securities analysts more confident that the program is well managed.

There is no way to overstate that a company or organization must know its market—the likes and dislikes of its public, special concerns, the extent to which constituents are loyal versus waiting for something better to come along. A well-crafted plan is drawn from inside knowledge of a subject, derived from sources that will be honest, objective, and provide information that will be useful in meeting objectives.

It is not unusual to hear a spokesperson for a company say that the public is excited about the company's new products, services, or message and wonder where the spokesperson is getting such information since rumors (or common knowledge) indicate the very *opposite* to be the case. The spokesperson in such circumstances is obviously trying to put a good face on a bad situation and in saying what management wants to hear is trying also to portray the company in a favorable light by engaging in the worst kind of spin, perhaps taking a single (or minority) opinion and suggesting it is a reflection of public sentiment.

This practice is sometimes referred to as the "everybody knows" variety of research, in which the only true science employed is exaggeration. In this example the spokesperson is not only not convincing anyone that what he or she is saying is correct, but is causing people to reflect on how much the illogical statement is out of sync with reality.

A real-life illustration of such an incident occurred when a tobacco company spokesperson told a reporter from a national publication that the company's very expensive corporate advertising campaign describing its philanthropic activity was being well received, with the result being that the public thought of the company in very favorable terms. A sad irony is that in the very same edition of the publication that carried the spokesperson's remarks was an article reporting on a new survey in which the public ranked the tobacco company 59 out of 60 on a list of socially responsible companies.

The Value of Genuine Market Research

Executives who choose not to spend money on research studies occasionally find arguments that seem to justify their decisions—when research generated for publicity purposes is interpreted by the media and some members of the public as frivolous or even silly.

For example, a major article that appeared on the front page of the features section in a Sunday edition of the *Chicago Tribune*, under the headline, "You really *are* what you eat," asked the questions, "Are you sweet? Saucy? Hot stuff? Condiments offer clues to who you are."

The accompanying story treated sauces, salad dressings, and condiments as providing true insights into consumers' personalities, as well as their tastes. (People who prefer French dressing are shy and less witty than others; those who like blue cheese dressing are middle-aged males who think they are witty and are concerned about exercise, but are more likely to watch TV. Someone who likes horseradish is a risk-taker, adventurous, and daring.)

While at first glance the story seems like good fun, a nice piece on sauces and dressings, and just a step down from the newspaper's daily horoscope column, its sponsor, the Association for Sauces and Dressings, claims it offers true and accurate information.

According to the newspaper, "Surveys such as this one commissioned by the association linking personalities and preferences for salad dressings, confirm that you can tell a lot about people by the condiments they keep."

The same article quotes a category manager of a food company insisting, "Yellow mustard is fun, inclusive and family-oriented, whereas a Dijon person is slightly more sophisticated and likes to cook."

This spokesperson, according to the newspaper's account, "identified a brown mustard person as someone 'serious about a good meal and a good sandwich.'"

Obviously most people reading a story such as this in one of the most prominent newspapers in the United States would find it good for a few laughs. Others, having perhaps a bit less of a sense of humor, would take it as evidence that market research is not to be taken seriously.

An unfortunate reality is that many of the most respected and successful companies in the world pay huge sums of money each year to "research" companies that generate this type of data, insist it is based on "science" and diminish respect for serious psychographic studies. Such companies are a later incarnation of the "trend shops" of the 1980s that positioned themselves as research firms, claiming to be able to observe teenagers and predict the types of products they would buy in the year ahead. Despite having an uncanny ability to convince sophisticated business leaders to pay them millions, their accuracy was approximately equal to that of TV psychics.

There is validity and integrity to psychographic research, which measures how people respond to specific social and cultural influences, but mustard preferences rarely, if ever, find their way into such studies.

Serious research can be entertaining, but its conclusions should actually provide information of value to a company or organization. For example, a study, sponsored by the *Nation's Restaurant News* and conducted by the Retail Intelligence Group, surveyed 1,003 consumers nationwide, who eat breakfast, lunch or dinner away from home at least twice a week. The study showed that restaurant patrons are "generally comfortable eating familiar foods, but different age groups respond to food in totally different ways." The theory behind the study was that more restaurants understand their customers' generational differences, the more they can target their efforts—in menus, marketing, pricing, etc.

After surveying seniors, baby boomers, members of Generation X, and teenagers, the study concluded that, "Perhaps the most important finding was the more familiar and trusted brand names a restaurant offers, the more consumers believe it (the restaurant) really cares about its customers. Some 46 percent of those surveyed expressed that belief."

Survey respondents also said they felt brand names used in restaurants was an indication that:

- The restaurant cares about its customers: 46% overall; leading group: teens, 53%
- Offers better quality food: 42% overall; leading group: Gen X, 46%
- Is upscale: 38% overall; leading group: teens, 43%
- Is a place you'll go: overall: 36%; leading group: teens, 43%
- Can charge more for these items: 26% overall; leading group: Gen X, 28%

More than one respondent in four said they would pay more for a meal or beverage that included their favorite brands.

Older baby boomers and seniors—the over 50 group—are more receptive to brand products in a restaurant. About one in three would be more interested in dining at a specific restaurant if it offered more food and beverage brands. Perhaps surprisingly, the *teen* group, once inside the restaurant and scanning the menu, is more likely to show the greatest enthusiasm for brands. Some 69% of those polled said they are most influenced by food brands when ordering. Nearly three out of four said they seek branded foods to satisfy taste cravings.

And 80% of teens said that, "at restaurants they go to regularly, they would be willing to try new dishes if they were made with brand name products they know and trust."

According to the study

- Teens, more than any other generation group, are influenced to revisit restaurants because they have seen grocery-branded food and beverage items served there.
- Juice brands are most important to Generation Y and least important to baby boomers (Top brand: Tropicana).
- Coffee brands in restaurants are most important to seniors and least important to teens (Top brand: Folgers).
- Known brands of bottled water, particular brands of ice cream, and popular brands of soft drinks are most important to teens, least important to seniors (The brands of choice were Evian, Breyer's ice cream, and Coca-Cola, respectively, according to the survey).
- Specific brands of tea are most important to older baby boomers and least important to members of Generation Y (Top brand: Lipton).
- Condiment brands are most important to baby boomers and least important to teens (Top brand: Heinz).
- Cheese brands are most important to teens and least important to Generation Y (Top brand: Kraft/Velveeta).
- Meat brands are most important to seniors and least important to teens (Top brand: Jimmy Dean).
- In the chicken/poultry category, the brand was most important to seniors and least important to Generation Y (Top brand: Tyson).
- Bread/rolls brands are most important to older baby boomers and least important to Gen X (Top brand: Wonder Bread).
- Among grains, brands are most important to baby boomers and least important to teens (Top brand: Uncle Ben's).

Upon reviewing the results of the survey, one food industry consultant commented, "People love novelty in watches, but not in food. Food is emotional and this is a real challenge in food service."

An added observation: baby boomers admit to being more conscious of status, such as the images associated with certain brands. Generations X and Y claim to be less concerned with brand image, but their buying patterns contradict this, especially in the categories of clothing and shoes. If the survey is to be believed, these groups are every bit as brand-conscious as their elders when it comes to foods.

Estimates are that there are more than 75 million baby boomers, 60 million seniors, some 70 million members of Generation X, and nearly 60 million in Generation Y.

Many people in management, particularly in the food industries, though in other fields where generational marketing is a factor, would find such data as this not only fascinating, but extremely useful in the decision making process. In preparing a public relations program, an understanding of consumer tastes and preferences is invaluable.

An objective of research is to provide information a company or organization can use to understand its consumer and constituent base and improve itself, and, accordingly, improve its position with its public.

It is also a reality check.

If research indicates the public has a problem with a company, its products or service, corporate conduct, positions on social issues, how it interacts with its various constituent groups, the credibility of its spokesperson, or any of a myriad of other issues, the company's management should be aware of this before it gets the news the hard way—a story placed by a disgruntled employee, a discrimination complaint, etc.

If the company is perceived as much better, much worse, or absolutely indistinguishable from its competitors—basically believed to have no corporate image at all—the management should know that too. Whether it chooses to take steps to change public perceptions or to ignore the information completely is management's choice, but it should at least be an informed choice.

Management could ignore any negative criticism and risk the consequences as several major airlines and other large corporations chose to do throughout the 1990s, only to incur the wrath of employees, creditors, and customers who, by the start of the 21st century, decided they'd had enough. Few were sympathetic to airline management and, as a result, the image of the entire airline industry suffered.

The very concept of relating to the public is an interactive proposition. A company or organization, through effective public relations at all levels—employees, investors, customers, regulators, the media—seeks to influence attitudes and decisions, but it must also *listen* to what its various publics have to say. Clearly, at times what the public wants or expects is unrealistic, and company representatives can remain detached and hope criticism goes away or they can provide explanations as to *why* such expectations are unrealistic and offer a counterproposal or idea that will tell the public that the company cares and wants to remain on its good side. In doing so, the company and its management stands a much better chance of earning the public's respect and good will than if it had done nothing or responded with a show of "attitude."

Research is a valuable tool for public relations practitioners at virtually every stage of a program—planning, monitoring its effectiveness, and certainly in evaluating the results.

Using Research to Uncover the Facts

Critics have said not only that research will tell you what you already know, but that it can be manipulated and interpreted to produce whatever conclusions the researcher desires. Both of these statements can be true in some situations. Research involves a human component, and at times, under different circumstances, people do lie, mislead, and manipulate the truth. Experience has shown that in most instances, truth emerges and returns to bite these people in the worst places.

As in the example of the tobacco company noted earlier, to insist something is true when all evidence and common knowledge runs to the contrary—even citing the results of a bogus study—will not make something untrue true. A company spokesperson insisting a company is appreciated, admired, and respected when independent surveys and news reports tell an opposite story will not result in the company being appreciated and respected. Organizations that have manipulated information in the past to create a conclusion favorable to their positions find the result to be only further damage to their credibility and reputation.

At times people are not truthful when answering researchers' questions, providing instead the responses they think the researchers want or offering comments they feel will make them appear more intelligent or otherwise better informed. This is especially true in internal corporate surveys where employees are asked for their opinions of management or their co-workers and find they fall from favor if they offer even "constructive" criticism. Professional research organizations are aware of such situations and their potential for providing faulty information and they have the skills to cut through misinformation and interpret tentative responses.

Positive information collected from surveys and focus groups can be more than research when it is incorporated into a company or organization's story, such as noting an extraordinary customer satisfaction rating or a high rate of referrals from long-time supporters and sometimes even referrals from competitors.

Creating an image, maintaining an image, or *changing* an image requires creativity and skill, but the ability to succeed in such an effort depends to an enormous degree on the accuracy and reliability of the information that underlies and drives the plan.

Companies and organizations need to know:

- What is the profile of the public or segment of the public that is the target of the company or organization's effort?
- What matters most to this target public in terms of its expectations of a company or organization it chooses to do business with?
- What does this targeted public—customers, former customers, potential customers, regulators, stockholders, potential investors, employees, the media, or other entity— think of the company on its own and relative to competitors? Each of the groups listed brings a potentially different perspective and different concerns to evaluating the subject.

- How does the subject measure alongside rivals or competitors in terms of perceived integrity, experience, credibility, and dependability?
- Is the subject considered innovative, solid, predictable, or boring? Does it matter? (Even companies or organizations regarded as boring or predictable are often rated high on integrity, quality, and dependability.)
- Is the public more concerned about price or the perception of quality, value or image?
- Does the public know or care where the company or its management stands on social responsibility issues?
- If any members of the public swore they would never do business with the company again, what happened to make them feel that way?
- Has or would anyone recommended the company or its products or services to a friend?
- How is the company perceived by or among its competitors? (Even within business and industry, some among others are widely regarded as setting the standards—the best or the worst—in the business.)
- If the subject is not a company or organization, but a person, a cause, or issue, where does the public stand on a scale of *not interested at all* to *strongly opposed* or *strongly supportive*?

These are only some of the questions and types of questions that market research can answer—and no image campaign should be undertaken without this information.

Taking Action after the Facts Are in

If a company learns or confirms it has an excellent image with the public, it can exploit that point and build on it—making it even better, using it to enhance its equity position, increasing its recognition of loyal customers, supporters, and employees.

If, on the other hand, a company learns from its research that its public has some less than positive—perhaps even extremely *negative*—feelings or perceptions about it, then it would certainly be in the company's best interests to set about changing those perceptions.

Public relations professionals, once they define the nature and degree of a client or company's negative perceptions, can develop a plan to specifically address them. But this issue of *nature and degree* is extremely important. In some instances, such as immediately after a company is the subject of a devastatingly negative story in a newspaper, magazine, or TV report, a company will perceive that it needs to shore-up its image and launch an expensive campaign—when, in fact, its problem was not with its image but only with that one story.

To launch a high profile initiative could be a huge overreaction, bringing additional attention to a negative story that much (or most) of the public might have been unaware of. If the basis of the negative story is correct, however, it should be for management and the PR experts to determine if the situation is isolated, widespread and ongoing, or perhaps a problem that has already been resolved. In any event, the importance of having reliable information regarding public perceptions before making significant business decisions and budget commitments cannot be overstated.

And if research reveals that in fact a company has *no image*—that awareness of who the company is and what it does is extremely low—the objectives of the proposed campaign become more obvious.

It is absolutely possible for an organization to be successful, self-sustaining and profitable, but to keep such a low corporate profile that it is unknown outside of the small circle to which it provides its service. In terms of its image, the company might as well be a generic product in a supermarket—there, but largely unnoticed. When a retailer wants to sell more of a generic product, the strategy and tactics run toward brightening-up the packaging, moving it to a more visible position, and bringing it to the attention of a larger public that might not have previously considered the product because it was unaware if it.

Types of Marketing Campaigns

Even among management, distinctions related to marketing campaigns are not always clear, but they are important distinctions nonetheless:

- *Corporate* programs focus on a company or organization, its management, strengths, history, size, mission, and reputation. This is the area of greatest concern to financial analysts, investors, labor, regulators, and prospective merger or acquisition partners.
- *Product* or *brand* programs put the emphasis on that which a company produces, manufactures, distributes or markets to its public. Consumers, vendors, and business-to-business companies are most interested in these programs—in relating to what the company actually has and offers.
- *Image* programs (or *corporate image* programs) are often among the most effective and enduring, but least understood approaches by management executives. This is in large part because corporate decision-makers are accustomed to evaluating facts, but image programs aim for an appeal to emotions and rely less on facts to achieve this. The objective of a typical image campaign is to make the subject seem anywhere from very interesting to irresistible and to influence how the public *feels* about the subject, often in unquantifiable terms. When the public indicates that it *likes, loves, respects, admires,* or *appreciates* a product, company, organization, or individual, it is difficult to immediately measure the impact of such feelings, but they tend to be very good for business, particularly over a long period of time. For someone to say he or she has "always liked" a particular company or product is a stronger endorsement than to simply like it at a given time and that translates to brand loyalty, brand equity, greater stability, and more business over time. All constituent groups are concerned about this affect, though some people, particu-

larly on the financial side, are uncomfortable with their inability to measure feelings as a budget line item.

Creating Imagery with Words

There is a lot of truth to the old expression goes that "a picture is worth a thousand words." The highly successful Marlboro cigarette ads for years showed only brilliant color photographs of a cowboy in wide, panoramic scenes set in the great outdoors, occasionally on horseback, mostly appearing to be doing nothing. The ads, without the standard 100 words of ad sales copy, drew upon people's own fantasies and a sense of what it might be like to be in a place such imagery suggested—open spaces and freedom. The cowboy was the embodiment of rugged individualism and self-reliance. No words were needed.

Newport, another successful cigarette brand, was less at home on the range but loved the water. Its ads, again with little or no copy, presented scenes of young people enjoying themselves at the beach, relaxing beside a stream, approaching a waterfall. . . .

Most fashion and fragrance ads succeed by putting elegant clothes on beautiful, often exotic, frequently mysterious, apparently uninhibited, wildly self-assured (or delicate and seemingly vulnerable) models. Most ads have no copy at all, only a logo or a designer's name. The idea is to invite the viewers of the ads to step inside the magazine, newspaper, billboard, transit poster, or mailer and to *see themselves in this picture*—to imagine themselves taking on the imagined lives of the people in the ads—to be free like the cowboy, carefree like the fun-loving kids at the beach, passionate and self-indulgent like the fashion and fragrance models . . . from the word "imagine" come away with "image" and feel it, experience it, enjoy it, absorb it, embrace it.

These often very expensive, highly artistic examples of photographic art in advertising convey all a company may want to say about its subject in few or no words. The photographer's imagery helps to create a brand image.

Rugged masculinity, taming the untamed west, *think of Marlboro.*

Summer at the beach, clean fresh air, *think of Newport*.

Elegant, sensual, powerful, passionate, *think of* <u>(insert any of about a hundred designer brands of clothing or fragrance here)</u>.

More conservative clients and company executives tend to react to suggestions of mounting an image campaign with a term that is itself rich in imagery: harrumph.

This is the part of management that wants to see facts, benefits, advantages clearly spelled out with percentages and dollar signs in bold type, and discount coupons or trial offers used as the hooks to bring in business *now*. Don't ask a consumer to "imagine" anything—tell them what you are going to tell them, then tell them, and then tell them what you just told them.

Despite the enormous success of an approach that uses strong visual imagery to convey a message powerfully, there will always be executives in the room who don't understand the concept. What, after all, do mountain ranges and canyons or beaches or streams have to do with selling cigarettes? Why would anyone stick the surgeon general's warning on a picture of a waterfall? And if we have to pay the media for all that space, how about 200 words on how terrific the product is!

The short answer is that some people cry at movies and laugh at pratfalls and love classical music . . . and some don't. When research determines what consumers like and what will trigger a positive response, the marketer's efforts should be geared to appealing to those *likes* as directly as possible with as few encumbrances as possible.

So the photo is very effective. And it may indeed take the place of a thousand words to convey the message the company wants to send.

But what about public relations, where the PR specialist does not control the space in the magazine or newspaper where the company's story will appear? Can a photograph included in a press kit achieve the same powerful level of imagery conveyed in a billboard above the downtown shopping district? What about the care devoted to developing message points, making value statements, and offering a unique selling proposition?

Certainly the cover of the press kit, catalog, annual report, or brochure should attempt to address the point of conveying or reinforcing a corporate image at every opportunity—and if a high profile image ad campaign is running, collateral materials, as well as the press kit that collects them, should reflect that same look and imagery. But for an overall PR strategy, depending solely on photography to establish a position and drive it home is not advisable.

The fact is, the truism about the photo and the thousand words works equally well in reverse. That is: sometimes a *word* is worth a thousand pictures. Automakers learned this decades ago when they began seriously examining the value inherent in their product names. "Chevette" said nothing to anyone, but the *Impala* was graceful, sleek, and fast. The Plymouth "Belvedere" suggested mid-range boredom, but the *Fury* was power unleashed.

Through the years, many cars came to look exactly like other cars, but the ones people chose to buy had names that conjured images the car buyers wanted—images beyond anything drivers were likely to actually get to experience—*Explorer, Expedition, Caravan, Navigator, Bronco, Range Rover. . . .*

The government of the United States brought in people who understood the power of imagery. Battles and wars were more than that; they were *Operation Desert Shield, Operation Dessert Storm, Operation Iraqi Freedom. . . .*

A law that drew the wrath of civil libertarians as it *limited* certain activities and allowed access to otherwise private information was dubbed the *Patriot Act,* and an action that lessened environmental controls was called the *Clear Skies Initiative.* Whatever one might think of government officials or politicians of any particular bent, it is nonetheless interesting that after decades of criticizing Madison Avenue's methods of influencing the public, politicians have recognized how effective those methods can be and have applied them in the most aggressive ways.

Terms such as institute, foundation, collective, cooperative, and think tank—even when representing an organization of one or two people—conveys an image and a mental picture of a group with suggested intelligence, power, and depth with just a single word.

The words *liberal* and *conservative*, as polarizing as they have become, speak volumes to groups on both sides of an issue or cause.

In a non-political context, terms such as *free-spirited, liberated, humanitarian, independent, socially conscious, humanist, new age,* and *outside the box* are examples of small words that create large pictures. The images those pictures inspire could be quite different from one person to another, which allows people to accept and interpret imagery within their individual comfort zones.

Creating a Corporate Image That Builds Bonds and Brands

Some people believe that putting the focus on image in the context of business is frivolous and unnecessary for a company that offers a good product at a good price to a well-identified market, and that might be true—for those people. Every business has to believe in the program it develops. But to define a brand, product, company, or an individual with an image that goes beyond facts and the required value statement, and aims to reach the public on an emotional level, is an ambitious idea, well grounded in the principles of good business.

A company studies its research and determines that a large percentage of the public it wants to reach lists social responsibility as high on its list of concerns. So the company agrees to underwrite the expenses of running a homeless shelter or a food pantry in its home community or to support an environmental program or other good cause, seeking to set itself apart from competitors and promote an image of itself that resonates with the public.

But that image must be true to the subject. Some companies advertise that they will exchange or replace merchandise for any reason or no reason; others take an "all sales are final" attitude. Obvious and known polluters won't be very convincing in press releases insisting they care about the environment. To be concerned about an image is to be concerned about how the public perceives a given subject. That subject—a company, organization, or individual—cannot be indifferent to service, ethics, and the public good and claim it cares about its image.

Warranties, liberal exchange policies, free delivery, early bird specials, discounts for seniors and students, free parking, gift wrapping, courtesy vans, extra perks for families (coloring books, caps, T-shirts, kids-stay-free at hotels), priority seating for frequent customers are all examples of ways that various businesses seek to shape their images and keep people coming back. Banks over-focused on the idea of personal bankers and a variety of VIP plans and customers realized that virtually every customer was being told they had special status and the status concept was meaningless. A better approach might have been just to say, "Every customer is a VIP customer."

But as many banks experienced problems in the 1990s, instead of aggressively promoting programs to attract more customers and encourage new business development, they eliminated community good will programs as cost-cutting measures, began charging for services that were previously free, and business declined even further.

As the air went out of the technology balloon and huge numbers of companies were in trouble, the public witnessed an avalanche of information about company closings, downsizing, and cutbacks of every sort. PR people were pitching stories that tried to either put the best face on a bad situation—such as how their clients and companies were not affected by the economic downturn—or find a way to exploit the headlines of the day, such as by reporting how their clients and companies were struggling, but valiantly pressing on in an economy that someone else had messed up.

These are both adherents of the "any publicity is good publicity" philosophy of public relations, which offers no one a reason to want to do business with them. People like to wear the caps and T-shirts with the names of winners, not *whiners*. Creating a good image involves connecting with people on terms favorable to them.

Consider the issues and qualities that are important to the targeted segment of the public. Think about the Unique Selling Proposition, about what makes the subject different enough and important enough that the public should care about it—and should *want to care about it.*

Now think about the words and pictures that convey the message that best connects the company or organization to the public. Reflect that message in every aspect of the program—literature, press releases, event participation, sponsorships, white papers, speeches, ads . . .

Be aggressive and initiate contact. In competitive times, people will not likely come around asking what companies stand for when so many companies are willing to be defined by that information out front.

Pretty much every company or organization or supporter of a cause or issue covets the designation "most talked about" if it is applied in a positive way. The method of earning that description is not to continue coveting it, it's to start talking.

SUMMARY

- The *image* is what the public *perceives* the subject to stand for.
- A consumer's choice of a popular brand name product over a generic or "house brand" product reflects the power of marketing and the consumer's response to the popular brand's image.
- Research indicates people make their final purchase decisions based on considerations of image and reputation.
- Executives are often reluctant to commission important market research because they believe it is assumed that they should already know all there is to know about their particular market or industry.
- An objective of research is to collect information that can be used to understand a consumer or constituent groups and improve a company or organization's position with its public. It is also a reality check.
- A business must believe in its program and create an image that goes beyond the value statement to reach the public on an emotional level.
- An image must be believable relative to its subject and marketers must be aggressive in promoting that image when initiating contacts.

References

Robert L. Dilenschneider, ed., "Public Relations: An Overview," in *Public Relations Handbook,* Fourth Edition (Chicago: The Dartnell Corporation, 1996).

Sue Vering, "You really are what you eat" *Chicago Tribune,* June 22, 2003.

"Generational Preferences and Food Brands," a 2002 study sponsored by the *Nation's Restaurant News* and conducted by the Retail Intelligence Group of Tampa Florida.

7

Taking Stock: Understanding Investor Relations

Under usual circumstances, the language of public relations is not terribly complicated. The idea of developing a strategy, writing a press release, generating awareness, pitching a story to the media, delivering a speech, or preparing for an interview are all concepts that are self-explanatory or can be easily comprehended. The markets, most particularly the securities industry, are a world unto themselves with its own language and rules. To develop an investor relations program, it is helpful to have a sense of what this other world is about.

Investor Relations: Not PR As Usual

Investor relations (IR) is a very specialized form of public relations. While the objectives may be similar to those of some other types of PR programs—principally to provide information and influence decision-making—there are legal considerations that require specific knowledge that is not essential to the PR representative of other types of privately owned organizations. The operative term here is "privately owned"—when a company is owned outright by a person, a family, a group of investors, or another company, as opposed to the company whose stock is traded over-the-counter, on the NASDAQ trading system, or on one or more of the stock exchanges trading around the world.

Communications that result in members of the public buying or selling stock in a public company—or believing they are in possession of information that might encourage others to take action regarding a stock—have implications not applicable to other PR activities.

The stock exchanges and the National Association of Securities Dealers (NASD) have rules, as does the Securities and Exchange Commission (SEC). Investor relations people need to know these rules.

At the start of the year 2003, some reports estimated that as many as 70 percent of the people in the United States were "in the market." While that number, if it is accurate, certainly represents a huge percentage of the public, a closer look reveals that a large percentage of that 70 percent, particularly smaller investors, are owners of shares in a variety of mutual funds. While owners of mutual funds certainly qualify as being "in the market," it is a position distinctly different from owning hundred of thousands of shares of stock in one or more companies.

Other people only own stock in the companies they work for and, in many cases, they have received the stock as part of their compensation packages. And that stock usually has certain restrictions, the most common of which is that it cannot be sold until a specific date or anniversary. In other instances, the stock might be held in trust accounts that have other types of restrictions attached.

In many cases, employees, executives, and other investors have options—the right to buy a specific number of shares of stock at a fixed price within a fixed period of time—and information that affects the value of the stock will have a similar impact on these options.

But regardless of how many people actually own stock or under what circumstances, the responsibilities of the investor relations specialist need to be taken very seriously for more than the usual reasons having to do with professionalism. Theirs are not publicity programs that compare the various virtues of brick to aluminum siding or reveal the types of people who choose brown mustard over yellow. If an IR person seems somewhat more humorless than the press agent, it is for good reason. People's life savings or retirement accounts might be invested in the stock of companies the IR professional is representing, and the information released, more often than not, has to do with what that investment is worth.

There are also major distinctions between the types of communications a company can and will disseminate when it first decides to go public (issue stock for sale for the first time) and the ongoing process once that has been achieved.

The ongoing communication between a company's management and its shareholders is guided by a different set of specific requirements as to what must be reported and at what intervals. Some companies go well beyond the required reports in an effort to maintain better-than-good relations with stockholders and to create a sense of stability both in how the company represents itself and in its stockholder relationships.

But there's another reason for promoting stronger relationships between stockholders and stock issuer, particularly in the case of mutual funds. That reason is *redemption*—of the non-religious variety.

Just as owners of shares of stock in a company watch the daily (and sometimes *momentary*) reports of gains and losses and will sell the stock at what looks like a profitable time to limit losses, owners of mutual fund shares check *their* closing prices and will sell—or *redeem*—fund shares for the same reasons.

Fund managers are aware that a huge number of redemptions in any given day, particularly if the fund has declined in value, is likely to trigger *further* declines and loss of value. So just as stability is important to owners and issuers of stock, funds and investors in the funds understand that a steady flow of communication with shareholders by letter, e-mail, newsletters, alerts, reports, broker communications, and through the media, results in a better informed and, thus, less trigger-happy investor who might impulsively sell on the slightest price movement in the stock or fund.

The IR and PR Process for an IPO

When a company's owner decides to take the company public, the pivotal event is the initial public offering (the IPO)—the first time investors are given an opportunity to own part of the company. The process begins with the pre-registration planning stage and ends with the closing of the offering.

Coordinating PR and IR Efforts

In the pre-registration stage the investor relations person's (or people's) work is rather mechanical, though ongoing parallel public relations efforts are likely continuing in order to keep awareness and interest in the still privately-owned company high.

It is extremely important at this time that IR and PR be carefully coordinated for two major reasons. First, PR efforts should be attempting to engender positive feelings toward the company and present a shining image, while being mindful that regulators will be noting the activities of the company and its representatives, making certain that these activities are appropriate and within the limits of acceptability as registration draws nearer. Second, a company only has one initial public offering, and if it goes badly, that will become part of its history and the public record, noted by researchers, regulators, and others in the investment community perhaps forever after.

During the registration stage the company's directors authorize the IPO, underwriters assemble to begin their work, and the lawyers and accountants complete the necessary filings under procedures set down by the Securities and Exchange Commission.

The Business Plan

A public relations plan is extremely important to keeping a program on track and on budget. How the PR plan dovetails with the organization's overall marketing plan is also extremely important. Certainly, the business plan is essential to setting up, focusing and funding the operation, but at no time is a business plan more essential than as the company begins to go public. It is a pivotal document that presents the company, its management, products, market, present and future in a single document that must stand up to intensive scrutiny.

As with a marketing or PR plan, the length of the business plan of companies will vary widely. In the 1990s, the proliferation of "dotcom" companies often began with some presenting business plans in fewer pages than some companies devote to internal memos. A business plan should include minimally:

- Statement of business objectives.
- Clear descriptions of products and services.
- A competitive analysis and comparison with *specific dollar value and market share data.*
- A total market analysis—including history and growth, current status, and future projections both short-term and long-term.
- A positioning strategy.
- A marketing plan.
- Management profile in detail, emphasizing accomplishments and competitive strengths.
- Detailed financial information covering all real and potential costs allocated for research, development, fixed and variable operating expenses, benefits costs, licensing, legal, marketing, and management fees.

It is also recommended that the business plan provide an "executive summary" that offers a concise overview toward the beginning of the document, detailing the highlights of the company's story. Such a summary might be only two to five pages and present:

- The Company: A brief paragraph or two describing exactly what the subject company is and does.
- The Opportunity: A concise description of why the company expects to be successful and profitable and what need or desire it addresses.
- The Total Market: The size and characteristics of the real and potential universe in which the product will be positioned and compete.
- The People: Brief profiles of the key individuals whose presence and participation assures the likelihood of the plan succeeding and affords credibility in a competitive environment.

The Objectives and Strategy

Much as with the creation of the overall marketing plan and the public relations plan within it, formulating a strategy and outline is important to keeping efforts focused and coordinated, from pre-registration through completion of the IPO to the emergence of the organization in its final form as a public company.

The objectives of such an effort typically would be to communicate the company's message to the financial community in particular and to the public (prospective investors) in general, and to establish a presence through ongoing communications with specific designated publics.

The Pre-Registration Phase

Some investor relations professionals recommend formulating and implementing the plan to the greatest degree possible *before* the beginning of the registration process. Since under normal circumstances lawyers, accountants, and governmental agencies are not usually accused of moving at the speed of light, this is a well-considered recommendation.

In reality, if a company is at some point considering going public, gearing the public relations efforts to that ultimate conclusion is useful and logical. PR people can "precondition" the market among prospective investors by keeping the company visible, promoting a sense of its being aggressive and active, and creating a positive corporate image.

To create goodwill in high-profile situations is to have a public more favorably disposed to one day investing in the company than if it had chosen to be not only privately held but *private* in presenting itself to the investment community or the market at large. Investment analysts are sensitive to public sentiment, recognizing the value of a company depends in no small part on how it is perceived (loved, hated, ignored) by the public.

Good PR is good for business, but for an IPO to be announced at some point in a company's future, it is essential.

But once the actual process gets underway, the rules of the game abruptly change. The SEC requires a moratorium on any activities that could be construed as conditioning the market. During this period marketing efforts virtually come to a halt.

During pre-registration a process known as "pre-registration house cleaning" takes place and the company undergoes a makeover of sorts, from the kind of organizational structure that might be fine for a privately owned company (which would be any kind of structure the owner wanted) to a type required of a public company—typically more suitable and responsive to its investors and secure from such improprieties as insider trading.

Articles of incorporation are revised to reflect the organization's new status; financial reporting methods and controls are developed or revised as needed; employee benefit plans are reviewed; and any outstanding tax issues are resolved. The necessary policies and procedures are adopted.

Investor relations specialists typically have a major role in this process and should also be involved in developing the company's overall communications strategy. The program should involve public relations, financial relations, and a lot of document checking and conversations with lawyers, much of it with the whole world watching (figuratively speaking). The meeting and conference reports that were a nuisance in earlier days are now imperative.

During pre-registration all communications programs should be carefully reviewed (advertising, employee newsletters, public relations fact sheets and handouts, etc.) to make certain that all components of the program conform to an approved communications strategy outline. It is particularly important at this time that everyone involved in the communications process stay "on message" and that both written and spoken communications be carefully managed, until the SEC lifts its restrictions on marketing activities. For this reason many companies use video or PowerPoint presentations to insure consistency and conformity.

Investor relations specialists need to be absolutely clear about statutory prohibitions that dictate the limitations of all activities during both the pre-registration and the registration periods. The company's message—a critical element of any PR program—takes on added importance in presentations to the financial community. Research to determine public and private perceptions of the company or organization's strengths and weaknesses is more valuable to management than at perhaps any other time.

Know what people think of the company and address these perceptions before someone not favorably inclined toward the company does so.

While lawyers and public relations people tend to have a natural adversarial relationship (lawyers are inclined to provide as little information as possible, while PR professionals' whole purpose is built upon disseminating information), this is the time when it is absolutely necessary for them to work closely together and to communicate with each other.

Lawyers need to brief IR and PR people on the applicable securities laws and legal limitations on what can and cannot be said. IR professionals need to know what members of the media and the financial community are going to want to know and get legal guidance in preparing message points and presentations that address such questions within the limits imposed.

In many respects the company's IPO is a more detailed version of a business plan, such as the one an owner of a business might have presented to a bank or investor when seeking a start-up loan. Such basic points as what the company does, the size and scope of the market it seeks to reach, breadth of competition, amount needed to fund a specific range of operations and activities over a specific period of time, short-term and long-term objectives, benchmarks and time line for performance evaluation, organization and management structure and experience of senior managers, existing contracts and commitments—both *to* the company and on the part of the company—and any additional real or potential resources or relevant factors that will contribute to the company's achieving its objectives.

What are the economic and market conditions at the time of the IPO and do they work to the advantage or disadvantage of the company in achieving its objectives?

With the exception of the technology boom of the 1990s, when a seemingly endless number of new businesses were launched and there seemed to be no limit to available funds, most companies historically find their IPOs reach a market preconditioned to view chances for success very conservatively.

The business plan was the document for the banker; the IPO makes the same case on a larger scale, asking more people and institutions to provide the funding to undertake ambitious efforts through their investments, knowing that virtually all new businesses should be viewed as mixtures of risks and opportunities.

The Registration Phase

When the IPO emerges from the pre-registration phase to being "in registration" the company's attorneys have filed its registration statement with the SEC and obtained permission to go forward—technically, the government agency never actually "approves" anything; it issues a document stating that it "does not disapprove" of the effort to go forward—implementing its plan, then closing the initial public offering.

The move from one phase of the process to another (from pre-registration to registration) is not like simply throwing a switch and watching it happen. Ask several lawyers and it is likely they will give several different answers as to when a company is actually "in registration." Its board of directors might hold a meeting and declare it so, or it might issue an intent-to-file press release, or the company may consider that the selection of a principal underwriter, or similar such public declarations constitute being "in registration" and thus subject to disclosure requirements and prohibitions as specified under the Securities and Exchange Act.

The IR Professional's Role in the IPO

Entire volumes are published on the subject of taking a company public or preparing for an initial public offering. They cover every nuance and all the steps, such as preparing the registration statement, managing the due diligence process and investigation, developing necessary additional pertinent documents, reaching agreement among underwriters, preparing sales documents for syndicate members, and generating the myriad of letters, memoranda, other legal forms, and agreements that clearly spell out costs, fees, commissions, and details—from preparing a variety of resolutions from the board of directors as they relate to the IPO to the producing and placement of "tombstone" (formal financial notice) ads for the IPO to appear in newspapers and other media.

This chapter, however, focuses on the role and responsibilities of the investor relations person, assuming that others have decided the company is—or is about to become—a public company and there is a need for someone to fill that role.

If public relations and investor relations were pivotal to the launch of the IPO, nowhere was this more evident than in the obligatory *road shows*, the presentations offered over breakfasts, lunches, dinners, and assorted conference tables, tightly scheduled in key financial centers across the United States.

The objectives of the presentations is to build relationships and enthusiasm for the IPO and the company, showcasing its management as more than names and titles on a prospectus or a registration statement, but rather as savvy, bright, experienced visionaries—or attributing to management whatever qualities are the hot buttons of the financial community. This is an opportunity for an investor relations specialist to excel.

Usually the road show team includes the company's CEO and/or

CFO and members of the underwriting group. It is the investor relations person who must make certain these executives present the company's story in the best possible light, using all the skills and tools that define effective PR: information packets with the prospectus, press releases, and other relevant documents; a properly arranged and lit room with a functioning video player or computer setup, monitor, and functioning sound system such as the group and setting might require, with ample opportunity for personal interaction, all while moving briskly along to stay on schedule.

Here the investor relations specialist is also writer, host, event manager, public information officer, and roadie—sometimes all at once. The critical point is, after the Road Show moves on to the next town, the leave-behind packet of information must be complete, accurate, and represent the best the company can be, and that the Road Show team, particularly the CEO, appear competent and totally buttoned-up.

The know-your-customer rule (in this case, the know-your-audience rule) is key. The IR professional and his or her associates must make certain that the most influential people are present to assure the success of the effort (and ultimately of the IPO) and that the presenters are clear about what these individuals came to the event expecting to hear; what reservations, if any, they might have about the company; and what major issues or concerns must be addressed by the team in order to make the best impression and create a favorable opinion of the company.

It is especially in Road Show situations that one of the most essential skills of the IR/PR professional is put to the test—the ability to think ahead, anticipate needs, and envision in every situation the potential "worst case scenario" and plan accordingly. This really should not require a crystal ball or mystical gift. A clear knowledge of what those attending the session will want to know, besides the obvious information provided, can be determined simply by *asking them* in phone conversations prior to arriving in their towns. Direct questions, such as whether or not they have had a chance to look at the company and is there anything in particular they want the team to be sure to address, will make the connection more meaningful for everyone.

If the overall aim is for the company's Road Show team to appear in control and buttoned-up, it is essential to convey a clear competency, credibility, professionalism and, perhaps above all else, the ability to take charge and solve problems as the company might encounter them. These are issues of *perceptions* and managing perceptions is a key capability of an investor relations/public relations professional.

Managing an Ongoing IR Program

Creating and managing an ongoing investor relations program is important to public companies in that it is a reflection of a well-operated communications mechanism that serves people who have invested money in a company to help it not just survive, but grow and pay a good return on investment. While PR professionals often must painstakingly review with clients and executives *why a program is being implemented and how the company will benefit from it*, an investor relations program is not likely to be mistaken for a publicity stunt. It is a serious information and communications program.

If an investor sells his or her shares in the company when the stock is at a low point, it is a sign of possible reduced value in the company—or *the perception of reduced value*—and the ripple effect from that perception cannot be good for anyone.

The SEC requires newly public companies to file interim reports (called 10Qs) no later than 45 days after the period covered by the report, which shows unaudited financial data and other information reflecting occurrences during the quarter. A more inclusive and comprehensive report, the 10K, is filed annually within 90 days of the end of the company's fiscal year. The 10K is important as it contains descriptions of the company's businesses, property, and financial condition.

While the legal and accounting departments are largely responsible for the preparation of these documents, investor relations people should be involved as:

1. They need to stay current on the company's business and financial status.
2. They are—or *should be*—sensitive to concerns of influentia members of the financial community and the business

press, and might want to elaborate on certain references in the narrative.
3. The reports are filed with a government agency and become public documents.

IR professionals should be prepared for inquiries from stockholders and/or media. Copies of the reports should be sent by mail to the company's list of portfolio managers and analysts.

The Annual Report and Shareholders' Meeting

The company's annual report, in addition to being a legally required document, offers a versatile platform for advancing an image and influencing decision-makers, even when the numbers aren't all good.

Many annual reports are six-figure projects (even before printing costs). Lush photography shows the company's facilities and management in scenes that suggest a story of operational strength—a living history of a company in motion, projecting an image of power, energy, and success.

A page for the president's message and another for the chairman's letter provide opportunities in a controlled editorial environment, with a tone of confidence and competence, to address directly shareholders, potential shareholders, financial managers, brokers, the media, employees, other potential partners in business or ventures, and an unlimited array of other possible groups and individuals. The annual report does indeed include the company's financial statements, but it is also an elegant corporate image brochure, designed to create a positive impression and advance an image.

And sometimes the report makes a sharp turn in the other direction. Many companies send a message to analysts, brokers, and shareholders that the company's management runs a lean and mean operation. No color photography or heavy, glossy paper stock—just a message about a very serious company that holds down costs wherever possible and has its priorities aligned on the side of the investors. Such a presentation is itself a form of corporate image building, only it is selling an image positioned differently.

The look and tone of the annual report should not be an isolated positioning statement but should be consistent with the image of the company, reflected in literature, its web site and anywhere else where the image is presented visually.

The annual meeting is normally the physical drop-off point and official release date for the company's annual report, though the vast majority of annual reports are mailed to shareholders, brokers, analysts, and the media on a specific date and then disseminated as a document to support the company's presence throughout the year. The meeting offers yet another platform and opportunity for the IR/PR team to advance the image of the company and its management, presenting both as well organized and solid in a speech, transcript, press release, annual report, special edition of the company newsletter or magazine, small group discussions on issues—with transcripts or highlights made available later, and interviews with the financial and trade press.

Monitoring the IR Program

The ongoing investor relations program, once it has satisfied the necessary legal requirements for disclosing relevant financial and other information in a timely manner, can be as broad or narrow as resources and the desire of management require.

Joseph A. Kopec and Art Gormley are seasoned specialists in investor relations who take note of discretionary investor relations activities—those areas not required by law—such as meetings, publications, and creating relationships. They observe:

> Investor relations, by its very nature, is an outreach business. It seeks to go beyond mere obligatory reporting of information to a pro-active approach toward marketing the company's securities. . . .
>
> Establishing and monitoring these relationships is accomplished via internally generated publications and written materials, exposure of the company through the media, ongoing telephone communications and meetings that present opportunities to communicate face-to-face. Media coverage of

the company can serve to spark the interest of new groups, and help maintain viability and recognition of the company.

That summary suggests that the practice of investor relations is virtually the same as public relations as it is commonly perceived and no special knowledge is required.

Not true.

Privately owned companies and public companies both want to create relationships and generate awareness, but they operate under very different rules. Whatever is said or written by someone associated with a public company has the potential to move the company's stock. If that happens, an individual or institution with a position in the stock—particularly one that could be part of a long-term strategy—might very well file a complaint with the Securities and Exchange Commission or the National Association of Securities Dealers or a lawsuit.

Ridiculous? Maybe to some people—and that point can be brought up during the subsequent investigation or trial. Even a price movement of a small fraction of a point can translate to millions of dollars of valuation to a publicly traded company.

A partner retires from a partnership and the organization continues going on without missing a beat; but a CEO retires from a public company without having created a seamless succession or transition plan and, whether or not operations are affected at all, a number of the company's shareholders are uncertain how the change will alter the value of the company and fear possible disruption, so they put their shares in play.

Such a scenario is not just hypothetical or an overstatement of the possibilities. Throughout the 1990s stocks fluctuated wildly— some closing up, some down—for no apparent reason. The chairman of the Federal Reserve called the vastly overvalued markets with heavy upside trading "irrational exuberance" and extreme decline provided no more rational explanations. Such market volatility, which affects the ability to raise capital and fund operations, was quite different in privately held companies, which were not subjected to the same stock market roller coaster.

Rumors, fears, uncertainties, and possible announcements about almost anything are too often what makes stocks go up or down, sometimes resulting in instability in the executive suite.

Who speaks on behalf of public companies, what is said, and how it is said does indeed make a difference. A public relations program administered by an investor relations specialist will be particularly sensitive to such matters, as well as how every public comment is interpreted by securities analysts, brokers, shareholders, and prospective investors.

Speeches delivered by—or interviews with—the CEOs of public companies must be vetted, showing particular sensitivity to not only what is said, but how it might be heard and what repercussions could result. Outspokenness in a leader that is admired by much of the public can create a ripple that drives a stock price down. Investor relations practitioners must monitor closely such speeches and interviews, providing counsel that can head-off a great deal of grief before the next annual meeting of shareholders.

SUMMARY

- Investor relations is a form of PR requiring specific knowledge of the markets, the securities industry, and laws and regulations that apply to the dissemination of information in an appropriately timely manner.
- Communications that result in people buying or selling stock—or believing they are in possession of information that might encourage others to buy or sell a stock—have implications not applicable to other PR activities.
- There are distinctions as to the types of communications a company can and must disseminate when it issues stock for the first time and the communication process it maintains once that has been achieved.
- The communication between company and shareholders is guided by specific requirements for what must be reported and at what intervals.
- Some companies go beyond what is required to maintain

good relations with stockholders and to create a sense of stability.

- IR people must be very clear about statutory prohibitions that dictate the limitations of activities during the pre-registration and the registration period.
- The investor relations program, after satisfying the legal requirements for disclosing relevant financial and other information, can be as broad or narrow as requires.

References

Joseph A. Kopec and Art Gormley, "Investor Relations" in Robert L. Dilenschneider, ed., *Public Relations Handbook, Fourth Edition* (Chicago: The Dartnell Corporation, 1996).

8

Employee Relations: The Power Inside

Clearly every company or organization has more than one "public," but beyond recognizing the existence of these publics, it is necessary to have a plan to reach them. Perhaps it is obvious to note the importance of maintaining good investor relations—of keeping investors informed and satisfied that a company is being managed well and remains a good investment. Ongoing communication with investors is a major part of maintaining a stable, well-run organization. As important as it is to send a message to investors and the outside world that the company is in good hands, it is equally important to make certain everyone within an organization supports its mission and feeling and showing a commitment to achieving its goals. Maintaining good relations with one's "internal publics"—one's employees—is as important as doing so with investors and other external publics.

All in the Family

It is probably fair to suggest that, unfortunately, too many executives of too many companies do not regard their employees as a "public" in the same way they think of customers, prospective customers, or investors—segments of the public they know they need to reach, impress, and win over. But, as with investors in public companies, the government of the United States requires that companies provide their employees with certain information, mostly relating to benefits.

There are really two issues interwoven here that might be described as the theory and the practice. The first (the theory) appears when management subscribes to the belief that when employees feel really good about the companies and organizations they work for, they work better and the company profits. In that regard, management initiates a program based on respecting its employees and creating an atmosphere that reflects that respect and the benefits that go with it.

The second point (the practice) is the more literal employee relations issue that allows once management has accepted the concept and the program, employee relations professionals communicate that story to the employees and any secondary publics that need to know. There is also the matter of equality within the workforce in that legally and ethically employers cannot discriminate in how employees are treated, yet by the very nature of the positions within an organization—vice president of sales, director of human resources, factory worker, shipping clerk, etc.—all employees do not have the same educational backgrounds, nor do they relate to, or appreciate, certain company issues in the same way. An employee relations program must reflect such distinctions without discrimination.

New Century, Same Old Communications

Despite the fact that consulting firms specializing in employee issues (mainly compensation matters) came into prominence in the 1970s and showed how well-run internal programs could reduce recruiting costs, lower absenteeism, and workplace accidents, and generally result in a better-run business environment that reduced the company's operating costs, the usual employee communications today seem largely like the legally mandated government fliers that were posted on the company bulletin board in 1955—except now many of them are sent to employees via e-mail and posted on the company's web site.

Employee communications seem to deal largely with safety issues and potential hazards in the workplace, emergency evacuation plans and procedures, charitable appeals, and other "notices" that could just as easily pertain to a group of faceless strangers passing through the building as tourists.

Most companies that have newsletters, holiday parties, picnics, sponsored bowling or softball teams still usually relate to employees with deliberate detachment. The newsletters, whether printed or electronic, tend to maintain a tone where employers speak and employees listen; they include profiles of someone who plays chess or owns a motorcycle and birthday greetings to Marge in accounting "who seems to have worked here since before forever."

Of course, some people contend that's all fine—*better than fine* actually, as it is more than the law requires the employer to do. They point out that companies that insist on presenting a sense that all employees are just one big happy "family" later encounter problems when they have to announce cutbacks or layoffs or the elimination of entire departments, or face tough negotiations on new labor agreements or the promotion of one individual over someone else who was expecting to get that promotion or—just as troublesome—the recruitment of new managers or supervisors from *outside* the "family."

Such sentiment does not come only from the task masters in the executive suite. Many employees today avoid forming "relationships" with their work and colleagues, preferring to do their work, collect their pay, and maintain a clear separation from their jobs and the other parts of their lives. These are people who proudly point out that their jobs and careers are not their lives and, as such, do not *run* their lives.

Many others of course insist that the folks at work are their best friends and that makes their work all the more satisfying.

Clearly, there is great potential for problems at both ends of the spectrum, but the fact is, whether the employer is serious and strict or warm and cuddly, it is not necessary to embrace either extreme position.

Turning Employees into Company Advocates

Fueled more by the economic aspects (high cost to the company in mostly tough economic times) as well as privacy and legal considerations, too few companies choose to focus on employees as a segment of the public that can become quickly activated, involved, and motivated to support the company's marketing effort in ways both direct and indirect that equate more to a change of attitude than a physical form of participation. Such an approach has not only proved to be effective in marketing terms, but has been shown to improve company morale, reduce turnover, reduce labor/management conflict, and contribute to overall efficiency in terms of productivity and cost reduction.

Of even greater significance is the fact that public relations professionals understand:

1. No one knows more about a company—its blemishes and beauty marks—than its own employees.
2. In especially difficult economic times, with many businesses downsizing and others closing altogether, employers need the support of a committed workforce, and employees need to understand the extent of their personal stake in not only helping to keep a business alive, but in

helping gain or maintain stability, to do well, if only to protect their own jobs.

3. In good times, being associated with a company with a high profile and a good reputation is always regarded as a good career or employment credit.

4. When times are tough, as when a company is in the throes of a major economic downturn, financial loss, or business crisis, the media and members of the public will get their sense of what the company is really all about by focusing on its people—seeing and hearing from the company's employees. Whether this occurs through a spontaneous encounter with a member of the press, a question from a friend or neighbor, or an impression conveyed through body language upon entering or leaving a building, a company's employees can make the organization look very good or very bad.

For all these reasons, employers and employees should want to work well together, support each other's interests, and avoid an adversarial or us-against-them type of relationship.

Management Commitment: Where Effective Programs Begin

Employees need to be responsive and do their part, but the responsibility ultimately rests with the employer, who has the power to set policies that define the quality of the relationship.

Small and medium-size companies should be able to communicate efficiently and personally with their employees and create a bond at least as strong as that which they hope to achieve with customers and investors, a relationship based on the recognition of value.

For any size organization, but particularly for larger companies (even global operations), consulting firms specializing in employee benefits management and communication have programs that address specific considerations of different types of employer/employee relationships. Obviously what's a good working policy for an international corporation will not likely be appropriate for a firm with seven employees.

The techniques for communicating benefits can be expanded to include other types of communications activities that promote ways in which employees take a more active role in the relationship and the company and employees relate better to one another.

Richard Bevan, an employee relations specialist, notes:

> Communication is more than symbols or messages. It is the vital process through which the organization survives, adapts, and thrives.
>
> Employee communications can be oral or written, face-to-face or remote, one-on-one or in groups, verbal, visual, or electronic. People continually communicate—with customers, with other external publics, among their immediate work groups, with managers. They talk and they listen; advise and respond; generate ideas and develop attitudes and loyalties.

One consulting firm took an "anything goes" approach to packaging and presenting information employees needed to know. Recognizing that much of the company's literature appeared to be somewhat technical, formal, and dry—which is to say *quite boring* even by the standards of some of the people who created it—the firm created a comic book that provided the same information in a lighter, more entertaining presentation that was read, talked about, and enjoyed. The same firm also produces CD-ROMs in which summaries of benefits are presented visually in bright, enhanced presentations with links to sources of additional information.

Management very often tends to compartmentalize such systems. That is, if a consultant can create a comic book, a video, a CD, or DVD to explain employee benefits, why not apply the creative process similarly to other employee communications? Such vehicles also offer methods of sharing with employees the company's vision, goals, philosophy, commitment to causes, and sense of community. This is not to suggest a corporate philosophy be the subject of a comic book, but that management often underrates the importance of having employees on their side, sharing their commitment, and feeling good about being part of the organization.

Most examinations of the subject of employee relations tend to focus on *employee communications* and that is certainly important, considering the entire concept of public relations is communications-centered. But the larger issue is the commitment of management philosophically to the program. Without question, this is not as easy or as black-and-white an issue as it might seem to be.

The company's management must accept that there is enormous value to the organization in employees closing ranks with their leaders and recognize the common good that comes from a less stressful, less adversarial relationship. Conceptually, it sounds very good to theorists and philosophers who believe in the principles of synergy.

But in reality is such a situation practical or even doable? Isn't it the historic role of good management to be fair, but reward excellence, weed out deadwood, and emphasize maximum productivity at the lowest possible cost? Isn't conflict inherent among the players?

Certainly many labor unions became powerful and effective by putting all their weight behind the rights of workers, always at the expense of profit and by reducing the power of management. And some would justly respond that it was management's greed and indifference to fairness and the safety of workers that created a need for unions in the first place. In the 21st century there are still large factions passionately facing off over the matters of employer control versus the rights of the worker, and as long as there is human nature, that argument might never fully be reconciled.

The company, after all, has everything at risk, but needs a workforce to succeed. Workers can hold out, refuse, reject, bargain hard, but the fact is they need the jobs.

It falls to management to address the philosophical issues with human resources specialists, its own board of directors, and perhaps representatives from a highly skilled consulting firm that understands this area of business and can offer unique but viable options.

But if management by this time either does not accept the idea of an employee relations program that supports, encourages, and recognizes the value of pursuing a positive, harmonious work environment or sees the value conceptually but cannot deal with the cost in dollars or loss of control, then this is a good chapter to skip.

Clearly many organizations operate profitably and productively with an impersonal employer/employee arrangement based on a simple pay-for-work philosophy that asks no more of either party.

Research shows, however, that, as noted, the harmonious workplace where people feel valued and respected is where the best caliber of worker wants to be. The result of that is a company that experiences lower turnover among employees, less absenteeism, fewer on the job accidents, higher morale, higher productivity, pride, loyalty, which in turn results in the company earning a reputation as being a good place to work, which means lower recruiting costs and a higher level of skilled employee that generate more favorable public relations for the company overall. That seems to be a pretty strong case for why management should care about their employees. It is a policy that is good for business.

Types of Media for Internal Communications

Business has come a long way from the days when a company's personnel department published a newsletter (which marketers called a "house organ"). While research indicates that employees prefer personal conversations with supervisors, given the pressure of maintaining productivity schedules and the potential large numbers of employees a supervisor must see (even just ten people—a small number by large company standards—is a lot of people for a supervisor to meet with in a single day), that is not always a practical or desirable approach, especially for the employee who is last on the list of people to be seen.

The better system is to let the type of information to be communicated determine *how* it is to be communicated. Obviously, some information will have great urgency, some none at all; some perhaps would require a degree of delicacy or discretion, where other company news could be painted on banners.

Fortunately, choice and variety of formats is seemingly endless, yet there are three basic categories: print, electronic, and person-to-person (or on-site).

Print communications alternatives are basic, versatile, adaptable, functional, and can address virtually any need with:

- Personal letters to all or certain employees
- Reminder cards
- Table-topper notice cards
- Posters
- Brochures
- Newsletters
- Bulletin board postings
- Post-it notes
- Magazines
- Newspapers
- Commemorative certificates
- Event programs
- Souvenir books
- Briefing documents

It might feel as if *electronic* communication forms have been with us forever, yet in many respects they are still in their infancy, as individuals and businesses each year find new applications using the Internet, intranet, and other systems for:

- E-mail
- CD-ROM
- Voice-mail
- Conference calling
- Video conferencing
- Tapes and DVDs
- Presentation software
- Designated chat rooms
- E-bulletin boards

In all likelihood, this list will be two e or three times as long by the time this book is printed. Such is the nature of technology.

In-person, on-site, or in a combination of on-site and video-conferencing, alternatives include:

- Meetings of all employees to address specific information
- Small group meetings
- One-on-one meetings
- "Town Hall"-type meetings for specific subjects and group interaction
- Round table discussions of task forces and committees

These lists offer a starting point for considering what might be the most effective means of communicating with employees on a particular subject, for a general update, on a regular basis or as-needed, using the method that seems most appropriate for the specific subject or a combination of methods. The comic book example noted earlier is clever, but obviously would not be appropriate for every topic with every company. The same could be said about the CD-ROM. The point is that communicating with employees in ways that promote respect, loyalty, and improved relations does not have to look like a legal notice circular from the federal government.

The Personal Touch and the Adult Approach

Of no small consideration to an employee relations program are political issues and matters of positioning. It would be presumptuous to suggest that employers and employees should emulate the emotional bond of parent and child, but the parallels exist in terms of the type of respect, support, encouragement, accommodation, and loyalty both would hope to achieve in the working relationship—including the often challenging element of communicating those qualities. Sometimes the parent, who was once the guide and teacher, is reluctant to let the child grow up; and sometimes the child, eager to demonstrate strength and independence, becomes less communicative, which causes strain in the relationship. There is still the sense of—and respect for—authority, but the lines of the hierarchy are often blurred, particularly as the parent moves back and forth in the roles of authority figure and friend.

Joseph A. Kopec, a Chicago-based public relations specialist, advises employers to "be willing to share truly useful information with employees. Do not feel that providing either detailed data, financial results, or negative news will destroy your credibility. Most employees are mature and sophisticated information users. . . . Be willing to send more information and let employees decide how best to use it."

He urges employers to avoid "corporate speak" and use plain, direct "employee speak"—language employees not only understand, but are comfortable with.

By treating employees as a "public," employers are more likely to show employees respect and appreciation for what they bring to the effort.

Effective and Efficient Communication Vehicles

What is the best method of communicating with employees in terms of effectiveness and cost-efficiency?

Executives still ask this question of consultants and public relations specialists as if there is any one answer that fits every situation.

PR professionals who work with the media know that as media is a plural term, there is no one system that is *the* preferred method of every reporter, editor, writer, columnist, or producer. Some media members insist on personal contact; others want to review media kits with pages of background material. Still others will not take phone calls and do not have the space or interest in creating piles of media kits, preferring exploratory e-mails to which they will reply if they have any interest in the subject.

Similarly, communications vehicles must be utilized in the ways that will allow them to be effective. Newsletters and magazines must be read; tapes must be seen and heard; e-mails must not be automatically deleted as presumed junk mail or puff pieces.

Employers generating such instruments often perceive they are doing a good job and being responsive to their need to communicate with employees when they are actually, in some instances, doing something worse than nothing. They are presuming they are communicating, but if the recipient of the communication does not accept and process the information, the gap only widens.

The situation is much the same as that of a company that prints and distributes a million copies of a free newspaper and tells potential advertisers it has a circulation of a million readers. Perhaps *no one* has read the newspaper, perhaps all million "readers" have read it from cover to cover, but there is no way to know. And claiming to know is simply delusional.

The fact that management approves funding and production of a magazine, video, a company newspaper, CD-ROM, or a "members only" web site does not mean the program is responsive to the concerns of its audience or, as such, will be effective (or worth the cost).

As noted, research indicates employees prefer face-to-face personal contact with supervisors, but that's not always possible or realistic. It is also fair to suggest that, even if that is the preference of the majority of employees, it still does not reflect the preferences of the *other* employees and a good employee relations program must try to reach everyone, not only the majority.

A solution to this is a program that incorporates a combination of vehicles and methods that can include something as basic as well-placed employee "suggestion boxes" of a bygone era (that are still used under a variety of more contemporary names, such as "team information input channels") into which employees can also place comments and signed or unsigned statements of concern or grievance. Company management would then publish a newsletter, magazine, or other vehicle on a regular basis and print and respond to what employees put forward.

Companies routinely set up hotlines and online contact mechanisms so customers an offer comments, express their complaints, or ask questions. A similar system for employees would let them know that lines of communication are open to them, even if they wish to make their feelings known anonymously. As in the previous reference, a companion or follow-up printed piece that offers employees "inside thoughts" and management's response is a way to tell employees their opinions matter. While they might not get the answers they want, management is not turning a deaf ear but is explaining its position and showing *why* whatever was requested or recommended can't happen.

Just as in sales, where the "know your customer" rule rules, it is imperative for employers to understand if employees prefer something printed and mailed to their homes or something accessible through technology—a web site, e-mails, CD-ROMs, or other type of interactive program.

Many people are required to use a variety of technology products in the course of their work, but on their personal time they prefer something they can read on a bus or train on their way home. Others, of course, ignore and dismiss paper communications and *only* read what comes to them or what they can access through their personal computers.

Employers must take the pulse of their own workforce, as they would their customers, and not assume that employees are in agreement with them (or each other) on any or all issues. This point is important because of the large amount of misinformation that exists. Marketers are told each year that younger audiences do not respond to print and are fully acclimated to Internet-delivered information, computer games, DVDs, CDs, and CD-ROMs.

Research is necessary and valuable, but occasionally, as people who favor the expression "think outside the box" know, creativity can trump research.

How this translates to employee relations is to note that there exist dozens of tested approaches for employers and a blank page for a creative application of a new idea or a variation on an old idea.

As consultant Richard Bevan notes, "Communicators can choose from a wide and continually expanding range of media. The choice depends on the purpose of the message, its content, its urgency, and the intended audience—and the available resources. Available media range from a simple memo to an elaborate brochure, from a type-written newsletter to a full-scale newspaper."

For a minimal investment the simplest desktop publishing programs can now do in-house what once required a contingent of designers, keyliners, typesetters, and layout specialists.

Using Employee Input to Craft Successful Programs

Researchers routinely use focus groups to create a portrait of the market for management. A focus group composed of employees could offer an especially unique perspective to management on issues and matters the company might need to confront, while at the same time reinforcing to employees that their opinions and insight are valued.

In times of business crisis, employees—particularly those who have a long history with the company—can be called upon to offer comments that might be made to the public, creating a picture of the company in a larger context than the immediate crisis. Both the public and the media tend to hold in high regard the opinions of longtime employees of a company—people who are not part of a self-interested management structure.

Modern videoconferencing capabilities offer another way for even the most diverse, layered, and sprawling global organization to stage a "town hall" meeting that brings together many or all employees from various levels and various locations. When such an event can be executed smoothly it becomes not only a morale boost for everyone who feels connected to the organization, but it becomes also a PR event itself for the company. If technology is not completely "cooperative"—causing the production to be somewhat less than seamless—management still deserves a commendation for its effort to try to make it work. Either way, most everyone in the company will be talking about it for a long while, most likely applauding the fact that so many people in so many places came together to make it work (or try to).

In terms of format, rather than the traditional town hall-style meeting that many politicians favor, where a senior official basically takes center stage and holds court by answering questions (many of which are obviously scripted), consider instead a horseshoe-shaped table on stage with members of senior management and employees of the company seated side-by-side (alternating)—not across from each other as if they were debaters or on opposite sides. This setup appears to put management and personnel on an equal level, at least in terms of the respect accorded them.

They could then engage in a dialog on a short list of topics, addressing concerns and issues and offering comments that will help everyone arrive at a clearer understanding of why people *have* certain issues or why company matters are dealt with as they are.

This is not a grievance hearing or a public airing of dirty laundry. Participants can even meet earlier and receive a briefing to set ground rules so that no one walks away feeling as if he or she has been ambushed or embarrassed by the program.

Questions and comments can come from employees in the on-site gallery or via videophone.

If management is truly committed to the idea of having a successful employee relations program, where people feel they matter, this is one approach that can build a bond and add value to the relationship. Even without global hookups and videophones, the session could be held once as a test at one location and, if successful, presented at other locations, perhaps even taped for later viewing by all employees on a closed circuit feed or on the company web site, in addition to a printed version with highlights the session.

Employees at all levels know who signs their paychecks and who is in charge, but they also need and want to feel appreciated and valued as individuals. People who make up a company's workforce can bring operations to an immediate standstill. They can also, individually and collectively, make a company look very good to investors and the public, increase efficiency, and hold down costs. An employee relations program handled well is a very good investment.

SUMMARY

- When employees feel good about companies and organizations they work for, they work better and the company profits.
- An employee relations program must reflect such distinctions within the workplace without discrimination.
- Fueled more by the economic concerns, as well as privacy

and legal considerations, few companies focus on employees as a group that can become quickly activated, involved,
and motivated to support the company's marketing effort.

- Having employees take an active role in the company's PR
efforts is effective in marketing terms, as well as in helping
to improve morale, reduce turnover, reduce labor/manage-
ment conflict, and contribute to overall efficiency in terms
of productivity and cost reduction.

- People want to work where they feel valued and respected.
A company benefits in many way, including earning a reputation as being a good place to work, which means lower
recruiting costs and a higher level of skilled employees generating more favorable public relations for the company
overall.

- An employee relations program is good for business.

References

Richard Bevan and John N. Bailey, ""Employee Relations" in
Philip Lesly, ed., *Lesly's Handbook of Public Relations and
Communications*, Fifth Edition (Chicago: McGraw-Hill/
Contemporary, 1998).

Joseph A. Kopec and Art Gormley, "Investor Relations" Robert L.
Dilenschneider, ed., *Public Relations Handbook*, Fourth
Edition (Chicago: The Dartnell Corporation, 1996).

9

Publicity: Imagination and Energy

As previously noted, to most people, public relations and publicity mean pretty much the same thing: *hype*. As also noted, public relations is an umbrella term that covers a great many functions, including publicity, which is often thought to be all about style, no substance.

Nonsense.

Real Publicity:
Substance and Goals

Publicity is a process of managing information and bringing it to the attention of the public. Sometimes, without question, that involves *hype*—aggressive promotion and drum-beating—but the task of generating publicity does not have to be loud and excessive to be effective. It can just as easily be telling a client or company story to a newspaper editor over a quiet lunch in a fine restaurant. A thoughtfully prepared "white paper" on an industry issue could result in the publication of a story about a company or organization in a prestigious business journal. That's very good publicity . . . and no hype. While every major story placed by public relations people isn't going to change the world, the subject of a publicity effort can be serious, such as a hospital, a campaign to benefit a literacy program, a new approach to financial management, or any issue or matter of great substance and value.

When a campaign *is* about hyping a subject, such as promoting a new movie or a television special event, the objective is to generate interest and enthusiasm. By design the campaign should be entertaining and interesting enough to demand the attention of the public amid hundreds or even thousands of stories pitched to newspapers, magazines, radio, and television programs every week.

While it is reasonable to assume most public relations plans list *creating awareness* among their primary objectives, other goals typically include influencing the deliberations of regulators or legislators; favorably interpreting and promoting the results of studies or surveys; resolving community controversies or disputes; developing programs to support recruiting, repositioning, or reengineering; and supporting fundraising efforts or membership drives, elections, or referenda. All of these goals could benefit from well-orchestrated publicity.

Many public relations professionals say they would rather hire people with a "customer service background" than someone with a journalism or business background. With all due respect to journalists and business majors, the reasoning makes sense. While writing skills and knowledge of business are important, PR people are required to solve problems on an almost daily basis and to make certain that the situation is resolved in a way that alienates or angers the fewest possible number of people. Journalism school does not spend a lot of time in such areas. Customer service people do.

Although the billionaire recluse-industrialist-executive-aviator-inventor Howard Hughes was perhaps the most famous person to employ an army of publicists to reportedly keep his name and business dealings *out* of the media (a reversal from his position earlier in his career when he kept a high profile and was regarded as somewhat less *eccentric*), he was by no means alone in his hope to avoid hype.

Many CEOs and companies believe their strength lies in part in their ability to operate behind the scenes and away from press and public scrutiny.

So not every PR program is about awareness.

But for those that *are* about awareness, publicity is not only the name of the game, it is the game.

Hollywood: The Birthplace of Modern Publicity

The model for the modern publicity campaign was constructed in Hollywood—not by the artists, directors, or even the (often highly self-publicized) Hollywood agents, but by the masters in the executive suite. Certainly PR pioneers and legends, such as Edward Bernays and Benjamin Sonnenberg plied their trade brilliantly in the business world, but even their great vision lacked the wide-screen opportunities that would be afforded by licensing, merchandising, and technology. Once upon a time a movie was just a movie, but now it is a *franchise*—a brand in its own right—that moves synergistically with designers, manufacturers, marketers, and purveyors of every stripe.

The concept that Walt Disney seemed to have perfected in the 1950s by presenting a movie wrapped in a major marketing campaign that included toys, clothes, records, books, fragrances, school supplies, posters, key chains, bed sheets, and pillow cases, has been. extended even further by his Hollywood successors.

Initially, the merchandise and product tie-ins were limited to those that could be controlled by the owner of the subject property and could be logically connected in some way to the film. Later, the rule of maximizing returns would apply, and even competitors were invited to get in on the action if the right deal could be cut.

It took awhile, but other industries, now led by members of a generation that did not feel bound by the limitations of their predecessors, saw the possibilities. A product is not just a product. It is a brand and brands have extensions, often into product categories illogically linked to the core product.

Creative public relations professionals speak freely of *re-inventing*, *remaking*, and *revisionism*. And the key ingredient to making it work is publicity. Their very sophisticated model has become even more sophisticated and priorities have changed.

In most industries, the hope is to build brand equity and brand loyalty indicated by customers who return week after week and year after year. But the entertainment industry, unlike consumer products such as food, gasoline, and bathroom tissue, operates within an upside down pyramid system. Movies, books, records, and CDs enjoy their highest levels of interest and heaviest sales volume at their time of issue and find diminishing interest the longer they are in the marketplace.

There is an occasional "sleeper" that has a quiet introduction and low expectations, but through good word-of-mouth advertising, a marketer that gives it time, and shelf space that allows it to stay around for a while, becomes successful. And the success is extra sweet because it was not expected.

But such successes are the exception, not the rule. A few years ago, an album by singer Michael Jackson, for example, sold 4 million units with a list price of $18.98 within weeks of its release. That was more than twenty times as many copies as most other recordings released in the same time period, but since it was only about one-fourth of the number of copies sold of the singer's best selling album, it was considered a failure.

The success of the Harry Potter movie is measured not only in how much it earns, but by how much it earns against other movies released in the same season, regardless of their subject matter. Gross ticket sales of more than $100 million might be shrugged off and dismissed as disappointing if another film earns $110 million in the same season.

And much of the issue centers on publicity.

The Importance of Publicity in Business Today

Publicity overkill is a throwback to the "say anything, just spell my name right" idea that was wrong when it was the order-of-the-day in the 1960s and will still be wrong in the 2060s.

The Hollywood analogy to business continues regarding the celebrity status accorded corporate executives. Where once a CEO or company founder only cared to issue rosy earnings predictions to *The Wall Street Journal* or contribute an opinion to the *Harvard Business Review*, the modern CEO turns up in the pages of *People* magazine or on *Good Morning, America*, talking about his or her hobbies, marriages, views on health and fitness and politics. The theory is that a warm and likeable CEO will project an image of a company or organization run by nice people, so it is probably the kind of nice company that people will want to buy from, work for, and invest in . . . right?

Well, that's certainly a possibility. A CEO who seems to be a decent person with a desire to convey a positive impression on behalf of his or her company is definitely better for the company's image than someone with a reputation of being difficult to work with and unable to keep good people on the corporate team.

Publicity is not all smiling portraits with the family and the dog. It can seem to be superficial, yet reports (or even rumors) of executives displaying explosive personalities—on the job, on the golf course, or in the VIP waiting lounge at the airport—can suggest immaturity, instability, and volatility in the executive suite which, in turn, makes gossip columnists and Internet reporters smile and makes investors and securities analysts view a company with some reservations.

No research has (as yet) proved a news photo of a smiling CEO sends stock prices upward, but an air of confidence suggests a positive work environment that recruiters say talented executives prefer.

An old adage holds that *nothing succeeds like success,* and there is more than some truth to that statement in that people are indeed more inclined to invest in, work for, and do business with a company they believe to be successful, solid and welcoming. The corporate application of the Hollywood publicity plan has:

1. Encouraged many businesses to embrace the concept of having a good public image.
2. Encouraged the general interest media to believe that, contrary to opinions held for decades, business news is not inherently dull and therefore not worth bothering to cover.
3. Shown business marketers that news and feature story opportunities are virtually unlimited.

A better-known company is perceived to be a better company, and publicity is about becoming better known.

PR and Publicity Plans for Businesses Large and Small

If people in the business have indeed learned the value of publicizing what they have to offer and promise to do, the logical question is: *Are all businesses created equal when it comes to publicity?* That is, are the elements in an effective publicity effort the same for every business, from Fortune 1000 companies to a two-person consulting practice?

The answer is . . . *sort of.* (It should by now be apparent that relatively few questions about public relations or marketing elicit simple yes or no answers.)

A meaningful marketing program requires a plan. A successful public relations program requires a plan. And a publicity campaign—

an overt, aggressive effort aimed at generating awareness and interest—most definitely requires a plan, whether the subject is a company that is large or small, successful or unknown, manufacturer or restaurant, cause or issue, candy bar or candidate.

Aligning Tactics, Message, and Media

A publicity plan will largely focus on tactics, but the message to be communicated must be consistent with the messages and objectives communicated by other PR and marketing activities. Advertising, literature, events, and sponsorships should all be based on a consistent theme.

Not every business will have the same objectives or the resources to apply to achieving those objectives. Yet, the Unique Selling Proposition—what differentiates the subject from its competitors or makes it similar—is essential. Regardless of the unique approach any part of the campaign might employ, the core message that stays with the public must be consistent with other activities in the campaign and with the company's own image.

Awareness can come from many sources—word-of mouth, a conversation overheard in an airport or a waiting room, at the proverbial office water cooler, from a speaker's platform, a preacher's pulpit, or an Internet sales presentation.Most people, however, become aware of what they know through various media:

- Television
- Newspapers
- Radio
- Magazines
- The Internet
- Mail
- Telemarketing
- Point-of-sale displays
- Newsletters
- Posters
- Out-of-home marketing (includes billboards, restaurant table-toppers, cashier and counter displays and signage, transit postings, and general signage in every conceivable location)

Sometimes people seek information about a subject, but far more often the information is presented to them in summarized forms, and they are free to absorb or discard it as they desire.

The Role of the Publicist

Despite the vastness of the news media and common assumptions, most of the information the public receives is not unearthed by intrepid reporters, but is information brought to the reporters, editors, columnists, producers, or news managers. The person who is bringing them information is almost always a paid representative—a publicist or public relations professional.

Often—*very* often in the case of small businesses—the question arises as to whether or not a public relations agency is really necessary. Can't a CEO or someone else on staff approach the media or handle press inquiries?

The theoretical answer is *yes,* just as a CEO or someone on staff can paint the office, deliver mail, and spend seemingly endless hours dealing with the phone company. Obviously, in very small businesses, that's what happens, but in most successful or aggressive companies of almost any size, responsibilities are allocated among people whose time and talents can be put to their best uses. As with the recognition that legal work should best be left to a lawyer and financial matters should be handled by accountants and business managers, public relations is also an area that requires specific knowledge and skills.

The question then becomes not *can* a CEO or someone on staff handle PR, but *should* a CEO or someone else not experienced in the various aspects of public relations have responsibility for a function that can have a significant impact on the growth and survival of the business.

If the preference within the company is to forego an agency relationship and have the PR function managed by an in-house person, that person should very definitely be a public relations professional and not another professional, such as a lawyer or researcher who takes on PR duties to save the company money. It is in such situations that great damage can be done. Publicity and PR are a relationship business and as such should not be considered as an afterthought.

PR Professionals and the Media

What do members of the media receive from PR professionals? How do they get it? How does the publicity process actually come about? The basic tools of the trade include the:

- Press release
- Press kit
- Backgrounder or fact sheet
- Bios and profiles of executives and designated spokespeople
- Photographs appropriate to the subject
- Additional materials specific to the subject or profession, such as legal filings, disks or CD-ROMs, product demos or samples, copies of surveys and studies

Information reaches the media through any of several ways:

- Press releases and unsolicited letters or e-mails.
- Unsolicited voice-mail messages.
- Press conferences.
- Press briefings.
- Special events.
- Demonstrations.
- Publicists who know and have relationships with members of the media, know what they are looking for, and already know the right reporter or producer who might be willing to review and present the company's story.
- Publicists who, over a friendly lunch or other encounter with media members, pitch ideas for stories about clients or their companies.

Certainly some publicity does in fact come about because a CEO or the head of a company's marketing department play golf together or their children go to the same schools or they strike up a conversation while waiting for a table at the Union League Club or they met at a class reunion or an alumni fundraiser, but such occurrences are predictable.

A great connection, spontaneous or personal, is frosting on the cake, but the *actual cake* is the plan.

In public relations, as in most businesses and professions, relationships can be a key factor in a program's success. PR professionals typically maintain ongoing communication with media people. This works to the benefit of clients and companies in that the PR specialists know:

- The types of material that certain writers, editors, and producers are always looking for or will accept.
- In what form or with what supporting material a media source will accept information and pitches.
- Deadlines and production schedules for various media.

As media people are reassigned to other beats, are transferred to other bureaus, or change jobs altogether, PR people do not normally lose contact with them, but use such changes as opportunities to expand their circles of media contacts and connections.

Basic Publicity Tools

But whether relationships are old or new, the skills and tools required for success remain the same.

The Press Release

The press release is the essential tool of the publicist. It not only provides the information relevant to the pitched story, but it also provides a basic "hook"—the element that turns a collection of facts into a story.

It is important for the publicist to differentiate between a *news release* and a *press release*. In the *news* version, the material is just that: *newsworthy*, timely, and containing all pertinent facts and at least a degree of impact. A *press release* is not necessarily time sensitive, nor does it have apparent impact. It is, however, a story with elements both interesting and perhaps valuable to a consumer of information.

Whichever version is issued should adhere to standard press release form that tells *who, what, where, when, why,* and *how,* in pyramid form, listing the most important points first, followed by explanation and details. Even as some media relax what have long been the journalistic standards, PR specialists should expect editors to look at form as a way of measuring the knowledge and professionalism of the provider.

Regarding relaxed standards, the "Internet generation" has produced practitioners who either never bothered to learn the long-accepted format for material submissions or assumed that a new electronic medium justified changing all the rules . . . without telling anyone.

Radical departure for the sake of radical departure (or, in some instances, to wrap text around unconventional logos and letterhead designs) has tampered with a presentation format that evolved for practical reasons and has been used for more than five decades. The format was adopted for easy readability and editing.

The *press release* or *news release* should:

- Be typed, double spaced, approximately 250 words per page.
- Have contact names, titles, phone numbers, and e-mail addresses of up to two people who will be available to provide additional information.
- List an after-hours phone contact and number.
- Indicate at the top of the page if the information contained in the release is "for immediate release" or is to be held back until a specific date or time.
- Have a headline that clearly and succinctly presents the subject of the press release.
- Note a dateline—the point of origin and date of issue for the information.
- Present the facts of the story in their order of importance in, ideally, 500 words or less (two typed pages).

EXHIBIT 9.1: SAMPLE PRESS RELEASE

Press Release

Contact: Joe Marconi
Marketing Communications
708/246-7102
For Immediate Release

**FUTURES INDUSTRY EXECUTIVES
LAUNCH NEW FIRM**
*Cadent Financial Services delivers
operational innovation, individualized service
in a boutique environment*

CHICAGO, NOVEMBER 6—Cadent Financial Services, the company formed by several senior-level futures industry executives, is now fully operational. The firm, a registered futures commission merchant (FCM) and exchange clearing member, brings together some of the industry's most experienced and respected professionals from both the operations and management sides with a very sophisticated client base.

"Nobody's doing what we do," said Ryman Flippen II, Cadent Financial's CEO. "Cadent's total focus is on creative solutions and timely delivery, which is unique to specific types of customers in today's market. Our boutique nature, depth of experience, and contacts within the FCM community are designed to provide customized solutions to larger clearing firms that might prefer to focus on executing their business model, while outsourcing their resource-intensive operational needs. This should enable both the firms and Cadent to increase their respective value propositions."

Mr. Flippen was previously the CEO of Intermarket Solutions/CFS and vice chairman and a principal of

Lind-Waldock, a leading futures trading firm where he was a major force for the past 17 years.

"Cadent is in an excellent position at a time of great change in the futures business," added Thomas J. Konopiots, Chief Operating Officer of the new firm. "We have access to the best technology; an extensive, experienced floor operation; and we approach the business with methods that integrate our experience with an open system architecture to provide speed, flexibility and strength in a highly synchronized boutique environment. That flexibility sets us apart." Mr. Konopiots also was a Lind-Waldock executive and a principal of the firm for 20 years before stepping down as COO in 2001.

"Service to a variety of constituencies is our defining factor. We provide a powerful resource to the FCM community as well as to the professional trader and that's what clients are looking for today," Mr. Flippen notes. "Cadent is well positioned to deliver superior solutions. We have no legacy issues or encumbrances and instead have perhaps the cleanest digitally-based operation in the industry."

The new firm's management team also includes chief information officer Linas A. Jucas, previously senior vice president for technology with NQLX following eight years with Commerz Futures—most recently as senior vice president and chief information officer. Chief financial officer Michael S. Plemich was formerly the controller for Lind-Waldock from 1997 to 2003 after 10 years as controller with TradeLink LLC. Kurt F. Lightcap, a former associate director of Barclays Capital in New York and a former vice president of operations for Refco, Inc., has been named senior vice president for clearing operations. Stacy Lightcap assumes the post of senior vice president, trading operations. A member of the Chicago Mercantile Exchange, Stacy worked with Refco, Inc. from 1985 to 2003, having also served as vice president, CME operations. Cheryl Fitzpatrick, a respected industry veteran, has joined the firm as General Counsel. She had previously served as Senior Counsel with Alaron trading, a CME clearing firm. Paul Fry, formerly with Refco, Inc., was named Senior Vice President of Risk Management for Cadent. Michael Popilchak assumes the post of Director of IB Services. He had previously been with the Rosenthal Collins Group, a leading FCM.

"Cadent may be the industry's newest FCM, but the experience and quality of the team we've assembled speaks to the level of quality we are prepared to deliver today," noted Mr. Konopiots.

"We don't aspire to be the biggest operation in the business, "Mr. Flippen insists, "but customers' needs have changed and Cadent's mission is to provide the type of service today's markets require."

Cadent Financial Services LLC is a clearing member of the Chicago Mercantile Exchange and transacts business on all major international futures exchanges. The firm's offices are located at 150 South Wacker Drive, Suite 1310, Chicago, Illinois 60606. The phone number is 312/384-1100 and web address is www.cadentfinancial.com.

———

Fact Sheet

The Company

Cadent Financial Services is a new kind of firm for financial institutions and other sophisticated traders. Established in 2003 by a group of veteran futures industry professionals, our boutique nature, depth of experience, and long established relationships within the FCM community enable us to provide customized solutions to larger clearing firms that might prefer to focus on executing their business model, while outsourcing their resource-intensive operational needs. This approach should allow both the firms and Cadent to increase their respective value propositions.

While Cadent provides a full range of services and a complete product offering—state-of-the art technology, open architecture to accommodate various trading platforms, a precision back office, and a solid trading floor operation that includes the most experienced brokers and traders on any major exchange—it is the customer that defines the terms of the relationship.

The Market

Sophisticated traders with an understanding of the market and its uses know that for more than a century, futures have been used to manage risk while exploring a wide range of opportunities. Cadent Financial Services is unique. As its name suggests, Cadent is sensitive to the rhythm of the market—to its tempo—and to maintaining a sense of balance.

No one can predict the direction of the market. Futures trading is not for everyone. Sophisticated traders can outperform other traders because they know the market and have the resources to follow through on their decisions.

Technology, the introduction of new products, and the expansion of global markets have created new opportunities for sophisticated traders—and heightened the need for a strong organization with a solid understanding of the markets. That's Cadent Financial.

The Mission

Cadent Financial Services' mission is to deliver creative solutions through an individualized approach, accommodating the demands of even the largest financial institutions with superior order execution and clearing services at competitive prices.

Like the old line about the weather—*everybody talks about it, but no one ever does anything about it*—everyone in business promises service, but few ever actually deliver on those promises. Cadent Financial is built on a promise to deliver an extraordinary level of service. The firm's management is committed to delivering the quality service they would demand for themselves.

Customers choose the services they need and want, from traditional order execution only and clearing services to full facilities management.

The People

Cadent Financial Services management team and brokers, traders and professional staff—separately and together—bring an unparalleled level of knowledge of the market, trading experience, operational expertise and skill to providing customers with uniquely tailored services developed according to customer specifications.

Some publicists use press releases as vehicles for self-indulgence or to impress their clients or employers, issuing long, highly detailed documents of perhaps five single-spaced pages—five times the appropriate, recommended length. It is not that editors don't want information, but too-long press releases simply clog and slow down the system. Editors have neither time nor inclination to immerse themselves in the details of a story before it has even been accepted for presentation.

The recommended two pages or less should provide the essence of a story. An accompanying backgrounder or fact sheet can add further pages of details and elaboration if needed or desired.

Almost as bad as the too-long press release are publicists' attempts to make their press releases "stand-out" by printing them on poster board or writing them in calligraphy or in crayon or in print that must be read while wearing 3-D glasses.

Editors pretty much hate such novelties. They are stunts that don't seem to take the business of gathering and presenting information seriously. More importantly, press releases that are unusual sizes and shapes are not what a busy editor is accustomed to receiving and, while they certainly get some attention and stand out from the other press releases, that might not be for the better.

As a rule, editors have their systems in place—the way they work, organize their files, set material aside in stacks or piles or a particular place. They are usually not amused or impressed by someone who expects they will set aside their routine to deal with this burst of creativity and cleverness. Why take the chance of irritating someone whose help is being sought?

Sending press releases that are written on chalk boards or mirrors or boxes or t-shirts diminishes the recognition that the process exists to convey information. To send editors coffee mugs or caps or other promotional items is fine, but a press release is for the file, to circulate, to copy, or to write on. There are times to be cute and delight in not taking life too seriously, and times to focus on content. The press release is about content.

Finally:

- Know and respect deadlines for press releases. Sending information late or outside of the production cycle is unprofessional and annoying to editors and colleagues.

- After including a contact name and phone number for anyone needing additional information, make certain that such a contact person is available and at that number. Nothing annoys reporters, editors, and producers as much as being blocked by a recording or having no one on the job when they are seeking clarification on a deadline.
- Keep facts factual. Don't overstate or hype the content of press releases. A release is not an ad or a brochure. Be honest in comments and content. Overstating value or misrepresenting statistics is an invitation to critics and competitors to correct the record and look good at someone else's expense.

The Press Kit

Much like an annual report, which many companies and organizations use as a corporate image brochure, (which, by its very physical appearance, makes a bold statement) a press kit can be understated or glitzy and can speak for a company with just its *look*.

The basic elements in a press kit are the most recent press release issued, photographs, and a backgrounder. Other inclusions should be based on (1) who the recipient of the kit is and (2) what objective the kit must achieve. It is not necessary that every kit contains everything a company has available or that every kit contains the same material.

While some companies strive to outdo one another in creativity, using oversize folders and moving parts, a standard press kit is a two-pocket folder containing the most current information available—usually a current or recent press release—in the most visible position in the right-hand pocket.

The left pocket is left to history; that is to say, it includes a corporate brochure and a fact sheet, history of the subject, and any relevant previously- issued press releases. In the right pocket, behind the current release, should be photos of the CEO or anyone who is quoted in the press release, information on the current management team, relevant current product/service/event information with appropriate related photos, if any, and perhaps a CD, CD-ROM, or diskette for media people who prefer to review and maintain files in electronic form.

In that same regard, an electronic version of the press kit should be posted as a permanent part of the company or organization web site. It is recommended that the elements of the press kit be formatted into a simple, basic, user-friendly design that loads quickly, not a wide screen or animated presentation that requires special software or a great deal of waiting/loading time for viewing. The graphics should not rely extensively on color or elaborate art to make its point.

Web sites of successful companies typically feature dramatic visuals with the theory and good intentions that they will stand out and look great.

That's commendable. But the gifted men and women who design and build web sites have been unable historically to grasp the fact that (1) not everyone loves computers as much as they do; (2) some people are only coming to the site for information, not for an animation festival or light show; and (3) the speed of downloading images and the color, quality, and resolution can be appreciably different from one computer to another.

Since the producer of the press kit material to be displayed does not know if it will be viewed on a new PC with sophisticated software and a high-speed connection to the Internet or on a notebook or laptop that is six years old (or more) and attached to a modem, it should not be assumed that any and all viewing will be equal in quality and under the best of circumstances. In fact, it should be assumed that resolution will vary, as will loading time.

Consider, for example, the function performed by the print version of the press kit: reporters and editors can skim through it instantly and stop, study, or bypass material as they choose. An electronic press kit should be no less easy to use. The press kit should support the objectives of the plan, but it does not *have to* include everything just *because it can* include everything. A company that develops a series of a dozen brochures to describe its many audiences and how it relates to each, does not have to include the entire content of all the brochures simply because they exist and might impress someone.

Remember the "know your customer" rule and include only

material that is necessary and useful in the press kit. If more information is needed or desired, it can be requested.

Whether printed material is packed into pocket folders or displayed on personal computer screens, it is important that the material be carefully constructed and presented as much for the image it promotes of the company or organization as for the information it offers.

Backgrounders and Fact Sheets

The *fact sheet* pretty much tells what it is. Just as a press release is built upon a logical journalistic format, providing essential information that tells *who, what, when, where, why,* and *how,* the fact sheet basically provides the same information, but in more of a grid or bullet-point format rather than in narrative style. It provides information-at-a-glance in the easiest possible reference style.

A *backgrounder* is a similarly factual "crib sheet" that a publicist prepares for inclusion in a press kit or for use as a briefing document that provides reporters, editors, or interviewers with enough background information on a subject to conduct an interview intelligently. A backgrounder is usually no more than a few pages and includes a brief history and highlights of a company, organization, issue, or person's career.

Bios and Profiles

The biographies and profiles of executives or principal members of a management team, as included in a press kit, can take a variety of forms. In some, all senior members of a company or organization's management will be listed on a single page, with their names and titles in bold typeface and a sentence or two about each of them. Perhaps a small identifying photograph will appear on the page next to the individual's name.

Other companies present each member of the management team on his or her own page with more information provided about that person's responsibilities, background, and noteworthy career achievements. The best choice of format should be determined by the overall size of the organization, the extent it wants to highlight or showcase particular individuals and areas, and the impression the company wants to convey.

There is also a flexibility factor to consider. If the company or organization tends to be of a type where people come on board and stay, updating the page poses no great problem. But if the company tends to have a high turnover or if people are elected or volunteer to serve only a year, the group page will probably be at the printer for changes more often than it is in the press kit pocket.

In terms of presentation, the material should be interesting, factual, and useful. Executive bios are not resumes. Think of a hardcover book that includes a dust jacket biography of its author— usually not more than 75 words, crisply written, emphasizing the person's strongest credentials and most significant accomplishments.

Photographs

Pictures tell a story, and a press kit is a representation of a company or organization's overall story. Each individual photograph should tell a part of the story. The kit should include reproduction-quality photography related to the subject. Most media prefer using reality photos rather than posed studio portraits referred to as "beauty shots." Even fine work of this type still tends to leave a company CEO or founder looking stiff and resembling a retired undersecretary of commerce.

People prefer to see casual poses or "working" photos where the subject of the photograph appears to be doing what he or she does— talking on a phone, meeting with colleagues, standing in a business setting such as a conference room or an office doorway, or pausing at the entrance of the company. Such pictures present the person as alive and well, which is a good message to send out.

Be careful about staging "natural looking" photos. Very often a leafy plant that went unnoticed or the corner of a picture frame hanging on a wall can appear in a finished photograph as if it is protruding from someone's head. Relaxed, natural facial expressions, such as those of a person in conversation, are better than somber expressions or exaggerated smiles.

A smiling photograph of a CEO is not appropriate if the newspaper decides to use it with a story about a corporate crisis or a poor earnings report.

Limit the number of photographs in the press kit to those of senior management and/or anyone quoted in an accompanying press release. This is not a yearbook, and individual photos of five managers and a new employee are a waste and are likely to convey an unprofessional, unfavorable impression with editors.

Do not use group photos unless they are specifically requested and only then when it makes sense, such as the co-founders of the organization or family members who are part of senior management or a CEO and a chief operating officer together in a "press conference setting" as if they are delivering an important announcement.

Group photos of the entire management team belong in brochures, annual reports, ads, and in background photos on the company web site, not in press kits. For a while it was thought that group photos were supposed to suggest teamwork and that the company had a management that worked together, but few publications are set up to handle group shots well so individual "head shots" should be the rule.

Again, as with brochures and documents, don't overload the press kit, particularly with photographs that, if not clearly relevant to a particular subject, can convey a sense of self-importance that works against a subject's own interests. Include as much information as necessary to provide a reporter or editor with an at-a-glance picture of the subject.

Cadent executives each have 20 years or more of futures industry experience, much of it acquired while holding senior level positions at some of the leading firms in the business.

The Strategy

If the press release, press kit, backgrounder or fact sheet, executive bios, and photographs are the tools of the publicity campaign, the strategy portion of the publicity plan is the guide to how to use those tools.

The objective of the public relations effort is to generate awareness, which can be accomplished in any number of ways from press releases to appearances on call-in radio shows, speeches to trade associations, even providing testimony at hearings of regulators and legislators. PR professionals should always be alert to opportunities, but in most instances, it will be necessary to *create* opportunities.

Depending on the subject, company, organization, product, candidate, entertainer, issue, or cause, there are formula approaches to attracting media attention—or attracting crowds that will then attract media attention. In any season, there always seems to be a single topic that totally dominates the media's collective consciousness as a lead story, cover story, or long-running headline.

Consider how at specific moments in time, virtually every conversation seemed to begin and end with references to AIDS, the O.J. Simpson trial, singer Michael Jackson, *Star Wars*, the Unabomber, Beanie Babies, the 2000 election, "hanging chads" in Florida, Harry Potter, Monica, 9/11, the Tall Ships, Enron, Martha Stewart, Iraq, SARS . . . One by one, they were everywhere in the media all the time.

And there were those who noticed and, for better or worse, weighed in on the story of the day with criticism, comments, rebukes, support, and interpretations before the circus left town and everyone went on to the next bit of "breaking news." But before that happened, experts, pundits, and spokespersons—and occasionally, someone who actually seemed somehow related to the story—offered a comment and a contribution to AIDS research, legal defense funds, organizations that work to end child abuse, spousal abuse, or world hunger, programs to support literacy, safe sex, protection from terrorist attacks, and various other causes.

Church groups said Harry Potter books encouraged witchcraft; lawyers and brokers appeared daily on talk radio shows and cable news TV programs to explain "insider trading."

Hundreds of companies turned public relations and advertising budgets into September 11 memorial funds, not all of them handled in the best of taste. Individuals and businesses sought to ride the wave of the story that had captured the attention of the media, the public, and the world, if only for a moment in time.

When no opportunity appears likely to generate publicity relating to events of the day, PR specialists again can rely on methods that have proved reliable through the years. Here are ten such examples:

1. Develop a study or survey on a trend or issue of the day that relates to a particular industry or commodity and release a summary of its conclusions to the media with a comment from the company or organization's CEO or another source, which then creates an opportunity for the CEO to comment on both the results and the earlier comment.

2. Organize an industry "leadership conference" (or on a smaller scale, a "leadership breakfast") with the CEO as host and moderator and an invited list of local business executives or representatives of civic organizations. Set a single topic for discussion. Let it be timely and important and send whatever recommendation might result from the event to the person or agency that might be in a position to act on it. Make certain that some of them are associated with companies that are local advertisers, as the media will be more inclined to cover an event in which their advertisers are participants.

3. Issue a carefully considered quotable comment (a "sound bite") on an issue or controversy (insider trading of stock, utility price hikes and gouging, cutbacks in educational funding, an environmental matter). It can be a statement posted on the PR newswire or a letter to the editor of the newspaper or an op-ed piece.

4. Announce the company or organization's sponsorship or participation in an event of almost any type—a musical arts competition, theatre series, lecture program, environmental clean up, restoration of old or neglected property, food drive, fundraising effort for a charity, renovation of a park or public garden, etc.

5. Establish and present an award for excellence, citizenship, community service, scholarship, courage, talent, or artistic ability. For an extra spin, name the award to honor—or invite to present it—a local dignitary, hero, or celebrity the media cannot resist covering.

6. Have a contest.
7. Announce a joint charitable or social program created with a well-known or prominent company.
8. Release an exchange of correspondence with a notable person in the arts or government and donate the letters to a school.
9. Organize a protest, letter-writing campaign, or demonstration aimed at bringing attention to an issue that affects a particular constituent group.
10. Award a scholarship and a career to a young person in need. Grant a college education to a deserving young person and assure that person a position with the company or organization upon graduation.

These are basic formula approaches that virtually assure the company publicity. If nothing on the list seems especially interesting or consistent with what the client or management wants to do, a seasoned publicity professional should easily be able to generate a list of ten additional ideas and ten more after that. Remember: with formula ideas that it is not necessarily originality that counts, it is getting public attention. What typically occurs is, as an idea is being developed, some element of uniqueness to the current application surfaces.

The publicist who dismisses an idea with a remark such as "That's already been done" or "That been done to death," must have been home sick on the day the lesson was taught about not giving up on something that works or trying to be new and different for the sole purpose of being new and different.

Retro marketing campaigns, nostalgic ads, re-makes of films and revivals of plays still find acceptance from an appreciative public if the ideas were good at the start. Songs continue to be written using the same notes of the musical scale that were written to write other songs. Races are run by people going over the same track that's been used by winners thousands of times before. It is the *content* that must be different to make something unique, not the process.

One of the simplest and perhaps least costly ways to get attention from the public is by using the "Letters to the Editor" section of local newspapers and national magazines. If this approach seems flat and threadbare, consider that in a typical year the *New York Times* will likely publish letters from hundreds of readers, bringing attention to a situation or taking exception to something that has been said or written by someone else. Among these readers will be people most of the public doesn't know, but just as likely the letters will be from Bill Clinton, Jimmy Carter, Henry Kissinger, some well-known figure from the arts or entertainment, or the chair of a public company or foundation. These columns attract attention when they appear, but more importantly, they begin a dialog on a subject that will continue on TV and radio programs, in other publications, on the Internet and around dinner tables.

Any newspaper will serve this purpose, from the free "home shopper" to an online publication or *The Wall Street Journal.* Magazines can include the full range of possibilities from *Time, Newsweek, Playboy, Rolling Stone,* and *People* to trade publications such as *Electronics News* or regional titles like *Crain's Detroit Business* or *Los Angeles* magazine.

The public relations process comes in when it is not assumed that the whole world was watching and reading the day the publication appeared, so the subject letter is "merchandised"—photocopied and sent on to members of a specific, targeted public. That mailing could be made to a personal or company mailing list of investors, customers, credit card holders, or select members of the media with a cover letter from the letter's author *or* from someone else with an interest in the letter's message and a desire to see it carried further and a dialog begun.

Next, a press release can be directed to certain columnists and specific media people with a known interest or history of writing or speaking on the subject, noting that a letter to a publication has stirred interest (and perhaps some controversy) about a matter that appears to be generating wide support or, at least, discussion. Editors, columnists, reporters, and producers see and hear the phrase constantly, but still must be sensitive to anything that "appears to have stirred widespread interest."

Ideas that work become known as ideas that work for a good reason.

The Internet

For years people have been describing the Internet as a powerful tool with enormous potential and no one has ever disputed that. Rarely a day passes that someone in conversation or in the media does not make some reference to having received a noteworthy e-mail or having been sent something from a web site or found an item online that was worth sharing or mentioning. This should suggest the Internet is a gift from heaven for publicists.

One day that truly might be the case. Some major obstacles remain to be overcome: *spam,* and the ability to quickly navigate, evaluate, and master *tens of millions of web sites.*

Other huge problems for Internet marketers include the absence of truly protective processes to safeguard the public from *hackers gaining access to bank account and credit card information, financial data, and personal records,* and *blocking the planting of computer viruses in the PCs of unsuspecting Internet users.*

Virtually every company, organization, nonprofit group, special interest group, hate group, club, brand, and association—from the post office to the Pope—has a web site.

For publicists, it would appear that securing a placement for a client or company's message on the web site of CBS News would be a pretty good placement indeed. The prestige of the news organization provides recognition, credibility, and the *perception of awareness.*

Certainly to PR people this would fit the profile of a good hit and clients would be told that they should be pleased.

Maybe.

The issue is that CBS News Online is *not* CBS News. It might very well have an overlap of some of its audience with the TV and radio powerhouse, but as an Internet site it might also have an audience that is totally an Internet audience and as such has little or nothing in common with the audiences of the broadcast entities that share its name.

While the web site might well register thousands or millions of visitors per day, it is still difficult to measure the degree of influence or impact a reference on the site affords a subject.

With traditional media, merchandising a PR placement is very important. To be seen on CBS television (or NBC, ABC, PBS, or CNN) is to publicists a successful hit, without question. And there is also considerable mileage to be gained from repeated references to a subject's having been "seen on TV," as television is the acknowledged influential driver of public opinion. The phrase has currency, and each time it's referenced the currency earns interest.

"As seen on CBS Online" might one day have such value, but until a definitive profile of the site's typical visitor is established, along with a sense of how great an influence the site has on that person's decision-making, a placement on a web site—even one with the same name as a media powerhouse—remains in the column marked "another media reference."

The exception to this dismissive wave at the Net is an affinity site where known members, subscribers, or patrons are committed to using the site as their place to find and exchange information electronically. Book lovers, gun collectors, sports fans, political activists, etc., can be counted on to visit their web sites of choice several times each day and exchange information. For the person, organization, or company that wants to reach that targeted public, a web site such as this is the cyber equivalent to a gathering in a town square.

Certain web sites have been known to become large and influential. Some sustain their status by linking with other carefully chosen sites with similar demographic and psychographic audiences. Others run out of steam and disappear quickly.

Companies focus on creating traffic to their web sites, rather than being listed or profiled on the sites of others. While that has a definite value, consider:

1. The company's own web site, since it is owned and operated by the company, is basically conceded to be a marketing vehicle very much like a brochure, catalog, ad, or commercial.
2. To generate traffic to the site requires itself an advertising and PR campaign. Search engines are helpful, as are links from other sites, but creating awareness and impact means *directing* people to the site in the same way PR

campaigns, ads, and promotions direct traffic to retail stores or other locations.

As with the perennial debate over which is more effective, advertising or PR, a story placed in a credible publication or program has a far greater return on investment than many alternatives and that is true as well for online stories and references.

Online magazines, such as *Slate* or *Salon.com*, report solid numbers in terms of their visitors to their sites, but their ultimate impact remains debatable. The greatest measurable benefit is in merchandising the fact that a placement within the magazines' electronic pages appeared. While information is sketchy as to actual influence, at least some online publications do a good job of marketing themselves and keeping their names out front.

Spam combines the intrusiveness of telemarketing with the desirability of fourth-class mail. Spammers so greatly alienated the public so quickly that the outcry for legislative controls only increases its negative perceptions. It does little to raise awareness and simply works the averages, indiscriminately sending millions of low-end promotions for high margin, low interest products. In the first few years of the 21st century, the largest contingent of spammers were pornographers. Unquestionably, spam turned off people to e-mail marketing before its potential could be adequately tested. Its existence downgrades the image of the Internet as a marketing medium. Yet the Internet remains a powerful tool with enormous potential, once it completes its shakeout and maturing process and controls are in place to safeguard the public.

As a publicity tool, the Internet should be a part of the marketing mix, but should be managed with care. It should most definitely *not* be the primary instrument of communicating with the public, as the downside risks still outbalance the benefits.

Publicity is generating attention and awareness, but *other people's publicity* invariably gets the attention of PR practitioners' clients and company executives—all of whom are familiar with the questions, "Why didn't *we* get that story?" and "Why weren't we even *mentioned* in that story" or, worst of all, "We have ten times the knowledge and history of the company profiled in that story, and it would seem from reading it that we don't even exist!"

Ouch.

Accounts are lost over such remarks. In truth, the media can't be everywhere, do everything, and know everything. They count on public relations people to bring interesting, useful, worthwhile information to their attention. The field is competitive, but for the creative, aggressive, efficient PR pro, the door is open.

SUMMARY

- Publicity is often synonymous with "hype" but it is about managing information and bringing a subject to the attention of the public.
- A publicity campaign should generate interest and enthusiasm.
- A brand today might encompass a wide range of items, from toys and clothes to books, fragrances, key chains, bed sheets, and pillow cases, all sharing a single logo and identity and creating a wealth of opportunities for publicity.
- The public respects and supports individuals and companies that demonstrate ethics, integrity, and god business judgment in public matters. It is an issue of style versus substance.
- Just as a marketing program requires a plan, a PR program and a publicity campaign require a plan, whether the effort is on behalf of a company, a cause or issue or candidate.
- Basic tools of publicity include a factual press release (free of hype), press kit, backgrounder or fact sheet, bios and profiles of executives, photographs appropriate to the subject, and any additional materials specific to the subject.
- Depending on the subject, there are formula approaches to attracting media attention or attracting crowds that then attract media attention.

10

Choosing a
PR Agency

Why do some companies and organizations
have public relations agencies, while others have an in-house **PR**
staff, and still others have *both*? If a company or organization is satisfied that its in-house staff has all the experience and capability
needed to perform its public relations function, then this chapter
could serve as a useful checklist. The question of whether or not to
hire an agency or what to look for when hiring an agency depends on
several considerations, such as:

- The objectives of the PR plan
- The time allotted for achieving those objectives
- The range of capabilities and human resources available
- The budget

Determining the Organization's PR Needs

Setting a clear goal or objective, time line, and budget are essential considerations in determining whether the organization's PR needs can be met with existing staff and resources or if retaining an outside agency is the right course. If the decision is to hire an agency, the information in the four points noted above becomes the basis of the client-agency relationship.

Under the PR umbrella are a number of areas of specialization. Many companies insist on hiring a "full service" agency when their needs would be better served by specialists. A public relations plan should be aimed at reaching specific publics and the requirements for doing so can include any or all of the following:

- Media or press relations
- Government relations
- Investor or shareholder relations
- Customer or client relations
- Employee relations
- Event management

Some people in an organization might never have worked with an agency before. Perhaps the company itself has never employed an agency and the individual to whom the agency will report is new at this sort of thing—a situation not unrealistic in even some very large companies. It is important to understand the distinctions between *publicity, press agentry,* and *public relations.*

Publicity is about "publicizing." It is a form of promotion that focuses on getting out a story or an announcement aimed at a specific audience or public.

Press agentry is the specific area of media relations that provides information to the press, responds to media inquiries, and makes qualified experts available for comments or interviews.

Public relations can include both publicity and press agentry, but is a far more encompassing area that can include:

- Strategic planning
- Media training and coaching
- Reputation management
- Crisis management
- Speechwriting
- Arranging and coordinating appearances/speaking engagements
- Advance work for speeches, appearances, and presentations
- Lobbying
- Creating and producing:
  —Literature and collateral material
  —Biographies and backgrounders
  —Video tapes and audio tapes
  —Annual reports
  —Special events
  —Publications, such as newsletters and bulletins
  —Research reports, studies, and "white papers"
  —Hotlines and other interactive vehicles
  —Presentations customized for specific or general audiences
  —Awards programs
  —Contests and promotions
  —Company, product, or issue web site

Public relations is not lying or managing news. *Spin control* is presenting information accurately and in the best possible context, thus reducing the degree to which negative inferences might be drawn from it.

Companies and clients should understand these differences and distinctions and know that PR, whether in-house or through an agency, cannot "kill a story," "bury a story," or turn bad news to good news. It *can*, however, take advantage of most opportunities for exposure to influence public opinion.

It is important to establish early on in a client-agency relationship who will be responsible for various aspects of the program. Some companies or organizations have an in-house public relations vice president, director, or manager. Others have PR committees, which may or may not include public relations professionals. Some have all of the above. When a decision is made to add an outside PR agency or to totally "outsource" the function, guidelines should be created to define who will be responsible for each phase and task of a program, project, or campaign to avoid duplication of efforts and conflict.

The Case for Hiring an Agency

If the determination is that the company or organization has sufficient in-house staff and experience to run the program, it is probably not necessary to read any further in this chapter. But even if an outside firm is only being brought in to assist, it is important that everyone have a clear understanding of the value of such a relationship.

Management will often ask that the role (and the cost) of an outside agency be justified. A qualified PR firm can:

- Provide an outside, objective perspective to a challenge or issue
- Add experience and expertise in specific areas
- Provide overall coordination of resources
- Strengthen industry links and community relations
- Offer experienced professional crisis management
- Provide a broad range of specialized, expert professional services and contacts more cost-effectively on an "as-needed" basis

The Agency Search

There are a number of reasons why a company or an organization might want to hire or change public relations firms:

- A new leader wants to make a fresh start with a new team.
- The company becomes dissatisfied with an agency for any number of reasons, from poor service to frequent changes in the account team to questionable billing practices.

- The company and agency disagree over strategy.
- One party outgrows the other or the relationship changes so it is no longer viable. Either the account becomes too large for the agency or the company reduces its budget and requirements to the point it can no longer afford the agency's services. Or, the agency grows, acquires new business, and can no longer afford to handle companies of comparatively smaller size.
- Conflicts. The agency acquires a new client that poses a conflict or merges, acquires, or is acquired by another agency that represents a competitor of the client.
- Money. Clearly this is one of the most unpleasant reasons to make a change. A client may feel that it is not getting its money's worth or that it is being overcharged. An agency can resign over slow payments or nonpayment of its bills.

Sometimes there are simply misunderstandings over assignments, responsibility, or costs. Changing agencies can be costly. Don't file for a divorce if a marriage counselor can help solve the problem.

As the company begins its agency search, it is in everyone's best interests to be clear about what they want out of the relationship. Create a working document—an outline—along much the same lines as a marketing plan or PR plan would be developed:

1. *Prepare a situation analysis.* Know where the company or organization is in its industry, both alone and relative to the competition. What are the major problems that must be considered or overcome? What resources can the internal staff or agency draw upon?
2. *Define the objective.* Be realistic and be specific. Quantify goals.
3. *Allocate responsibility for achieving the objectives.* Define precisely the responsibilities for the public relations department and the public relations agency.

A company or organization must define its goals, specifically with regard to what the agency will be expected to do. All prospective agencies—as well as the company itself—will benefit from having a concise profile of the company and its mission. The Counselors Academy of the Public Relations Society of America (PRSA) recommends that an informal backgrounder be developed that includes:

- A history of the organization (size, products, services, date founded, etc.)
- Mission, aims of the organization
- PR needs as they are presently perceived
- PR expectations
- Any special PR skills or resources being sought
- A summary of current or past PR efforts
- Requirements for collateral materials, advertising, etc.
- Budget parameters, if any
- Initial length of contract with the firm selected
- Special circumstances that might affect any aspect of the PR program

The next step in the process is to form a search committee. Ideally, a search committee should consist of no more than three people with a clear understanding of the PR function. The head of public relations (or marketing) should chair this committee. Too often, an executive vice president, vice chairman of the board, or other corporate officer will be named to a search committee to give it an appearance of greater importance (or because these people don't have a full plate of daily responsibilities). Often this only slows down the process and takes it off track. Stay focused. Determine:

- Is the account "corporate," for a product, service, institution, or other?
- To whom will the agency be accountable as the client contact and will that person have direct decision-making authority for public relations matters?
- What is the *real* budget? Look at what has been budgeted for PR for several years and compare that figure to what was actually spent. If there is a variance, try to determine why. Did the agency go over budget? Was there a change in the business climate?

- What actual services will be required from the agency? Strategic planning? Publicity? Writing? Event management?

The Agency Profile

Apply these questions to determine what the organization really hopes to find in an agency:

1. Is knowledge of (and experience with other clients in) the industry an important consideration to you? If yes, should the agency have had such experience during the past year?
2. Should the agency be regarded as a specialist in a particular area or discipline?
3. How important is it that the agency has won awards for its work?
4. How important a consideration is the age/experience level of the people assigned to work on the account?
5. How important is the agency's size in terms of billings, number and location of offices, number of employees, or number of other clients?

It is not always necessary that the agency is physically located in the same city as its client or that it even have a branch office there, *but it helps.* While most business will by done by phone, e-mail, fax, messenger service or FEDEX, it is cost-effective for regular meetings to have a local connection.

Being immediately accessible for a face-to-face meeting is preferred, especially when a problem occurs. However, if the best agency to meet the company's needs is across the country, conference calls are the next best thing.

Qualifying Prospective Agencies

The most efficient ways of targeting prospective agencies are:

1. Consult the web sites and/or published directories of PR agencies and public relations trade associations and compare their profiles to the one you have created of your

ideal agency (O'Dwyer's Directory of Public Relations Firms, published by J.R. O'Dwyer Co., Inc., in New York, is regarded as the definitive guide among PR professionals).

2. Contact members of the media who cover the company or industry and ask for recommendations of agencies they respect and trust.

3. Retain the services of a consultant who is skilled at screening, reviewing, and recommending agency selections.

Before contacting prospective agencies and with a *request for proposal* (RFP), narrow the list by sending all who fit the profile a qualifying questionnaire.

Creating a Qualifying Questionnaire

A qualifying questionnaire to prospective agencies can be as brief as:

- Who are you?
- In 250 words or less, tell us why you think we should hire you.
- Send us a representative sample of your best work.

Or it can be lengthy and include such questions as:

- Who are your current and past clients?
- How long have they been/were they your clients?
- What is your specific experience in our industry?
- Who would work on our account and what are their credentials?
- What has been your agency's turnover rate in personnel over the past five years?
- How are your fees determined?
- What is your normal learning curve or "ramp-up" period and when might we begin seeing the results of your efforts on our behalf?
- What references we can contact to create a profile on your agency?

Some agencies won't respond to questionnaires at all, others will respond in their own way, disregarding the questions asked, attempting to gain control of the process and guide the relationship. Still other agencies use any contact, no matter how preliminary, as an opportunity to position themselves. They will phone (sometimes often) requesting more information and asking to schedule a familiarization meeting or a "get acquainted" lunch.

Some clients respond favorably to these tactics, considering them a show of serious interest or "hunger" on the agency's part. It may be that, or it may be simply a ploy to circumvent the process.

In most instances, the best course is to consider all prospective agencies fairly and equally and not confuse aggressive salesmanship with quality service.

To those whose responses make a favorable impression, request a proposal and allow their ability to relate to a prospective client to demonstrate how they operate in a business environment.

The Request for Proposal (RFP)

Narrow the list of prospective agencies to a manageable number, ideally, no more than ten agencies, and ask for written proposals. If the response is satisfactory, move on to repeat the process with the next ten agencies. Your Request For a Proposal (RFP) should:

- Note specific problems, questions, or concerns the agency should address
- Describe any constraints under which the agency must work
- Provide specific information about budget parameters, other commitments and agency relationships
- Be specific about deadlines for both agency selection and the term of the client-agency relationship

Exhibit 10.1 shows a typical RFP.

EXHIBIT 10.1:
A TYPICAL REQUEST FOR PROPOSAL

Dear (agency CEO):

Ours is an established technology organization seeking to retain the services of a public relations firm. If you are interested in being considered for this assignment, please complete and return the enclosed qualifying questionnaire by no later than (insert date for return of questionnaire). It is our intention to narrow our search to a small number of agencies, meet with their representatives, and have our new agency in place by (insert date the arrangement would become effective).

While we are seeking a locally based agency or an agency with a branch office in the same city as our own corporate headquarters, we anticipate running a national campaign and program. Our PR budget for the current fiscal year is $(insert annual PR budget).

In an effort to help us select the most qualified agency, please help us determine if our organizations would be a good fit. Thank you for your cooperation; we look forward to your reply.

Sincerely,

Presentations and Meetings

After reviewing written proposals, narrow the list to three to five agencies (or groups of three to five agencies) and schedule meetings with each of the candidates. It is important at this stage to put each of the finalists on as "level a playing field" as possible.

Ideally, meetings should not exceed 90 minutes in length and should be scheduled at the same time of day, one per day, on consecutive days—*at the agencies' offices.*

There are good reasons for this. The search committee should see each agency at its best, on its "home court," and get a sense of its unique atmosphere and work environment. These visits will also show the "personality" each firm wants to convey. While this process is time-consuming, tiring, and may be a hassle, it is an important part of making the best choice and that takes some effort.

Agencies make a lot of presentations. Have a list of questions that are of particular concern to people within the company or organization, but allow each agency to set the agenda for its meeting with the search committee. This is their opportunity to impress a prospective client under conditions most favorable to them. Challenge them to do so:

- Judge them by how well organized they seem.
- Does the presentation seem tailored to the company or organization and its industry or does it appear to be a generic pitch the agency would deliver unaltered to all prospective clients?
- Note the interaction between members of the account team and management.
- Do they appear confident and comfortable with their subject, their material, with the company people, and with each other?
- Do they strictly adhere to the time restrictions?
- Do they have thoughtful questions *for management* to answer?
- Is there a focus, logic, and continuity in their presentation?
- Did they exceed your requests by offering creative recommendations?
- Did they indicate that the company would be an important client to them and that they really want the company's business?
- Do they answer the questions *directly and succinctly*?

The Moment of Truth (or, at least, Choice)

Evaluate prospective agencies according to these criteria:

- Do they understand the company or organization's objectives?

- Are they responsive and service-oriented?
- Do they *listen* at meetings and respond with solutions?
- Are they creative?
- Can they provide services, contacts, access, or expertise that is not available elsewhere?
- Is their work for other clients getting results?
- Are their fees competitive with other agencies?
- Do they seem to know their business?
- Are they honest? (Checking references here helps.)
- How important a client will the company be to them? It is not necessary to be the agency's single largest client, but don't believe that all clients receive equal treatment. The size of an account is directly related to the quality and amount of service it receives.
- Do the people who will be working with the agency feel comfortable with them? Never underestimate the importance of good "chemistry" in client-agency relationships.

The last point may be among the most important. If management or the company people feel comfortable with the agency people, have confidence in them and are impressed with their competence and professionalism, then virtually any problem, setback, or misunderstanding can be resolved quickly and easily.

Upon making the decision, notify the agencies that were not selected with a telephone call before they read of the decision in the trade press or hear the news on the industry grapevine. It is good business to maintain a reputation for professionalism with other agencies that made a favorable impression. There might be a special project or additional needs in the future—or a reversal of fortune for the agency chosen might necessitate reopening talks with others.

Finally, place a phone call to the agency chosen and/or send a bottle of champagne with a note of congratulations. Invite the new account team to lunch to celebrate the beginning of a successful new relationship.

SUMMARY

- The question of whether to use a PR agency, an in-house PR staff, or both depends on the goals of the plan, time allotted for achieving those goals, budget, and capabilities and human resources available.
- Setting clear goals, time line, and budget are essential in determining if the organization's PR needs can be met with existing staff and resources or if retaining an outside agency is the right course.
- Prepare a profile of what an agency must be and evaluate potential agencies based on that criteria.
- A PR plan should reach specific publics and may require media or press relations; government, investor or shareholder relations; customer/client relations; employee relations, or event management.
- PR agencies should be assigned specific responsibilities, such as publicity; strategic planning; media training; crisis management; speechwriting; lobbying; producing collaterals or events; interactive vehicles; awards programs; or managing designated web sites.
- People working with an agency must feel comfortable with the agency team. Never underestimate the importance of good "chemistry" in client-agency relationships.

11

Public Relations and the Media

As mentioned previously, public relations draws on many different functions, and , in a sense, everything comes first. Is it the plan, or the creative or the media? Which of these is "the first among equals" depends on who is determining the priorities. In this chapter we'll give the nod to the media.

The view here is that no matter how well-planned or creative a program is, it will fail if no one sees it, hears about it or reads about it. Therefore, to assure reach and influence, the first order of business is to cultivate appropriate members of the media.

The Importance of the Media

The media.

On any given day in the United States, the mass media's representatives are cursed and courted. Separately and together, according to small organizations on the left and right and large organizations of every stripe, the media is manipulative, unfair, and biased.

And most spokespersons for media entities repeatedly assert that since extremists on all sides insist the media favors their opponents, they must be doing something right, which they clearly are or everyone would not be hustling so aggressively to secure precious minutes of media exposure.

Like the people who are fond of saying they are not experts, but they know what they like (and then go on at length as if they *were* experts), many clients and members of senior management profess to not understand media, but really believe that they do.

Most people watch television, read newspapers and magazines, see promotional posters, receive mail, or use the Internet, so the commodity that is the media is not foreign to them.

And it looks so easy.

How difficult, after all, can it be to answer a few questions about what you stand for?

The answer is that it is actually *very* difficult.

Ask people in the company or organization who think they understand media to answer the list of questions in Exhibit 11.1.

The fact is, to most people, working with the media *does* look easy. Yet, the overwhelming majority of people who find themselves contacted by a member of the media—even a telephone call from a reporter—become nervous, self-conscious, and highly ill at ease in such situations.

Interviews with journalists are often high-anxiety situations in which countless numbers of intelligent, articulate, capable men and women report they were "unhappy with how that went" and wait nervously to see how a writer or editor will represent what they said.

The correct answer to all these questions in Exhibit 11.1 is: *That is why there are public relations people*—to know and understand deadlines and production schedules, to know what media entities are likely to be friendly and which are virtually always trouble, which af-

---

EXHIBIT 11.1: KEY MEDIA QUESTIONS

- What does a producer of a TV news show do?
- What is the deadline for getting information in the next edition of *USA Today*?
- How does one get an op-ed piece published in *The Wall Street Journal* or *The New York Times*?
- What kind of lead-time is standard for stories that appear in monthly magazines? In bi-monthlies? On public access television?
- What are the rules regarding embargoed reports and press releases?
- How does one use information that was given "off the record"?
- How exactly does a PR expert "kill" a story?
- What is "deep background"?
- What is the protocol for offering the same story to more than one news organization?

---

ford the best opportunities for merchandising and extending the news cycle for a story . . .

Media Alternatives

Media alternatives continue to proliferate and often overlap, even when the economy suggests the opposite should be true. On the print side, where the choice is not simply newspapers or magazines, there are more than fifteen variants within those two categories and a lengthy list under each of those.

Electronic media is not just TV and radio, but the Internet and perhaps a dozen sub-categories that both broaden and fragment the audience, while fine-tuning the publics within narrower demographic and psychographic market segments.

Exhibit 11.2: Media Options

Today's ever-expanding media options include:

Newspapers:
- National newspapers
- National and regional feature publications
- National newspaper syndicates
- Ethnic and foreign language newspapers
- Foreign language editions of mainstream newspapers
- Special interest publications that coincide with conferences, conventions, meetings and trade shows
- Local newspapers—city, suburban, regional, community editions
- Professional publications (specializing in finance, law, technology, etc.)
- Home shopper-type free newspapers

Magazines:
- General interest weeklies, monthlies, quarterlies
- Business magazines
- News weeklies
- City magazines
- Fraternal and professional journals
- Lifestyle publications aimed at specific demographic audiences
- Ethnic magazines aimed at clearly defined publics
- Affinity publications for clubs, associations, and special interests
- Magalogs

Electronic Media:
Television:
- Network broadcast
- Local broadcast
- National cable
- Local cable
- Public access cable
- Closed-circuit
- Satellite stations
- Pay-per-view programming
- In-flight TV/video
- In-store point-of-sale video
- DVDs
- CD-ROM

Radio:
- Network
- Local
- College and university
- High school radio
- Satellite radio
- Syndicated programming

The Internet:
- Web sites
- Chat rooms
- Streaming video
- Weblogs
- E-mails

Out-of-Home:
- Billboards
- Transit signs
- Windows signs
- Marquees
- Posters in public waiting areas

- Bus shelters
- Point-of-sale displays
- Printed T-shirts, caps, buttons, bumper stickers, and car-toppers

---

Using Media Options

While virtually all the entries on the list above accept advertising, they are also the essential platforms for constructing public relations programs.

Generating media placement is a key step, but a single appearance or segment alone, or followed by others—shotgun style—might well be judged a success by a publicist, press agent, or media planner, only to leave the public thinking, "Wow! This person seems to be everywhere!"

Ideally the public would process these repeated exposures as knowledge of the subject the person is out there talking about increases, but too often, if poorly managed and loosely controlled, they become an exercise in over-exposure and the public is turned off and tunes out.

A key rule-of-thumb here is: Do not bring as much attention to the presenter as to what is being presented.

PR pioneer Philip Lesly once noted, "It is clear that as great as the change has been in mass communications in just a few years, much more change is ahead. Old methods of dealing with them, based on the press release and the quiet event, are obsolete. Today's methods probably will be obsolete before long. It will be one of public relations' greatest challenges to keep abreast of this multifaceted pattern." It is certainly true that PR specialists, as well as other marketing and advertising professionals, have a true passion for the word "new"—it probably appears more than any other word in advertising copy, press releases, and product packaging. From political awareness of the value of the term through such applications as the *New Deal, New Frontier,* and *New World Order* to the reformulated *new and improved* Tide, the implications suggest a finger on the pulse of public opinion and a desire to keep moving toward something better. It is the standard advisory to clients and company management:

- Public tastes change.
- The public tends to become bored quickly with what it perceives as older or stuck in "sameness."
- The product, the packaging, and the message must continually be kept fresh and *new*.

But with all due respect to the late Mr. Lesly, who certainly recognized this, the term "basic" has a great deal of power from which those things that are new derive. The press release will remain the *basic* vehicle for information, presenting facts to the media, though as time evolves it may indeed be called by another name.

The basic "pitch" to the media must be delivered in some form, and although reporters, editors, and producers might want the pitch delivered electronically (telephone, e-mail, CD-ROM, diskette) or in person over a fine lunch, ultimately the essential information—the basic pitch—must be reduced to a concise, comprehensive, factual document . . . the press release.

The Media List and the Media Plan

The plan has outlined the objectives and noted the strategy and tactics that will achieve those objectives. Creating awareness involves generating media interest, and that means first developing a media list and a media plan. There is a difference.

The *media list* is just that: a list. It can be a set of mailing labels with a list of telephone numbers and fax numbers and e-mail addresses. It is both an indication of the public relations person's professionalism and a way to increase the likelihood that the material sent to the media will be used if:

- There is certainty that the lists are specific and current. Never direct a press release, media alert, memorandum, or invitation to simply "business editor" or "producer" unless specifically asked to do so by the recipient. Use names of current recipients, not of their predecessors. Phone first just to be sure there hasn't been a personnel change since your last press release.

- Know the form in which the recipient (media person) prefers or requires information to be sent. Some editors, producers, and reporters will not accept unsolicited press kits if they do not have time or inclination (or the physical space) to review hundreds of packets that could arrive each week. Many prefer to receive e-mail pitches and written brief inquiries from which they will request information or call to schedule an interview if they are interested.

It would perhaps be an overstatement to suggest that the media *needs* public relations people—certainly few people associated with the media would ever hint that was the case—but astute media people understand the immense value of PR professionals as sources of information and as people who help them do their jobs more efficiently by providing ideas, access, and resources.

In working with the media, knowing how and whom to approach is very important. Reporters and editors do not appreciate having their time wasted, so PR people understand not to bring a feature story to a financial editor, even if the subject is a corporate CEO, unless the editor expressed a prior interest in preparing a profile on the CEO.

Just as editors with the larger book publishing companies will usually only accept proposals from literary agents they know and believe understand what they are looking for, many editors, reporters, and producers are approached by so many people so regularly that they need and appreciate the PR professionals who know what to send to them and how to send it.

The media list identifies everyone the PR person wants to be sure receives information, but if the PR person knows his or her job, it will not be sent out as a bulk mailing to everyone indiscriminately, playing the averages that if enough releases and pitches go out, someone will bite.

The *media plan* is much more than a list. It is basically a briefing document that contains information and details a client or management executive needs to know, such as the circulation and audience size, demographic profiles of the target audience of each entry in the plan, where it ranks among its competitors, and why its inclusion makes sense as part of the overall plan and its objectives.

A detailed media plan helps to:

1. Make certain that the information is not just about reaching an audience, but that it is about reaching the *correct* audience for the subject.
2. Reinforce the program by educating decision-makers.

It is not unusual for some executives at the top of an organization to be unfamiliar with many of the publications and programs that serve, reach, and influence their markets. To put it more directly, experienced PR people are accustomed to having clients and company management ask why someone from a media organization they've never heard of is interviewing them.

Like most people, they have heard of *The Wall Street Journal, Forbes, Fortune, Business Week,* the two best-selling trade publications, and business TV programs such as *Money Line, Wall Street Week* and *Squawk Box.*

General audiences know the major general interest publications such as *Time, Newsweek* and *People* and a range of slightly less general interest titles like *Rolling Stone, Variety, Vanity Fair, Architectural Digest, The New Yorker, National Review,* and the *Weekly Standard,* to name just a few. These are just a handful of media entities where management would be pleased to see its name.

Yet, interviews with lower profile but highly respected organizations, such as Reuters News Service or Bloomberg News and countless other fine venues, would be fine connections and excellent placements for CEOs or spokespersons in almost any industry, though many executives have little or no awareness or them and are unimpressed.

For every well-known publication in a specific trade, there are usually many less well-known vehicles, some of which have significant and devoted readers. The media plan spells that out and educates clients and executives, a public often overlooked by many PR specialists until it is too late.

Similarly, on the broadcast and cable side, many executives are unfamiliar with the programs and the people who are the hosts and anchors of these programs. Yet, these are media opportunities that offer significant reach and audience influence.

CNBC cable television, for example, has for years maintained an extremely small audience by TV standards, but it is nonetheless an audience comprised of many decision-makers with a real impact on the markets.

PR professionals should understand the value of securing placements in even lower rated programs and smaller publications where the cumulative affect of such visibility registers with quality audiences, and in making certain clients and management understand why these are worthy of their best efforts. These connections can also often be stepping stones to other, higher visibility media—as well as opportunities for executives to gain experience presenting their messages before microphones and cameras, in the usually brief period of time allotted for interviews. Viewing and listening to tapes of these experiences provides opportunities for executives to improve their presentation skills.

It is useful for public relations people to educate their clients and executives. The media plan demystifies the schedule and raises the level of appreciation and enthusiasm for it by identifying programs and publications, providing information on audience size and demographics, and helping clients and management understand there is a large and diverse media universe to be explored and cultivated to create awareness and influence attitudes and opinions.

An interview with a columnist for a small circulation local newspaper, a trade publication, a newsletter, or even a web site will not only reach the core audiences of these entities, but if merchandised properly by PR professionals—distributed with cover letters, follow-up comments, literature and phone calls—can spark the interest of *other* columnists, editors, and producers who would consider how a story on this subject might appeal to *their* audiences.

Just as clients and executives of a company see, hear, or read a story in which a competitor is featured and ask, "Why wasn't that story about *us*?," editors and producers see the same story as it appears elsewhere in the media and ask, "Why didn't *we* have that story?"

In both instances the answer is usually that an aggressive public relations person, representing a company or organization, took careful aim and pitched the story to members of the media that ran with it.

Other media will consider the story that has already been told, but a public relations person can extend its life, finding other angles to highlight so other media can appear not to have overlooked a story with something of value.

Cultivating and Maintaining Strong Media Relations

A company or organization that is very well known must be concerned about maintaining its image and reputation, cultivating an even wider public, and projecting a sense of being forward-thinking—not assuming that because it has achieved its success, that success does not have to be preserved and protected. Many organizations that once enjoyed number one status, relaxed their efforts and saw aggressive competitors overtake them.

Media relationships must be nurtured and cannot be taken for granted. A reporter, editor, or producer who is responsible for a company or organization receiving favorable treatment in a story does not promise to do so forever. Companies that achieve leadership status must remind the media on a regular basis how they achieved it, how they maintain it, and why they deserve preeminent roles in business.

Much smaller or younger organizations that are not so well known must also be concerned about their images and reputations and about their need to generate any media coverage or interest at all.

Once a company is able to break through, its public relations representatives have something on which to build. Often young, struggling companies that need media exposure to establish their presence will push too hard. Their management demands the PR people pressure media for attention—as the expression goes, *with a vengeance*—sometimes before their message has been tested and before they are ready for the market. That is, with no actual success stories to tell and only an idea and an organization of bright people—but no history, track record, awards, high profile customers, or firm relationships—they shout for recognition and attention from the media and, in the process, call attention to management's relative lack of sophistication and immaturity.

If and when a media entity, perhaps on a slow news day or as a favor to someone, affords the company some coverage, hundreds of executives of other companies notice and become convinced that generating publicity through the media is easy and they are entitled to expect nothing less than the same treatment.

PR people are creative (or at least they *should be*) and routinely develop imaginative approaches for presenting a company's message. But management must be realistic in such situations. Unless an unknown or less known company or organization is being led by a former head of Coca-Cola, IBM, General Motors, or Nike, the company does not deserve space in *The Wall Street Journal* just for existing. It still needs a unique selling proposition—a good, different, interesting story to tell.

More Mediums, More PR Choices

Whenever a new medium appears to be finding an audience and growing in popularity, its proponents and pundits invariably pronounce all that came before "over" and only appropriate for a display in the Smithsonian Institution.

TV was supposed to be the end of movies, radio, magazines, and even the daily newspaper. Despite the advanced form of intelligence that cultural observers like to display, the prevailing sense seems always to have been that it is okay to *say* there is room enough for all, but in fact there is only one choice per industry of what is "hot" and all else is passé.

The Internet was touted as the choice of a new generation, rendering all other media venues as secondary, if not totally obsolete.

Nonsense.

Marketers cannibalized their budgets to create "an Internet presence" at the expense of other media. After some five years of trial and error, which was actually more like trials and disasters, the Internet was pronounced important and useful, but pretty much another medium of information and communication alongside television, the telephone, and newspapers.

While TV and the Internet have each had their time as flavor-of-the month, creativity and solid work keep most media sectors alive and well. Audiences are more fragmented, usually driven by lifestyle, economics, and demographic considerations, and theoretically, that should only enhance the power of each fragmented sector to deliver the message to audiences.

Newspapers in Public Relations Programs

The newspaper in America has been pronounced dead on countless occasions, yet the industry remains strong. Some 10,000 newspapers are published in the United States alone. More than 1,700 of those are daily newspapers; nearly 8,000 are weekly and special interest papers. This presents public relations people with some very diversified options and alternatives for their messages—*if* they study the specifics of the medium and draw a plan that thoughtfully identifies where opportunities lie.

Public relations expert Dorothy I. Doty notes that, "In publicity, as in so many other things, there is a place for everything and everything should be in its place . . . It is up to you to decide upon the best place for your publicity. To make this determination, you should know as much as possible about the media you are considering." This means looking beyond the best-known media entities, even though they are the placements clients and CEOs covet most. Don't exclude these from the list, but recognize that since virtually everyone wants to be in *Time, Newsweek* and *The Wall Street Journal,* and on *The Today Show, Good Morning America, Oprah,* and *Larry King Live*, their editors and producers are being contacted by hundreds of PR people each week—all insisting they have a story that would be perfect for that audience.

Editors and producers typically have these overtures reviewed by their least experienced staff people, who reject nearly all of them. Meanwhile the more senior staff members of media organizations are looking at local newspapers, specialty magazines, and local programs for stories that other editors and producers have already designated as worthy of their attention and which now might be worthy of wider exposure.

Magazines and the Internet in PR Programs

The magazine business has a very rocky history. Most new ventures fail and nearly every success story is marked by periods of being up, down, and sometimes out. *Look, Life,* and *The Saturday Evening Post* once posted huge weekly audiences and a generation later, all were gone. *Redbook, McCall's,* and *Cosmopolitan* each underwent innumerable facelifts; celebrity-fronted vehicles named for TV personalities Oprah, Rosie, and Martha found the renewal route and investor interest as fickle as the average day's audience and as changeable as a network executive suite.

Yet, thousands of magazine titles flood racks, shops, and mail boxes each month, each offering something aimed at touching every interest from gun lover to gourmet chef, biker to animal lover, Beanie Babies to students of foreign affairs, social critic to crafts fan to just plain lovers. Whatever the subject or interest, there are magazines to appeal to all tastes—wine, cigars, yachting, health and nutrition, writing, romance, self-improvement, weight loss, technology, guitar, piano . . .

It is safe to conclude that whatever the product, company, issue, cause, region, profession, or special interest, at least one magazine exists to respond to that interest. The overwhelming majority of content in such magazines is provided by freelance contributors who usually write for (or contribute to) other publications and web sites—very often specialized publications or sites exclusively produced for the members of associations and groups and, as such, are not always noted in directories or on lists, even though their audiences could be considerable.

PR people need to check publications and web sites for not only the most visible special interest or trade media, but for the names of the contributors to these publications who may, in turn, provide information and access about additional possible opportunities.

Directories exist in printed versions and online and Internet search engines can provide considerably more information about lower profile publications and alternative web sites by cross-referencing entries.

The Internet is a useful tool for developing a media plan in that it not only can help to identify and reach narrowly-targeted special interest audiences quickly, but it can also provide information and access to *tens of millions* of web sites that seemingly include every subject, interest, and group imaginable.

Unfortunately, the reliability of the information found on some web sites is highly questionable. These sites appear and disappear quite suddenly, many of them top-loaded with erroneous or even fraudulent material. Many Internet sites, however, are operated by companies, organizations, trade associations, special interest groups, libraries, government agencies, and other honorable entities. Visitors must view web sites with caution.

It is not uncommon for an entity with an impressive name, such as United States Publications Institute, to be one person operating a web site from a kitchen table. Public relations people need to validate a web site's credibility before using its content or supplying it with information. Many publishing organizations have long had such a policy, but since web sites rarely involve voice contact with individuals, caution must be exercised that references are not faked—such as a fraudulent site providing a link to *another* fraudulent site that confirms its information—along with its bogus core content.

That warning noted, the Internet is still a force in media with its greatest potential still ahead, despite its elements of risk.

PR people must also evaluate the weight of certain Internet media in the media mix. For example, technology companies that would be delighted to have their presence noted in *Business Week* might actually prefer to have their story in that publication's online edition even more than its established and respected newsstand version.

The same companies might view articles, profiles, or items that appear in *MacWorld* or any of a myriad of other respected tech sites, as superior media placements as they not only are viewed by the companies' target audiences, but are accorded a certain high level of respect and status for having "made the cut" and been singled-out from their competitors.

As with more established media, the Internet performs a dual role of being both a source of information and, for public relations people, a provider of a vast array of vehicles on which to efficiently place information that could be accessed and viewed worldwide. But unlike newspapers or TV in similar roles, Internet sites are often indiscriminant or arbitrary as to standards of accuracy and fairness.

The web sites of established media organizations—ABC News, the Tribune Company, Forbes.com, etc.—apply similar standards to those of their print and broadcast operations. Certainly more successful on-line media, such as Slate, Salon.com, or TheStreet.com, will not accept just anything from anyone. But that cannot be said for a huge number of sites among the many millions of sites that exist.

Weblogs (commonly called "blogs") are usually described as diary-like personal web sites—as places where pretty much anyone with a personal computer and a modem can "publish" a newsletter, journal, magazine, or whatever they choose to call it. These simple, inexpensive setups have created a new tier of media operations that have virtually exploded in the early years of the 21st century.

What causes blogs to be taken seriously is the fact that companies began creating weblogs to launch and promote products and brands. Dr. Pepper, for example, drew national attention for its effort to create a "network of bloggers" in a viral marketing-type approach to marketing its new beverage product, Raging Cow. The company offered free merchandise, such as T-shirts, caps, etc., to bloggers—mostly young people who spend large amounts of time online—who help to promote the product.

In many respects this system is similar to other programs where people are enlisted to help in an effort and are paid in product rather than in cash. How viable a method of promotion or a marketing instrument "blogging" becomes has yet to be determined.

What is clear is that what has been called "new media" since the 1990s remains new because it is still very much evolving.

Reporter Steve Lohr, writing in *The New York Times*, noted in 2003:

> Book publishers, newspapers, magazines, television networks and movie studios—all would be digitized, some would disappear, but vast new opportunities would arise.

The shift to bits promised more than just faster and cheaper distribution of the same old information and entertainment. The digital age held out potential for a genuinely 'new media.' . . . But it hasn't happened."

Almost everyone agrees that the new media factor of the

Internet will be realized one day, but it is important for public relations professionals, their clients, and managers to also be aware that some companies have been convinced *the future has already arrived*. These companies cannibalized their marketing budgets and shredded their programs to focus almost exclusively on Internet communications. A decade later, their message reverberated through cyberspace, and missed huge segments of the market that had not yet arrived there.

New media is exciting, but it is not everything.

E-mail Communications in PR Programs

E-mail marketing seems in theory to be the logical extension and a great step forward for the direct mail industry and certainly an instrument public relations professionals should be able to put to good use. Like so much else, however, there is both an upside and a downside.

Just as the value and importance of direct mail has been undermined by junk mail, spam threatens to lessen the power and effectiveness—if not the very future—of e-mail.

For years spammers seemed to proliferate, sending literally millions of unsolicited e-mails, clogging the mailboxes of the unsuspecting public, and turning off many people to a very useful process.

The cause was not helped by the fact that spammers were so indiscriminant—offering cut-rate prescription drugs, cut-rate second mortgages, and an assortment of cut-rate products and systems advertised to enhance or enlarge the dimensions of various body parts, to people who were not remotely prospects for such products.

Adding to this was (and is) the fear that using e-mail of any sort would leave consumers vulnerable to being added to more spam lists and the very real possibility that unsolicited e-mails would result in destructive computer viruses.

How marketers in general can or should use e-mail to its best advantage is a large subject to cover, but one for which the model should be the direct mail programs developed for the non-electronic environment. For public relations, e-mail should be used to communicate with lists of people who have indicated this is their communications method of choice. To do otherwise virtually insures the overwhelming percentage of e-mails sent will be deleted unopened, unread, and useless—much like junk mail.

A key element to e-mail messaging is creativity—the creative headline and lead that makes people want to open and read the e-mail. This is a challenge as spammers have so often used exterior headings, such as "Important—open immediately" or "Urgent—do not delete," only to then reveal a tacky ad for low-end merchandise and services.

Spammers also use the tactic of creating bogus senders' names to make the spam appear as if it were being sent by a friend or someone the mailbox owner thinks he or she might know—fairly common names like Maggie Meyers or James Smith. This tactic even *further* annoys the recipient, much to the complete indifference of the spammers.

PR people should use their own or their company or organization names as senders of e-mail, as any attempt to be clever or especially creative is likely to put sender names unopened into the junk mail recycling bin. Other tips:

- Include terms such as "press release attached" in directing releases to the media.
- When communicating with specific segments of the public, refer to that with a heading such as "shareholder information attached."
- Have a code number or member ID word that will appear in the address.

Alas, "information for members only" has already been usurped by the spammers for junk mail.

A great advantage to using e-mail communications for PR is, apart from significant savings in production and postage costs, press releases, media advisories, media alerts, confirmation or event or press conference reminder notices, and other information can be delivered instantly.

Television in PR Programs

Television has long been regarded as the most powerful and coveted medium because of its reach, in terms of both its audience size and its level of impact, as well as for the cultural implications it carries.

For generations of people who grew up with television, to have their message or product or company appear or to actually appear themselves on TV, is a validation of status and importance.

Almost anyone can have his or her own web site or web log and creating a brochure or other printed piece can be done very inexpensively.

But not everyone makes it to TV, and to be seen on the same television screen that brought into people's homes presidents, kings and queens, rock stars, superheroes, and people who walked in space is still considered an achievement. This remains true despite the proliferation of cable channels that would theoretically lower the status of TV in the value equation. Some cable channels do indeed sometimes draw larger audiences than many of their wealthy, powerful broadcast counterparts.

If the porthole to print is the press release, what is the gateway into television? Is it necessary to be photogenic? Is it possible to control the content of a TV segment or interview? Are there any do-overs allowed for CEOs who are unhappy with the way their TV presentation and appearance turned out?

Despite its mystique, for public relations professionals, securing a TV placement should be no more difficult to accomplish than a print placement. Producers and their assistants and associates hold jobs that include the same functions as those of an editor. Indeed, many TV producers began their careers as editors.

The elements of the process are much the same, assembling all the ingredients to present a compelling story—only on a screen rather than a page, but still requiring a deft touch to bring it to life.

For years the producers and editors in the television industry were resistant to programming business news or features, limited coverage to only daily stock market reports ("The market closed up 26 points today and Wall Streeters are happy."). The charge was that business and financial news is not "visual" and TV is a "visual" medium that needs pictures and action. Obviously times have changed.

If the story allows for a prop to hold up or to show in a close-up a package of diet pills, a computer screen, a cellular phone . . . that was a bonus—but a CEO or corporate spokesperson with an announcement, no matter how important it was or what its impact, was ignored or rushed by with as few words spoken as possible in order to get to sports news or the film of the burning factory across town. It was TV—it had to be *visual*.

The success of TV "talk shows" changed the standards of the news. If audiences would delight in watching two or four people sitting on a sofa and just talking to each other for 90 minutes each night, they might accept news reporters announcing a misappropriation of millions of dollars by a corporate executive or an anchorman describing two giant companies agreeing to be one even bigger giant company.

A spokesperson with something to say, just standing at a microphone and saying it, is now the central element of TV news, sports, or "magazine" programs. Reporters introduce their stories by standing outside a building, in the middle of a bridge, in a hallway near the scene where a meeting is taking place—anywhere that offers a snipet of "visual interest."

But the story is about what is being *said*. News is presented as news has always been presented—*someone tells someone something worth knowing*. It just took television a few decades to catch on that visual was interesting, but an announcement that something worth knowing had occurred was worth more than a few feet of film or video tape. People wanted to know.

The "visual" element might be (and typically is) a person getting out of a car or entering a building or shaking hands with someone else. For this, a press release, backgrounder, and bio provide the necessary content. The pitch is the same as it would be for a print story: the unique selling proposition—what makes this subject newsworthy, useful, and interesting to know about.

People said for 40 years they never saw anyone unattractive on television as a reporter of the subject of a story. Just as the story itself had to be visual, the theory was that the people on television had to be nice to look at or the audience would not watch. While that's still true, for the most part, in entertainment programming, news and information has changed, and CEOS no longer are required to report to the make-up department before telling their stories.

What made the difference in television is that, in addition to producers and editors in the industry finally growing up, the corporate or organization spokespeople presenting their messages on television today are the informed sources, the experts, the foremost authorities, and they *seem* more buttoned-up and "ready for TV" because:

1. In many ways, *viewers* of television have changed. People view people on TV from a different perspective than the people they see on a train or in the supermarket. For their time on television, these people are "larger than life."
2. They are seen for only a very short period of time. Critical judgments and challenges are made over time, rarely from hearing a person deliver only a sentence or two.
3. Spokespersons on TV are presenting their messages in a very deliberate and controlled manner.
4. They have often been prepared as to how to look their best and rehearsed with a media coach.

Someone who is *well prepared* can handle a great deal of pressure and field tough questions in a composed, confident, professional manner. In some cases, a TV interview or segment is "live" and there is only one chance for the speaker to create his or her best impressions. In other situations, the segment is pre-taped for length, flow, crispness, and interest. It is unusual for the subject of the piece to have any role or approval in the editing so, even though the piece is recorded, it is important to get it right the first time to create the desired impression with the audience.

Meeting the Media

People can be confident and relaxed in conversation with friends and associates, but with a camera rolling, microphones in front of them, and a warning that just possibly the whole world is, even the most intelligent executives can freeze up and become self-conscious and forget points they have articulated a hundred times.

See Exhibit 11.3 for specific steps that can be taken to prepare for an interview. When meeting with the media, whether TV, print, radio or online, use this checklist to get organized and focused.

EXHIBIT 11.3: FIFTEEN STEPS TO PREP FOR MEETING THE MEDIA

1. Know as much as you can about the reporter you are talking with. Check examples of his or her previous work to get a sense of any predispositions or prejudices.

   It can be helpful to know if the reporter is favorable to a particular organization, rival, or point of view, has a history of "getting things wrong," looks for (or to create) controversy wherever possible, or has written flatteringly of competitors. It is sometimes possible to win over people and change their minds about a subject. At the very least, being well prepared and knowledgeable might keep critical references from an unfriendly reporter to a minimum.

2. Don't assume the reporter knows about you, your company or organization, your product, or even your industry. People assume all reporters do their homework, but that is not always the case.

   One mistake many executives and spokespersons make is to assume that all reporters do their homework and arrive for interviews well prepared with a list of thoughtful questions and insightful observations. Sometimes that happens, but don't count on it. More often, reporters have not prepared well for interviews, know little or nothing about the company, product, person, or issues the subject is ready to discuss, and counts on a public relations representative to supply the necessary input and information.

3. It is okay to set "ground rules" for your interview.

   While reporters are supposed to be the ones asking the questions, it is well within the prerogative of the person being interviewed to specify that for legal reasons or proprietary concerns, certain subjects can't be discussed.

4. Be prepared. Rehearse remarks before the interview.

5. Provide the reporter with a press kit or other written material that summarizes your message.

Some reporters take notes, others use tape recorders for interviews, and still others trust their memory as to what is being said. In any case, have a prepared packet of material to leave with the reporter. More often than not, he or she will quote from a press release or backgrounder, bio, brochure, or annual report as much as from the interview and the chances of accuracy are far better for it.

6. Provide "sound bites"—your best most quotable information in short, concise remarks.

7. Position yourself as the reporter's best source on the subject.

Be helpful and offer to put the reporter in touch with other experts who will support the message or argument being presented. Don't allow yourself to be drawn into related discussions about matters or issues that are not in line with the point of the story being presented.

8. Focus on facts. Keep comments brief and concise. Keep examples to a minimum. Avoid anecdotes.

In interviews, there is often the tendency to want to "give a little background on the subject" or "provide some history." This is a mistake. It tends to slow down the interview and draw attention away from current matters. Focus on facts and stay close to the subject at hand. Keep comments brief and concise to minimize chances of being misunderstood or misquoted.

9. Stay within your area of expertise.

10. Remember that numbers make good stories. Use statistics or growth or revenue figures as much as possible.

Statistics, rankings, percentages, dates and dollar figures add depth and color to a story. Inject numbers into the story whenever possible.

11. Be aware of gestures, tone of voice, and body language.

It is important to be conscious of gestures and body language during an interview. Reporters are attuned to a subject's ability—or lack of ability—to make eye contact. Even one's tone of voice in phone interviews can make a difference in how the subject is presented, suggesting the interview subject was unable to focus. An unfavorable story might include phrases such as, "the information told one story, but the speaker seemed ill at ease, distracted, preoccupied, and seemed unable to look the reporter in the eye throughout most of the interview." Be confident, relaxed, courteous, and alert.

12. "No comment" is never a good response to a question.

The phrase "no comment" has not only a harsh sound—even when said in a light tone of voice—but usually conveys an impression that the person being interviewed has something to conceal or that the reporter has touched a nerve and moved into an area where there might be a good deal more to uncover. In fact, the situation might just be that something is proprietary or covered by a confidentiality agreement. But rather than "no comment," the same point can be conveyed more diplomatically by answering, "It would be inappropriate to comment on that at this time, but I'll be happy to follow up with you when I get the information I need." The result is the same, minus the combative tone.

13. Visualize what your words will look like in print.

It is helpful to visualize or imagine how words will look in print. If the finished picture looks like something that a client or senior management would not want to see, don't say it.

14. Never go "off the record" with a reporter.

Going "off the record" with reporters takes people into very dangerous territory with comments often paraphrased as observations or attributed vaguely to sources that are not supposed to reveal the actual source. If the information could prove to be troublesome, the best policy is to just not say it.

15. It is okay to get assistance from a consultant or PR professional.

An interview, whether conducted by phone or in person, should be business-like, relaxed, and friendly, and all sides benefit. This does not mean an interviewer is climbing into the ring to do battle with his or her subject. It is very appropriate for someone from the company or organization's PR staff or PR agency to sit in on the call or meeting to both monitor the session and provide helpful information and assistance if needed. Some reporters don't like it, but most have no objection to it, realizing that the objective is for the reporter to get a good interview, useful information, and good quotes. If a PR person can help facilitate that, a good reporter won't mind.

Radio in PR Programs

Radio, like newspapers and TV, has been pronounced dead on many occasions, only to rise again. It is true that the consolidation of radio stations has led to more homogenized music formats and reduced the opportunities for public relations, but many options remain.

Local news is a highly overlooked area because the historic perception is that its resources are so tight, a station is forced to limit programming and coverage to only local events of major interest and importance. Certainly local news should be its top priority, but in many markets resources are not so limited that opportunity for coverage does not exist and, in situations where resources *are* limited, a PR person coming in with a story virtually packaged and ready to be put on the air is welcomed.

Often a local radio station will only have five minutes (or less) on the hour before going "back to format" with music, sports, religion, etc. Radio stations with any news programming at all still have someone designated as the news director and a creative recommendation from a PR specialist could result in a segment within a newscast— from cold weather tips on the noon news to tax preparation or advice on nutrition at 3 PM, home safety recommendations, or virtually any bit of information that can be attributed to a company or organization as a reliable source—with a phone number to call for more information provided.

American Public Radio, National Public Radio, Mutual Radio, and Westwood One are some of the networks and syndicators where talk radio thrives. Many call-in shows have themes from politics to technology, but particularly those with general interest "open microphones" formats are opportunities for PR specialists to present messages with value to the community or even to their "special interest" demographics.

Most colleges and universities have radio stations operated by students and open to recommendations and programming input from public relations people representing community interests. For companies aiming to reach this generation or demographic, the opportunities are many.

To generate awareness, media can take the company or organization message to more people in less time. The tools and procedures for dealing with media do not have to be complicated.

Almost every time the word "media" is used in planning meetings, the word "budget" is not far behind. Clients and management always want to know what the plan will cost and the short answer is that there is no short answer. Since every media plan is unique to that company or client and is developed along very specific, customized lines, there is no generic response to the question.

While there are costs, a *public relations* media plan is not the same as an *advertising* media plan in that print space and broadcast or cable time are not being purchased outright—usually for very big bucks—as with ads.

But the development and production of media kits, informational CDs, bound copies of surveys, studies, white papers and other literature, photos, press conferences and briefings, media tours (involving travel and related expenses), videos, and promotional merchandise all have costs. Once the media plan is fully developed, cost estimating and budgeting can proceed.

To manage such costs most efficiently, consider what elements or components can be used for more than one purpose, thus charged in part to budgets of other departments. Literature, studies, and white papers, for example, might also be used for business development, legal filings, recruiting, or other areas with budgets that can be tapped for part of the expense.

SUMMARY

- To assure reach and influence, it is essential to cultivate appropriate members of the media.
- Media alternatives proliferate and often overlap. In print, there are more than fifteen subcategories of newspapers and magazines; electronic media includes TV, radio, the Internet and perhaps a dozen subcategories that both broaden and fragment the audience.
- Segment the targeted publics into narrow demographic and psychographic market groups.
- The public should view frequent exposures as positive but, if poorly managed, they can result in over-exposure and the public is turned off.
- Tastes change and the public can become quickly bored with what it perceives as older and tired. The product, the packaging, and the message must be kept fresh and *new*.
- The *media plan* contains information a client or executive needs, such as the circulation and audience size, demographic profiles of each entry in the plan, where it ranks among its competitors, and why its inclusion makes sense as part of the overall plan and its objectives.
- Audiences are fragmented, usually driven by lifestyle, economics, and demographic considerations.

References

Dorothy I. Doty, *Publicity and Public Relations* (Hauppauge, NY: Barron's Educational Services, 1990).

Philip Lesley, ed., *Lesly's Handbook of Public Relations and Communications*, Fifth Edition (Chicago: McGraw-Hill/Contemporary, 1998).

Steve Lohr, "New Media: Ready for the Dustbin of History," *New York Times*, May 11, 2003.

12

For the Good of the Cause: PR and Social Responsibility

A company is engaged in cause marketing when it commits itself to a cause or issue with the intention of doing something good and worthwhile, advancing support and awareness of the cause and in so doing realizes there will be a benefit to its own business. To support a cause that is important to the organization's stakeholders is not gratuitous; it is expressing a desire to return support to communities that have been supportive of the company.

That support can come about in several ways: social investments, philanthropy, sponsorships, or partnerships with nonprofit organizations.

The objectives of public relations professionals include creating relationships with as many segments of the public as possible. In a perfect world, a unique idea would solve every problem. In the current imperfect world, until the unique idea springs forth, the pros will have to settle for reliable formula ideas that are effective and make sense. One such idea is to bring the subject company or organization to the attention of a defined segment of the public with whom the company shares a concern, interest, passion, or a *cause worth embracing*.

Doing Well by Doing Good

Cause marketing identifies a company or organization as strongly supporting an issue or institution. It is about doing well by doing good. Those members of the public with a strong feeling for that cause—environmental issues, literacy, the elimination of world hunger, support for AIDS research, finding a breast cancer cure, child welfare, etc.—then usually reward the company for its support with loyalty, which it is assumed will include additional future business, referrals, endorsement, and goodwill.

At least in the minds of people who compose certain market segments, the image and reputation of the company rises and, as has been noted, a good image and reputation is better for business than a poor one, contributing to a more satisfied workforce, lower recruiting costs, a higher quality of job applicants, more stable stock value, and community support. Cause marketing is growing as more companies find that participation in socially responsible matters is good for business. According to information released by the advocacy group Business for Social Responsibility, some 36 percent of consumers have a more positive feeling toward a company they believe is doing something to make the world a better place. Nine out of ten employees working in cause marketing programs say they are proud to be working for their companies.

Business for Social Responsibility (BSR) is a San Francisco-based global nonprofit organization that helps companies "achieve commercial success in ways that respect ethical values, people, communities and the environment." Here are just a few insights it provides:

- According to a 2002 survey conducted by PricewaterhouseCoopers, nearly 70 percent of CEOs worldwide agree that corporate social responsibility is vital to the profitability of any company.
- Environics International reported in 2001 that 49 percent of citizens across 20 countries selected ethical, environmental, and social responsibility concerns as the most important factors when forming an impression of a company.
- In a report released in June 2002, KLD Research and Analysis reported that over the previous ten years, the Domini 400 Social Index outperformed the S&P 500 by ten percent.

What this information reveals is that even those individuals or executives who might personally rank social responsibility low on their personal priorities lists can see that cause marketing is a very pragmatic policy that offers an excellent return on investment.

While for the most part BSR promotes partnerships involving businesses and nonprofit organizations, the concept can be employed on very modest and local terms—and not always for lofty causes with noble aims.

Years ago in Chicago, for example, the city announced it was ordering the closing of the Tap Root Pub, a long-popular tavern and gathering place. Patrons mounted a campaign to reverse the city's decision. Press releases were issued. Petitions were circulated. Fundraisers were held. Local TV stations and newspapers were contacted. "Save the Tap Root Pub" posters and bumper stickers were visible across the city.

Were dozens of people on board? Hundreds? No one knew exactly. But the cause was kept alive for more than a year, and the city finally agreed to work out a deal of some kind.

Clearly the cause was not a textbook example of social responsibility on a level with efforts to "save the rain forests" or raising funds for cancer research, but it did attract a number of supporters and sponsors who won the appreciation and loyalty of a community of Chicagoans who battled to save a beloved meeting spot.

Other causes have been mounted to save landmark buildings, schools, libraries, parks, and trees, Often the causes seem trivial—even sometimes selfish—but they have a constituency that believes in the righteousness of the cause and will be forever loyal to anyone who stands with them.

A local homeless shelter or food pantry, park cleanup program, or Little League team sponsorships are among the modest examples of what many small businesses do to show a commitment to their communities, doing well by doing good and earning support and goodwill along the way.

The Benefits of Social Responsibility

In 1993, Students for Responsible Business was formed and evolved into what is now Net Impact, a mission-driven network of, according to its literature, "more than 5,000 visionary new leaders." The group claims more than 60 chapters in business schools in cities across the United States and is supported by corporations, foundations, and individuals who "share the vision of creating a better world through business."

Net Impact, in applying the principle of networking for a very focused purpose, is taking the position that businesses and corporations do not have to choose between social responsibility—supporting causes that benefit those in need—and the capitalistic drive for profits.

The public relations benefits are as great for the companies as the more practical benefits are for the people the cause-related programs are designed to help. Each year rankings are published as to which companies are voted "the best places to work" and businesses receive awards for community service and stewardship, for helping to meet the needs of less fortunate people in society.

Contributing and raising money for good causes is important, but community service and raising public awareness of worthwhile causes are high in importance as well.

Some companies write checks to charities and issue press releases to make certain they receive credit and their generosity does not go unnoticed. Such acts are better than doing nothing, but that is how they appear and what they are: acts.

The companies that organize groups of employees to go out—both on company time and on their own time as volunteers—to clean-up the land along a riverbank or replant trees or participate in collecting food for hunger projects or working in homeless shelters or participating in environmental rescue efforts: These are people and companies that deserve to be remembered and rewarded for their unselfish contributions. And on the business side, their contributions pay dividends in respect and customer loyalty.

The Dangers of Cause Marketing

Some companies construct cause marketing programs on their own, while others enter into partnerships with nonprofit organizations that already have the knowledge, the organizational machinery in place, and are identified with a cause or issue.

Perhaps the most essential consideration a company must address before undertaking a cause marketing program is one of *belief*—that the company must be absolutely sincere in its commitment to the cause, fully aware that to make such a commitment will not sit well with all segments of the public.

In the early days of the 21st century, members of the public are outspoken as never before. Some consumers will not only stop buying products from a company with which it disagrees philosophically but will organize demonstrations, boycotts, and letter-writing campaigns to encourage others to dislike and work against the company as well.

Hopefully, a company that makes a serious commitment to a cause it believes in will gain enough new business and favorable publicity to compensate for any loss of business brought on by those who disagree with its position.

More important, it is necessary to conduct or study study research to identify which issues or causes are of great concern to a client or company's constituent groups. If management's greatest concern is to save the whales, but the company's stakeholders are more concerned about literacy, then supporting the whales issue will not likely offend customers, but it won't exactly help strengthen the company's relationship with those it wants to impress most.

It is not required that someone who wishes to do good works must receive a payback for such a commitment. But then such an activity is not cause marketing. It is a generous, caring gesture and contribution.

Matching the Company and the Cause

Announcing support of a cause can be risky if the public does not immediately recognize the company and the cause as a good fit. If the pairing does not look like a good match, it should at least not seem to be absurd, such as the retailer of erotic merchandise that offered to underwrite a children's nutrition program.

A watchmaker might receive a "thank you" for supporting a project to combat pollution, but the public will most likely not see a connection between watches and pollution, so the association will not seem a natural or logical match. This does not mean that the company should not go ahead with its support of a cause, but that it will have to repeatedly explain why it considers the cause important and sought to work on its behalf—why eliminating pollution should be a matter of concern to everyone, including watchmakers.

A brochure, an ad, or a press release could succinctly point out that *pollution is everyone's problem and all individuals and businesses have an obligation to do something about it, for the sake of our families, our communities, our futures. . . .*

Then the company should briefly outline the program and who will benefit from it. Such an expression of genuine concern can explain why an automobile company wants to help fund breast cancer research or the maker of spaghetti sauces, salad dressings, and popcorn contributes heavily to environmental causes.

In an ideal situation the partnership of a company and a cause would appear logical and obvious. When that is not the case, the company must overtly seek to identify itself with the average person—in this case, the "average person" being defined as someone fitting the demographic profile of the core customer or supporter the company or organization wants to reach—and mount an effort, alone or in partnership with another organization, to be responsive to issues and concerns that are important to that person.

In theory, (and if handled properly, in reality) this creates a connection between the company and the consumer.

"Rock the Vote" is an organization founded in 1990 by members of the recording industry who wanted to bring more young people into the election process. But the campaign's impact was most strongly felt when cable television channel MTV began running its public service spots, particularly those featuring the pop singer Madonna—wrapped in an American flag. Some people were outraged, but it brought a huge amount of publicity and awareness to the cause.

MTV's primary audience is younger adults, the very target "Rock the Vote" wanted to enlist to register and make its presence known. The cable TV operation and the cause seemed like a natural and good partnership. While other television organizations carried the "Rock the Vote" message, it is MTV's participation in the effort that remains the best remembered and most influential.

More importantly, the MTV image had been shaped years earlier as the maverick outsider in TV bringing rock music to television. It was aimed at the successor generation of the hippies and counter-culture public that advocated sex, drugs, and rock 'n' roll 25 years earlier. Now, solidly established as a TV powerhouse, MTV, like the magazine *Rolling Stone*, had to hang onto its core audience as it was growing older and still draw the younger audience that was coming up behind it.

The music was the edge, its centerpiece, but styles and tastes change. Producing videos for music television is costly and record companies were making fewer music videos. MTV needed to remain relevant to remain in the game.

"Rock the Vote" was the right thing at the right time for MTV. It was, like the music, about the collective power of young people as a dramatic force in the election of a country's leader. It was as relevant a cause as the network could want. The cause was a perfect fit for the company and the company fit the cause.

Meanwhile MTV's spin-off cable channel, VH1, took note and found its own cause in "Save the Music," a program created to benefit schools across the United States, where music education had become an early casualty of budget cuts in most states. VH1 held auctions and pledge drives, staged concerts, and sold merchandise in order to buy musical instruments for students and restore programs.

It should be noted that when a celebrity, whether from sports, entertainment or some other field, is used as a spokesperson for the cause or organization, the public might well identify that famous person with the subject and that association could continue through good times and bad. That is, the cause benefits by the celebrated person delivering his or her fans or supporters, but if the celebrity becomes involved in a scandal or is named in some negative news reports, that negative shadow can extend to the cause or organization as well. Support or endorsement from someone of prominence can help, but it can hurt as well if that person's reputation is tarnished.

Not every partnership of company and cause will be dazzling and obvious fun. Some are far less exciting but can still be effective for participants on both sides.

Office supply companies can donate basic school needs to local schools or create designated days when a percentage of sales benefit particular area schools; technology companies can donate computers and software to schools and senior centers, then teach both young and older students how to use and benefit from their new treasures.

The pairing of companies and causes such as these will reliably generate goodwill and good photographs for newspapers, sales brochures, and point-of-sale displays.

But these easy match-ups can also become double-edged swords, so obvious and logical that companies *can't* not become involved and, in a public relations sense, are so obvious that they are often dismissed by the media as filler or relegated to inconsequential status, rarely treated as if the partnership were important. The programs are reviewed as nice gestures and little more.

The more actively involved a company becomes in cause marketing, the more the media expects of them, looking for angles that are new and different. Generosity, time, and money receive respect, but *sizzle* gets major media attention.

Companies that become known as innovators are expected to continue being innovative, even in their efforts are on behalf of a good cause.

Starbucks, for example, continues to be a story that is difficult to ignore, no matter what aspect of marketing is under review. Starbucks became successful in a difficult economic climate, opening a chain of upscale businesses that are not coffee houses or restaurants, and have too limited a variety to qualify as a bakery or retail store.

Yet, the company built a passionately loyal clientele on very little advertising, relying to a large extent on word-of-mouth promotion, selling a strong cup of coffee (the smallest of which is called "tall") for about twice the price of a cup of coffee elsewhere.

Marketers attributed the company's success to its offering quality products served in pleasant surroundings with plenty of atmosphere and the correct mix of attitude and snob appeal at mass market prices. Starbucks was not a concept the market demanded, but was the result of smart marketers seeing an opportunity and positioning the product accordingly.

While critics initially dismissed Starbucks as a trend that would evaporate and called the product yuppie coffee brewed in designer pots, the public liked what it saw and tasted. Imitators scrambled to offer clones and knock-offs, none with the same edge or uniqueness (the very fact that they were Starbucks imitators was an indication of *its* uniqueness and their *lack of uniqueness*). People joked not about Starbucks being on every corner, but in some cases across the street or down the block from other Starbucks locations.

The company's public relations programs were well conceived. Starbucks listened to its customers and made use of what it learned. Perhaps most importantly, it learned who its customers were and what was important to them.

In 1997, the company created the Starbucks Foundation and as of 2003 it had awarded more than 650 grants totaling some $6.5 million to literacy programs, schools, and community-based organizations.

Branding Cause Marketing Programs

While some companies and organizations become partners with established and well-known nonprofits to both take advantage of the nonprofit organization's experience and expertise and to avoid staff and cost redundancies, others choose to undertake cause-related marketing efforts on their own. One obvious advantage is the ability to maintain total control of the program, though increasingly companies that choose this approach do so to *brand* the program—to put their name above the title, as it were, and make certain there is no doubt as to who or what entity will receive credit.

Some companies will try to have it both ways.

Lee Denim Day, for example, was a single well-promoted day during which the jeans manufacturer asked its customers to donate $5 to breast cancer research. No one questioned that this was a good and important cause, and Lee, normally identified with the more rugged types of western jeans—as opposed to the more costly designer-label women's jeans—clearly stood to identify itself with an image and message important to women.

But the contributions from Lee Denim Day ultimately were passed along to the Susan G. Komen Breast Cancer Foundation, an organization recognized as a leader in breast cancer research, education, screening, and treatment, and well-known for its own programs and numerous partnerships with other major corporations, including the Ford Motor Company. The fact that Lee put its name on the campaign did not seem to hurt the company in that it made clear its program was just about collecting money for the cause, not that it was actually taking an active role in cancer research.

Target House, on the other hand, a partnership between Target and St. Jude Children's Research Hospital, went a bit further.

The facility, a part of the St. Jude complex in Memphis, Tennessee, provides assistance to families of children undergoing treatment at the hospital. By all accounts, it is a perfect fit of a good company and a good cause, Target being a place where average families shop for family needs, often together.

But Target House is not actually owned and operated by Target Stores or its parent corporation. The giant retailer provides promotional support and a percentage of funding, and encourages its vendors and others who do business with Target to also support the cause on some level.

While a separate organization actually *runs* Target House, its support agreement includes a provision that the retailer's name be on the building and the public can make its own assumptions.

Purists might suggest there is a bit of sleight-of-hand involved, particularly since Target House is promoted on bags and posters in the pharmacies located in many Target stores. But the public has an overall favorable opinion of Target as a good corporate citizen, so such blurred distinctions would likely be considered legal technicalities that would not diminish that opinion.

At the same time, Target continues to support national advertising and public relations campaigns to promote its association with other good causes. One such example is the "Start Something" program, a nationwide youth program that appears to be a partnership between Target and the Tiger Woods Foundation. As with Target House and St. Jude Hospital, it is unclear from its advertising whether Target runs the program, is its primary funding source, or only one of many sponsors. People who want to know more are invited to visit the company web site. Further, photographs of Tiger Woods used in ads show the Nike logo prominently visible on his shirt and cap, though nowhere is Nike identified as a sponsor of the program.

While this is somewhat confusing, again, the impression conveyed is that this is all for a good cause and Target, at the center of it all, is on board to help. The campaigns for both Target House and "Start Something" are executed in a way that positions the retailer as involved in the programs, while not appearing to be grandstanding or engaged in expensive exercises in self-congratulations.

Other companies have tried this same approach, advertising their involvement with cause-related programs not exclusively their own— perhaps most notably the large tobacco company and the giant financial services firm—and in those cases, both appeared to be simply attempting to win favor by taking credit for good work that had actually been done by others, with only partial financial assistance from the companies.

The heavy-handedness of their promoted involvement left much of the public perceiving the companies' efforts were transparently self-aggrandizing. What could have been represented as generosity looked instead as if the companies were trying to grab more credit than they deserved—or had paid for.

The key point is for the company to know its market:

- How is it perceived by various segments of its publics?
- Would its identification with a good cause endear a company to some groups and, perhaps, force critics to rethink their negative opinions?

If the public perceives that branding a cause with a corporate sponsor's name will distract from the importance of the work—making it seem like a mere PR vehicle—a noble idea with a good business component to it could be dismissed as a publicity stunt and it could backfire, inviting *negative* publicity.

But if *not* branding the program—only strongly identifying it with a sponsor through ads, in-store displays, and promotions—were to be the strategy employed, the campaign could become even more successful.

Partnering in a program, borrowing a program, or going it alone, the essential element is to know what is important to the public. Remember:

- The "Rock the Vote" program was not owned by (or an original concept of) MTV—indeed, the program had significant support from other television networks, most notably CBS and FOX. Yet the campaign became so closely identified with MTV that the public *believed* it had begun there and the cable channel benefited mightily. Its name and logo were nowhere in the ads or literature. When 1996 proved to be a big year for registering new voters, "Rock the Vote" and MTV received much of the credit. The campaign was a good choice for MTV to back, given the concerns of its audience.

- "Save the Music" proved to be a good cause for VH1. In its first six years, the campaign delivered some $17 million worth of musical instruments to 750 public schools in 70 U.S. cities.
- Starbucks, as noted, donated more than $6.5 million to literacy, schools, and community programs and, following terrorist attacks in the United States in 2001, contributed $1.2 million on its own and collected an additional $1.3 million from its customers to aid the families of victims.
- Lee Jeans and Target Stores both understand the value to a company of positioning itself as socially responsible and concerned for its public and its community.

Making the Program Work

The public might be divided as to the things it cares about most, but every part of the public most assuredly cares about something. Virtually any organization, large or small, in any industry or profession, can likely find benefits in embracing a cause, particularly a cause that is important to its primary target market.

If the cause is something that can be undertaken with existing company staff and resources, the company can likely achieve even greater recognition by "owning" the project. But if the chosen cause is one that requires substantial expertise or resources not available in-house and the company wants its connection to the cause to be take seriously—not assumed to be merely cosmetic—a partnership with an experienced nonprofit organization is an efficient alternative.

Certainly any company can be a source of support to the United Way, the Heart Fund, the American Cancer Society, or the Special Olympics. But such programs can be carried out with a collection jar next to a cash register or checkout aisle or with a note in a pay envelope. They are general, mainstream programs that win a nod of approval, but rarely an outburst of enthusiasm from employees or the public.

The public is familiar with these causes, and while familiarity should not be considered a negative, it does not create a great deal of excitement or a sense of exclusivity with a particular company. Creating interest and excitement is the challenge of the public relations and marketing teams.

Environmental causes and specific, focused, community-based organizations tend to have a more readily identifiable constituency, membership, or list of supporters. Finding the right cause is the first step. Making the program work is next. To meet those objectives:

- Believe in the program. If the cause or the program could be regarded as simply opportunistic, its value will be seriously diminished.
- Be consistent. Support the ethical principles of the cause or critics and the media will note such lapses or inconsistencies.
- Have a plan. Just announcing a connection to a cause and waiting for the public to respond with praise won't do. Know what is expected and be responsive to public expectations.
- Be aware of laws and regulations. Know any and all legal and regulatory requirements that will apply to the cause-marketing program.
- Choose partners carefully. A company and a nonprofit organization partnership requires good chemistry among the people and the corporate cultures.
- Make goals clear. In a cause marketing partnership, both the company and the nonprofit organization must be clear about their own and each other's objectives and work in a coordinated manner—or the program could be compromised.
- Put agreements in writing. Written agreements between cause-related marketing partners minimize confusion and misunderstanding as to objectives, areas of responsibility, time lines, and costs. Be clear about who has ownership rights to program names and materials.
- Keep everyone informed. Be certain that everyone involved at all levels of the organization understands the goals and mechanics of the program, even if they have no direct line responsibility for its implementations.

- Promote volunteerism. Encourage volunteers to become involved with the cause.
- Create a Plan B. Have a contingency crisis management plan that anticipates what could go wrong and who will respond.
- Tell the truth. Be honest and positive in presentations.
- Prepare for the negative. Don't expect a totally positive response. Factions exist to view virtually everything critically and to dig deep for controversy. Expect criticism; respond with dignity.
- Meet problems head-on. If problems occur—whether with a partner, member of an organization, the media, or the public—respond quickly and directly. People respect those who acknowledge a problem and try to fix it.
- Never compromise the company's integrity. Don't take credit for someone else's work. That undermines the very credibility of a socially responsible organization.
- Give the program the same attention as any other project. Treat the public relations aspect of a cause-related marketing program as if it were any other PR project, such as an event, brand launch, IPO, or anniversary celebration. Have a plan that lists objectives, strategy and tactics, the time line and budgets. It is another element of presenting and defining the corporate or organization mission and message.
- Have the necessary PR tools ready. Press releases, media kits, backgrounders, photos, bios, videos and/or CDs, as for any other PR project, should be available to define the cause or position of the company or organization regarding corporate responsibility.
- Keep the proper records. Be certain to maintain legal and regulatory records as needed. Just as all publicly traded companies publish an annual report, many companies (Starbucks, McDonald's, Chiquita Banana, and others) publish a separate annual report on social responsibility. This document defines philanthropic activity, as well as fundraising, partnerships, and related activities. It is an

important document for both legal and accounting purposes, and carries enormous public relations value as a detailed background piece that focuses on specific programs and aspects of a business that has many noteworthy sides.

Cause-related public relations almost seems as if it is a redundant term. Knowing what is important to the public, carrying on the business of doing business in a socially responsible manner, and doing well by doing good are what PR is about.

SUMMARY

- Cause marketing is an effort through which a company commits itself to a cause or issue with the intention of doing something to benefit the cause and in so doing realizes certain advantages and benefits to its own business.
- People with a strong feeling for a cause usually reward a company for its support with their loyalty, which usually includes future business, referrals, endorsement, and goodwill.
- Contributing and raising money for good causes is important, but service and creating awareness of a cause is important as well.
- The major consideration a company must address regarding cause marketing is one of *belief*. The company must be sincere in its commitment to the cause and aware that such a commitment will not sit well with all segments of the public.
- Study research reports to learn what issues or causes are of the greatest concern to constituent groups.
- The more actively involved a company is in cause marketing, the more the media expects of them, looking for new and different angles.

13

Public Relations, Ethics, and the Culture of the Times

The Oxford English Dictionary defines irony as "the expression of meaning through the use of language which normally signifies the opposite, typically for humorous effect."

A bit wordy perhaps, but there certainly does seem to be an element of humor—*or irony*—in the fact that public relations, a profession that so successfully creates, manages, maintains, and changes the public images of other professions, organizations, companies, and individuals, finds itself with a rather serious image problem. And people are talking about it.

Public relations expert Thomas L. Harris observed that, in early 2003, two major Hollywood motion pictures were released in which the main characters were PR guys—and not very nice ones at that. In both movies the concept of ethics seemed to be part of a foreign language for which there was no English translation.

Critics described the respected actor Al Pacino's film, *People I Know*, as a "scathing look at the PR business" and the second movie, *Phone Booth*, with Colin Farrell, as a work in which the lead character is "the embodiment of an unethical, self-serving existence" who finds himself in a situation "where his lies, half-truths and obfuscation no longer matter."

It is unlikely that either film will achieve classic status, but it is interesting that the appearance of such films is invariably accompanied by references to one that did.

The Sweet Smell of Success is a 1957 movie that left a lasting impression as to what the public relations business is about. Reviewers praise the film with such terms as "sleazy," "amoral," "ambitious and self-serving," and "smarmy." Nearly a half-century after its release, this film remains not only popular, but considered the definitive inside portrait of the public relations profession.

In June of 2003 writer David Greising noted in the *Chicago Tribune*, "Not long ago, there was a simple phrase people could say with a straight face: 'Trust me.' These days, it's the setup for a joke . . . Too many top people have let us down in too many ways."

The Good, the Bad, the Unethical

All people may be *created* equal, but culturally and ethically the forces that move people to behave as they do are anything but equal.

For some people, the issues are decided well in advance. There are definitely things that honest and honorable people will not do. Professions that adopt codes of ethics do so with expectations that those who subscribe to such codes will not look for exceptions or loopholes.

Still, a question that drives many professionals and raises the ethical issue often comes down to: *How much do I need this account?*
Consider:

1. A client calls to say he or she has a great idea for a product and is about to enter into a joint venture with a Fortune 500 company to develop it. . . . Get the deal some publicity.

   The PR person has doubts about the legitimacy of the story, but no publicity means no client. So the story gets pitched and proves to be a non-story—one that was premature at best. The media pros are skeptical. Do they accept the story as fact, based on its coming from a reliable source? Do they investigate? Do they choose to take a pass on the story?

   In different media situations, it is possible that any of these responses could result. Rules are bent. The story becomes a possible minefield of half-truths. The idea is not actually fully developed, hasn't been tested, and funding has not been approved. The Fortune 500 company isn't actually on board yet, though it did acknowledge the client sent an e-mail or left a voice-mail discussing the idea. Perhaps the announcement *was* premature.
Perhaps.

2. A business executive retains a public relations specialist to publicize his memoir on how he became so successful in his profession. He is a decent fellow, he insists, with a good record, but critics and envious rivals have attempted to discredit him at times on his way up. He notes that his late father in his youth had low-level ties to organized crime, but the times were tough, he had to support his family, he did the stupid things young guys often do, etc. He was really a good man and a great father.

   In the course of pitching the story, the PR specialist learns that the client's father was not a naive lad who had committed youthful indiscretions, but rather was a ruthless thug and reported to be a known hit man for the mob.

Oops. Did the reporter check his facts carefully? Had the PR person *not* checked his facts carefully—or checked them at all? Did the PR person need the fee badly enough not to care?

Perhaps.

As noted earlier, some PR agencies promise prospective clients major stories in *Forbes* and *The Wall Street Journal,* knowing at the time that such placements are long shots or complete impossibilities. The company and its story did not warrant such a placement in a high-visibility national publication. But the PR agency needs the business and the client wants to believe that dreams come true and such a thing is possible. So the doomed relationship begins, and the agency is fired three months later when no story materializes in big media. The ethically challenged agency, meanwhile, collected and banked three months of fees.

Of course the reverse occurs when a client insists that its story is worthy of major national media because "the media covers less important stuff than this all the time!"

- Should the agency have told the client the story placement was not likely to happen because the story was not a qualifier?
- Should the agency have resigned the account?
- Would the client then find another agency willing to accept its money to pitch the same story?

Perhaps.

In these examples, the ethical bar keeps being lowered.

Who is *more* at fault?

Some PR agencies are staffed by experienced, talented people with proven skills and records of accomplishments. Some other agencies, however, are "bucket shops" where the account people are little more than telemarketers, calling lists of media people and reading the pitch from a card or computer screen, e-mailing and faxing press releases, playing the averages.

If a mediocre story is pitched to 25 reporters or editors or producers, might someone bite? If the process is repeated every day for four days, might one or two or three placements result, and isn't that what the client wanted? Is this really public relations?

The answers are yes, yes, yes, and no.

If someone fires a hundred shots and four hit the target, that does not make that person a qualified marksman. The media have the option of rejecting the message.

The PR representative has the choice of pitching the story "shotgun" style, refusing to do so, or attempting to persuade the client there are long-term advantages to creating relationships, being honest, maintaining integrity, building brand value, and realizing that people and companies that use "hit and run" tactics to gain short-term interest incur disdain over the long term and play a high-risk game.

New Ethics for a New Age

If the ethics of public relations professionals have come under question, it cannot be assumed that it happened suddenly overnight or that it was prompted exclusively by desperation on the part of a lonely few. It is, however, very much a reflection of the times in which they exist.

They have been described as the business side of "the *Me* generation" for their dedication to self-esteem, self-awareness, and self-absorption. In the 1990s, they and their philosophy emerged from profiles in business and lifestyle publications to become the new movers and shakers, celebrity CEOs, role models for one another and the CEO wannabes of generations that would follow.

This was a great time for public relations professionals. New companies were being launched at an unprecedented rate—most of them through IPOs. The new technology seemed to quickly change the landscape. Young chairmen, presidents, and founders of "hot" companies wore T-shirts, jeans, and running shoes to their offices, arriving in sports cars, high-end SUVs, and on motorcycles. It was the era of the rock star CEO.

Critics characterized them as being identified by their designer jeans , and their overt sense of entitlement.

The technology boom and proliferation of celebrity CEOs and dot-com companies represented not only a change in the appearance of the executive suite—or the look of business in general—it signaled a major cultural change. And new rules, new definitions, new standards of social acceptability.

Consider some of the touchstones that spurred and reflected cultural change:

- The Internet
- Blogging
- Wireless communication
- File sharing
- TiVo
- Cell phones
- Cable/satellite TV
- Viagra
- Enron
- PACs
- Gay rights
- Hooking-up
- AIDS
- The Drudge Report
- The Starr Report

Technology played an important role in the cultural changes, but the television ad that talked about the "new attitude" barely touched the surface in describing the shifts in economics, language, looks, and values. Consider:

- The trial of O.J. Simpson changed how millions of people felt about lawyers, news commentators, racial bias, and the law.
- Condoms were distributed in some public high schools, and condom ads appeared in magazines and on TV.

- A year after running as the Republican party's candidate for President of the United States, former Senator Bob Dole appeared in TV commercials for Viagra, discussing erectile dysfunction. He also appeared in commercials for Pepsi.
- The makers of Wow! potato chips noted on the product's package that it was a fat-free product . . . and people who ate it could experience anal leakage.
- Gay politicians, artists, writers, actors, musicians, clergymen, and business executives *came out*.
- A group launched an "I hate Starbucks" web site.
- Tobacco companies were required by law to produce anti-smoking ads, though their products remained legal to buy and sell.
- The technology boom ended, the dot-com "bubble" burst, stocks plummeted, tens of thousands of members of Generation X lost hundreds of millions of dollars worth of stock options as companies that soared a year earlier crashed.
- In 2002, the United States reported a record number of bankruptcy filings.

It is against this cultural backdrop that public relations professionals must generate awareness, excitement, and interest in clients, companies, and organizations, establish positive positions of distinction, and favorably influence public opinion.

Change in society is not only constant, it is a welcome occurrence and the lifeblood of marketing. The difference in the wave of changes that marked the 1990s and the start of the 21st century is the shift in cultural standards and values that make an examination of ethics and ethical behavior particularly noteworthy.

Seniors, baby boomers, generations X and Y appeared to be firmly in separate camps, sometimes overlapping in interests and in harmony, sometimes not.

While previous generations were distinctly different in styles of art, music, entertainment, fashion, and certainly in social and political matters, ethics was an issue that remained above controversy. Ethical behavior was a constant—issues were black and white, right or wrong. There was nothing that required interpretation.

Some people would suggest that the defining moment was when former President Bill Clinton, in discussing possible wrongdoing, insisted that the standard depended on what the word "is" is.

The problems of course started before that.

At some point in every political campaign a candidate must make a decision on whether or not to "go negative"—to attack an opponent on a very personal level, usually by misrepresenting the opponent's positions to such an extent that the opponent is forced to respond. Why do candidates continue to go negative in every campaign when the public insists it holds such tactics in low regard?

Because negative campaigning *works*.

Bad news is more interesting than good news, is remembered longer, and is what people tend to share with others—even after they've been told it's not true.

While all the research experts' questions are answered in ways that people think they are saying what the researchers want to hear, real life tells another story. Everyone says they want the truth, but what they *really* want is an answer or resolution to an issue that fits their purpose or point of view.

Further, the truth has become a relative thing. That is, people agree it is wrong to lie. But if being totally truthful will hurt another person's feelings, cause an argument, or compromise security, then a popularly held belief is that "the whole truth" becomes a negative force and can be modified for the good of the cause.

Dodging Responsibility: A Newly Accepted Practice

In public relations, "correcting the record" is a routine function of the job. Everyday the most respected and prestigious media issue corrections of their earlier work. Newspapers and magazines carry "letters to the editor" that are sometimes legitimate corrections of errors caught by readers and sometimes are opinions of readers as to why they believe what was reported as fact was wrong—essentially because what was reported conflicts with their own opinions.

For the PR professional, it is unusual to issue a statement reporting that "the CEO misspoke" or "the senator had been given incorrect information" or "the material cited was out of date."

Explanations such as these are intentionally vague and responsibility for errors or for disseminating incorrect information as fact takes a circuitous route until it seems to just evaporate into space.

In a culture and society where great importance is awarded to total candor, truthfulness, openness, and honesty, the public is accustomed to hearing official spokespersons for its leaders say, in the most casual and off-handed manner, "I might not have been totally honest when I spoke with you earlier."

Members of the media rarely blink when this phrase is repeated. This is a cultural fact of life. The public expects and respects honesty, but it also expects that for a variety of reasons and self-interests, public officials, business leaders, and almost everyone else, "might not have been totally honest" at various times in their public and private lives.

How the public reacts to these admissions has become extremely predictable: Supporters of the person who has acknowledged not having been "totally honest" are predisposed to make allowances— okay, mistakes were made. People are imperfect. Things happen. Let's just move on and put the matter behind us.

But people who are *not* supporters of the person who was not "totally honest"—competitors, rivals, members of opposing groups, or adherents to a different philosophy—are not so inclined to let the matter go quite so quickly. They'd like to know: what parts of what was said *were* "totally honest," which were *partly* honest, and which parts were not honest at all—even a little? Is this the first time the speaker was not "totally honest" with the public? Are any of the people associated with the speaker honest?

The most public examples of highly visible people caught in this position in recent years include:

- Martha Stewart, public personality and CEO
- Bernard Ebbers, former CEO, WorldCom
- Samuel Waksal, former CEO, ImClone

- Geraldo Rivera, TV news reporter
- Jack Welch, retired CEO of G.E.
- Stephen Ambrose, award-winning historian
- Joseph J. Ellis, award-winning historian
- Dennis Kozlowski, former Tyco CEO
- Donald Carty, former CEO, American Airlines
- Cardinal Bernard Law, former head of the Catholic archdiocese in Boston, Massachusetts
- The Catholic Church
- Jayson Blair, former *New York Times* reporter
- Sammy Sosa of the Chicago Cubs
- Tobacco company executives
- Pretty much every president of the United States since 1869

Notice the number of times the word "former" appears on the list. Despite the fact that nearly everyone noted steadfastly refused to admit to any wrongdoing in the face of overwhelming evidence to the contrary, for the most part they retain a large, loyal group of supporters who either refuse to concede their failings . . . or don't care.

In 2003, financial writer Floyd Norris reviewed three books in *The New York Times Book Review.* Under the headline, "Business Ethics and Other Oxymorons—three books about hubris, greed, corruption and incompetence," he examines the collapse of Enron, the demise of Arthur Andersen, and the corruption of the U.S financial markets.

Mr. Norris writes, "When the deals went bad, they could be hidden through financial sleight of hand and, in any case, the people who put them together would be on to new deals and new bonuses. Enron, it was said, was a company that valued the ability to bury bad news."

Enron had taken to calling itself "the World's Greatest Company," while it socialized with world leaders and helped write government policy until it was revealed that the company's management at the very highest levels had approved and engaged in allegedly fraudulent business practices on a massive scale. Shortly after its business activities were exposed, Enron collapsed, destroying careers and throwing thousands of lives—and the pensions of thousands more—into turmoil.

As bad as the Enron debacle proved to be—and it was bad on a truly epic scale—even worse was the message it sent to people across the United States and around the world. A large and powerful organization could violate so many rules and principles of business, and none of its hundreds of executives would raise even the most modest ethical concerns, much less moral outrage.

Worse still was the fact that Enron's outside accounting firm, the large and extremely respected Arthur Andersen, charged with certifying the company's financial reports, thereby casting shadows over the integrity of reports it had certified for thousands of other companies.

For young people, for people in a variety of businesses of all sizes, companies such as Enron and Arthur Andersen were as good as it gets. They were successful, powerful, had status, and tremendous wealth.

And apparently no ethics or principles when the chips were down.

Comparisons would be drawn between the collapse of Enron and Arthur Andersen and that of the dot-com companies and other technology firms that soared, took in huge amounts of money quickly, and crashed as technology, the culture, and principles collided.

But the comparisons were not exactly accurate.

The tech sector's collapse might have been predicted, a relatively simple matter of too much too fast too soon, as ideas and innovation flooded the marketplace, ultimately overwhelming it with more than could be produced, digested, and absorbed. Even a culture so hungry for innovation could only change so fast.

It might be said that the excitement the technology boom generated was made of pure energy and the reason the public ultimately didn't "get it," as the prevailing expression went, was because "it" wasn't as much *there* as it was a state of mind for inventors whose creations did not fully exist. It was not a sleight of hand or a massive deception.

Enron and Andersen were.

To the end, the ethically challenged executives of Enron and Arthur Andersen would insist they were not bad people and would attempt to suggest they were perhaps visionaries who were operating on a level so far beyond the understanding of lesser minds that most people just "didn't get it."

Of course, they should have known better. They were bright people to whom ethics was a subjective factor that allowed for a greater degree of flexibility where they were concerned. This is another cultural characteristic: the ruling class, or those who would aspire to be members of the ruling class, hold themselves to a different standard than that which applies to others.

Sportswriter Dan McGrath wrote of the baseball manager who taught a fading left-handed pitcher to throw a "spitter"—a pitch that had been illegal in professional baseball for about 100 years. The manager's advice to his player, if anyone should ask, was to not say it was a spitter, but a "Cuban forkball we'd been working on." Go ahead and use the illegal tactic, just call it by the name of something that has *not* been judged illegal.

"He leaned back in his chair, quite pleased with himself," McGrath wrote. "A roomful of sportswriters nodded. No one said a word about the skipper's business ethics, no one wrote a word about blatant deception. They viewed the southpaw as flawed, but a good guy. They'd been writing tributes to his gritty comeback and they were willing to rationalize bending the rules."

In July 2003, a woman in North Carolina wrote a letter to the editor of *People* magazine. It was published and read in part, "It gives me great joy to think that Martha Stewart may go to prison. She is a snob who has made millions from people who are completely out of her league and who wish to emulate her. Fortunately I am not one of those people. I can't wait to see how she can dress up her cell."

It reveals a great deal about a culture when a national magazine would print a letter from someone who, in all likelihood, does not know, nor has even ever met Martha Stewart, but first wants the general public to know a few things about herself—that she is not an admirer of Martha Stewart, that her "great joy" will come from seeing Martha Stewart go to prison (perhaps as much to be punished for becoming so successful as for her alleged insider trading of stock in a friend's company), and that despite her extreme dislike of the woman, she will gleefully follow Stewart's progress should she, alas, be sent up the river.

How might a public relations expert for Martha Stewart's vast conglomerate of companies win over this person?

Is this person a part of the Martha Stewart target demographic? What might be said on the matters of ethics, the presumption of innocence until proven guilty, or the rights of people to become rich by providing a product or service to the public?

What was Ms. Stewart's crisis management team doing when this letter was being written and published in one of the most widely read magazines in the United States?

Greg Burns wrote in the *Chicago Tribune* of a woman who sought to defend Martha Stewart by indicting all of society. "In a letter posted on Marthatalks.com, a web site the domestic diva launched for her supporters in the wake of her criminal indictment . . . [the woman] says she couldn't care less whether Martha cheated in the stock market. 'People do this every day, and no one bats an eye.'"

Citing her own experiences working for a northern California mail order company and her close-up view of the dot-com bust that shaped her ideas of just what people do, the woman told the reporter, "Everyone wanted to get rich really fast, and it all came crashing down. The standards of America and the world have probably been diminished. We don't know what the rules are."

The Cultural Context of the New Ethics

Some people have suggested that Martha Stewart, corporations such as ImClone, WorldCom, Enron, and Arthur Andersen, singer Michael Jackson, and talent agent-turned entertainment industry mogul Michael Ovitz, to name only a few, have triggered a national case of *schadenfreude*, a feeling of joy that comes from witnessing the misery of others—particularly the rich and powerful.

There certainly might be some of that, but it is just as likely that even more than clucking about how the mighty have fallen, is a sense that people such as Martha Stewart and Jack Welch, who positioned themselves as the reigning authorities and living embodiment of how to do things better than everyone else, should be held to at least the same ethical standards as everyone else. The sense of entitlement that seemed to be a proud characteristic of those members of Generation X who led the technology boom was apparently not limited to their generation alone.

Generally, people on the political left hear the voices of the top-rated conservative analysts on Fox TV News and roll their eyes in disbelief, dismissing the predictable liberal-bashing as fabricated nonsense. At the same time, people on the political right dismiss virtually the entire content of *The New York Times* as liberal propaganda. What is credible evidence of wrongdoing to people in one camp is subject to a wholly different interpretation by those in another camp.

In actual court cases and public forums, people accused of ethical lapses and improprieties blame their behavior on alcohol, prescription medicines, exhaustion, road rage, having been abused at earlier times in their lives, or—the most popular justification by far of bad behavior—*the media*.

Leaders who are among the most outspoken proponents of personal responsibility are often among the most experienced and adept buck-passers.

Cultural Phenomena or Facts of Life

Until the mid-1960s the role of teachers, government officials, and religious leaders in the United States was rarely subjected to challenge on the basis of honesty, integrity, or authority.

But the Vietnam War, the presidencies of Lyndon Johnson and Richard Nixon, the Watergate scandal, the Peace Movement, the campaigns for women's rights, gay rights, and human rights and an increase in the number of affluent, college-educated people, the proliferation of media, successful challenges to authority on a large scale—incrementally and cumulatively—changed the landscape of the country, society, and the culture. People no longer accepted that integrity in public and corporate life could be taken for granted and, if even one member of the general public disagreed with the rules or authority, it was no longer outside the limits of *anyone's* power to create a movement for change. Today:

- People agree to marry complete strangers on television for large amounts of money.
- Church secretaries are paid a million dollars to be photographed nude for magazines.
- People reveal their most intimate life experiences to cheering audiences on daytime programs . . . and a public that would have been shocked and outraged by any of these occurrences a decade earlier now buys the book, applauds the revelation, and accords celebrity status to the participants.
- The occasional religious or community leader who *does* express outrage is typically revealed to have skeletons in his or her *own* closet.
- The Internet provides access and the ability to move information.
- Internet access, a declining job market, and the soaring number of home businesses has created millions of new "executives" as individuals took greater charge of their lives . . .
- A wave of "reality" television shows has created hundreds of celebrities who are nationally known only for the fact that they are nationally known.

When the blatant theft of copyrighted material is called "file sharing," and legislators shrug and look away as the perpetrators become wealthy and celebrated, without notice, the rules have changed.

Parents who were taught never to disgrace their families now proudly beam as their children mischievously hack into corporate and government computers or run-up huge profits in the market by engaging in fraudulent stock transactions. Times have changed.

A thousand miles away, other parents file lawsuits to expunge their teenage children's records of criminal behavior, claiming such records could limit their ability to get into the more prestigious universities.

Huh?

Ethics and Interpretation

Historically, the prevailing sentiment has been that ethics, or a code of ethics that informs the public that a subject is trustworthy, was a good thing—good for business, good for a subject's public image and reputation, and good for marketing purposes, not to mention just being good for its own sake.

What is new to the discussion is that never before in the history of public relations have trust and ethics been so subject to reinterpretation. Subject to change though they may be, business and society still have rules and laws, and ethics is not yet a fully outmoded concept.

As businesses and organizations deal with larger segments of the public, ethics become symbolic of standards to which professionals agree in order to enhance the position and status of their profession, as well as to assure the public that some in the profession are committed to integrity. It is a plus, a value consideration.

Being a "subscriber to a professional code of ethics" is intended to distinguish the good guys from the bad guys to that segment of the public to whom, alas, such considerations still matter.

If a subscriber is found to have violated the code, others in the profession must move to exclude the violator from their ranks or the code becomes worthless as a distinguishing characteristic of good businesses.

Can an ethical person work for an unethical client or company?

The answer seems as if it should be simple, but it is not. First, as in the case of a PR strategist called in to develop a crisis management plan for a company that might be a good company caught up in a bad situation—a gray area—a coherent, well-managed presentation of the facts can set things right for the company, its stockholders, employees, and customers, as well as other segments of its public. The company has some problems. It is neither all good nor all bad.

There can also be the comparison made to lawyers who believe that even a person who appears guilty deserves to have the best available representation in order to be certain all sides of the story are explored fairly before judgment is rendered.

Finally, there is the unethical, unprincipled, dishonest company or organization whose management tries to buy representation from a well-regarded, first-rate PR specialist in the hope of getting a halo effect—a reflection of a good image that may overshadow a company with a bad reputation and give it a softer hue. The PR specialist who becomes involved in this type of situation risks a great deal, and there is virtually no justification for thinking the specialist can get away with selling his or her good reputation to a bad company for a fee.

The reason ethics should still matter, despite the fact that the playing field that never actually may have been level is now actually more of a *minefield*, is that, as with cause-related marketing, there are still large segments of the public, companies, and organizations that stand for something and are committed to making things better. Public relations people should:

- Encourage clients and companies to become part of professional organizations that have and adhere to codes of ethics. If the companies are already members, this fact should be exploited whenever, wherever, and as much as possible in press releases, literature, on business cards, letterheads, in ads, in bios, and on the sides of trucks, if possible.
- Draft an internal mission statement that incorporates a commitment to ethical conduct.
- Issue a call that others in the profession or industry sign-on to a code of ethics and publicize the fact that some do and some don't, allowing the public to consider the distinction.
- Be alert to lapses and violations by others in the profession or industry and move quickly and aggressively to distance, distinguish, and clarify the company or organization's position relative to such situations.
- Turn negatives into opportunities. While it might appear on one level to be inappropriate to benefit from the problems of others, as with so many marketing matters, it's all in the packaging. It is not appropriate to kick another company while that company is already in crisis or under attack, but it is *very* appropriate to use the occasion of such a situation to bring attention to ethical issues that are important to the particular profession or industry (and relate it to those

issues as they apply to the client or company). Perhaps suggest how the subject company of the controversy could have avoided being caught up in the problem and indicate what the company or person offering comment does to assure such situations do not occur. This is a standard public relations concept of identifying opportunities for comment as a means of generating publicity. Often what is considered bad news, such as a competitor's ethical lapses or improprieties, is considered by some practitioners— especially those holding law degrees—off-limits as it brings a company or organization into a story containing negatives. That's silly. Opportunities are to be identified, taken, and managed.

- Understand that context is important. Few people do not have something in their past (or present) that critics could not eventually unearth and possibly use against them. Be honest in dealings and honest in published (as well as internal) documents and communications materials so that anything that might be a potential problem has been accounted for.

- Know that recognition for a lifetime, career, or history of good works and ethical behavior does not guarantee immunity from criticism or a free pass against attacks in the future.

William Bennett served as a respected government official, educator, writer, and lecturer for more than two decades and his best-selling *Book of Virtues* and its sequels, read by millions, provided guidelines for morality and ethics. His message was essentially to do what is right, and his own life seemed to serve as an example. When the public learned he was a habitual gambler who had lost more than $8 million, critics ridiculed and denounced him as a hypocrite who preached one set of rules and lived another.

He could have avoided damage to his credibility and reputation by simply acknowledging that he had a problem with gambling. Instead, he said nothing until he was discovered, then dismissed criticism, saying in his case gambling was not a problem because it helped him to relax and he could afford to lose the money.

Many people found his response strained credibility and responded that numerous other methods of stress relief would have been more in keeping with the image he so carefully cultivated.

Clark Clifford had a distinguished career in government and served as an advisor to several U.S. presidents. Late in his life he also advised foreign banking interests and at one point accepted the title of president of a foreign bank's American branch. When it was revealed that the institution had very questionable and unsavory ties, his reputation was immediately tarnished and fifty years of good work was compromised—reduced to the suggestion that his name and connections had been bought by a high bidder.

Bolstering Image and Reputation in Today's Environment

Because the public associates a subject's image and reputation with good work doesn't assure that it always will. Good U.S. companies with ties to overseas sweatshops hurt their images (and their stock performance). Disclosure could have negated or reduced the damage, putting issues on the record and explanations in context.

These days:

- Creating or subscribing to a professional code of ethics and funding worthy causes help to position a company, organization, or individual on the right side, but the media and the public will only accept and embrace that image and support the subject based on what is actually done. If ethics are not fully reflected as a way of doing business, all else seems cosmetic.
- Ethics in the modern era seems to be subject to interpretation (or *re*interpretation) largely due to issues of ego, power, and greed. "Medical ethics" specialists, however, deal with issues that literally come down to life and death.

Their training encompasses medicine, law, philosophy, psychology, and theology to various degrees. At the other extreme is the person assigned to write the popular newspaper column "The Ethicist" that appears every week in *The New York Times Sunday Magazine*. He is a feature writer who, like *Dear Abby* or *Ann Landers* and hundreds of other columnists, dispenses advice and arbitrates disputes, rendering opinions on what is right and wrong *ethically*.

Ethical issues, theoretically, should not merely be matters of opinion, yet in many instances, that is exactly what they are—*judgment calls*. For this reason, public relations professionals are well advised to put missions, policies, philosophies, and standards in writing. Being flexible is important, but having a core base of principles from which to be flexible is both essential and virtuous.

For the public relations professional who believes his or her profession is getting an undeserved black eye and wants to do something about it, the recommended strategy is to *become a client*.

Thinking of one's own business and profession as a "client" means preparing a plan—a situation analysis, objective, strategy and tactics, time line, and budget to achieve the stated objectives. Consider the unique selling proposition and what about PR in general and a specific PR practice in particular has value.

Consider what negative perceptions people have of the firm and/or the profession. Mount a persuasive argument that counters the claims of critics.

If the objective is to create a positive impression of a profession, work to that aim without rationalizing short cuts and loopholes to ethical behavior.

Be honest. If the reason a campaign is needed to change public perceptions about PR is because terms such as those used in the film reviews noted at the beginning of this chapter (amoral, self-serving, sleazy, smarmy, etc.) have stuck, the damage must be undone and a positive image created to replace it, not another negative image to reinforce it.

Is it realistic to expect that a PR person can change a negative image of his or her profession or any profession when the societal and cultural trend seems to be moving in the opposite direction?

It is definitely not an easy task and perhaps it is not realistic—going against the tide rarely is—but for someone to whom such issues as ethics and integrity make a difference, the next time the phrase "everybody does it these days" is said or written, there will be the satisfaction that comes from knowing that really isn't so.

SUMMARY

- In business and in society in general, the ethics of PR professionals have come under question and the ethical bar keeps being lowered.
- The technology boom and proliferation of "celebrity CEOs" in the 1990s represented a major cultural change with new rules and new standards of what is socially acceptable.
- Bad news is more interesting than good news and is remembered longer—even after it's been proved to be not true.
- People say they want the truth, but *really* want an answer that fits their purpose or point of view. The truth has become a relative thing.
- Some people experience a sense of *schadenfreude*, a feeling of joy that comes from witnessing the reversals of the rich and powerful.
- A code of ethics informs the public a subject is trustworthy. It is good for business and good for the subject's public image and reputation.
- PR professionals should put missions, policies, philosophies, and standards in writing. A good PR program can help to change a negative image by demonstrating and maintaining ethics and integrity,

References

Greg Burns, "Stewart merely reflects lower standards" *Chicago Tribune*, June 15, 2003.

David Greising, "The rug pulled out from beneath our feet," *Chicago Tribune*, June 15, 2003.

Dan McGrath, "Throwing the fans an ethical curve," *Chicago Tribune*, June 15, 2003.

Floyd Norris in "Business Ethics and Other Oxymorons," the *New York Times Book Review*, April 20, 2003.

People Magazine, Letters to the Editor, July 14, 2003.

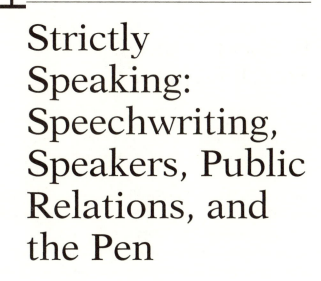

14

Strictly Speaking: Speechwriting, Speakers, Public Relations, and the Pen

While professionals in the various areas of marketing continue their search for "the Next Big Idea" that will (again) redefine the business, there are fortunately still tested concepts that work. What keeps these tested concepts from becoming tired and overused is the creative twist that each practitioner adds to the mix.

In public relations, every press release is different, no two media kits need be exactly alike, and media alerts and pitches all have their own uniqueness. And the company or organization executive, the scientist, athlete, candidate, technology expert, or financial wizard who delivers a speech to a well-considered audience of admirers, colleagues, or critics at a carefully-chosen venue, is delivering a speech that no one ever delivered before. In the process he or she is creating a list of PR opportunities that might include everything from disseminating and marketing transcripts to providing press releases and magazine excerpts to Internet chat rooms or radio to arranging TV interviews—all of which create opportunities for still more PR.

Delivering a speech, like writing a book, is a substantive end in itself, but it also becomes a vehicle to market—an instrument to extend and promote the message around which it was created.

Factors to Consider in Speech Preparation

When planning, scheduling, preparing, writing, and rehearsing a speech, keep this is mind: some people out there really want the speech to be terrible. They are prepared to yawn and to criticize it no matter what is said or done. In such cases, the critics of course are not actually finding fault with the speech, but have issues with what the *speaker* represents to them, and that is another matter that has nothing to do with public speaking.

In other instances, the critics' problem with the speech has to do with their own expectations. The presentation or the content fails to deliver what some people came prepared to hear. This is the same factor that accounts for why some people prefer jazz, rock, classical, or country music and cannot tolerate anything else.

In some situations, *where* a speech is delivered is as significant a consideration as *what* is being said. Choosing a proper venue is enormously important in that even if, in a worst case scenario, the speech itself does not go especially well or is poorly attended, the very fact that the speaker addressed a particularly prestigious group or spoke at an important conference or a highly recognized institution is a story hook that few editors or producers can ignore. The entertainer who "plays the Palace" or the musician who performs at Carnegie Hall enjoys the halo effect of the institution's prestige long after the performance ends. Speakers benefit in the same way when they appear on programs or at events at leading universities and professional conferences.

Of course, having the speech go well and avoiding the worst-case scenario should be a goal as well as booking the right venue.

Not everyone is a great or entertaining speaker, can write a great speech, or go out there and leave audiences cheering in the aisles. Content matters, presentation skills count, and practice doesn't necessarily make it perfect, but it helps.

Throughout the years speakers have used slides, overhead projectors, PowerPoint and laser presentations, music, and assorted props or "visuals" in efforts to hold an audience's attention. Any such devices are choices and preferences that add extra touches, but in its final presentation the speech is what it is. A transcript read a year later does not include the slides, music, ambient lighting, or fireworks. If the content is not there, the packaging becomes irrelevant to the presentation.

Steps to Assure Success

But just as the speech itself can be used as a formula vehicle to create visibility and awareness, certain steps can be taken to at least deliver a solid presentation that will warrant coverage and subsequent marketing.

Choose the venue carefully, not only for its image and prestige, but for the type of audience it will attract. In some situations people attend events known for having "a tough crowd"—a particularly critical, hard-to-please audience. If that crowd is won over, the speaker scores a major victory. Other events attract people who are simply glad to be there, and their audiences are not known to be especially discriminating.

The A-list platforms often schedule programs a year or two in advance of its taking place. Still, to many people with a serious long-term agenda, it is all part of the planning. While all organizations want to have timely topics and "hot" speakers, every industry conference and convention is an event that requires long-term planning, and the planners cannot afford to wait until the week before the event to schedule a speaker or promote his or her participation.

Whatever the venue, the speaker and the speechwriter should know:

1. The makeup of the audience to the extent that is possible:
   - What percentage attending the speech are CEOs or executive level versus middle management?
   - How many are outside or independent consultants versus in-house decision-makers?
   - What do they expect from the event?
   - What are some "hot-button" points to note or avoid?
   - What is the essential message the speaker needs to deliver that will send the audience away satisfied?
2. How the speaker's strengths and weaknesses in experience, reputation, and presentation skills are likely to play with this crowd.

Even seasoned presenters and performers continue to work with voice coaches, acting coaches, personal trainers, and other experts.

A CEO or other individual about to deliver an important speech or a series of important speeches should consider if any weaknesses or areas of possible vulnerability in presentations can be helped by bringing in professionals to assist.

Sometimes pride or ego can get in the way. It is good to remember that business leaders get help with their golf games or financial planning, so the same business leaders need not be reluctant to accept constructive recommendations in preparing to write or deliver a speech. And if the presentation is well attended and well received, no one needs to know who came to help as the speechwriter's role is one of the last bastions of anonymity.

It is always important that a speaker establish a comfort level with an audience, whether the occasion is a small club meeting or gathering or a major convention. This is intelligent planning.

Speakers or their representatives should request information well in advance (not the day of the speech) about the most significant concerns of the audience and include references that are audience-specific in the speech.

Obviously it is useful to know if the audience is composed all or partially of "lay" people who would be less familiar with certain terminology, references, or language unique to a particular industry or profession.

When, for example, a marketing executive speaks at a medical conference, it is appropriate to maintain a proper balance of marketing and medical references to let the audience know that the speaker knows both his or her business and theirs. Knowing that some of the audience members could direct or refer business or contacts to the speaker is a strong incentive for making a good impression in terms of both presentation and specific or focused content.

A good speech—the right topic presented to the right audience as useful information easily understood—can be a key element in achieving larger public relations or marketing objectives.

Speechwriting is a particularly artful process—even more so when the speechwriter is not the person who will be delivering the speech. All the capabilities of other types of writing are required, as well as an ability to mentally step into a role and deliver a performance through a pen—or a word processor, as the case may be.

Writing a speech that will be delivered by someone else involves getting into the mind of the person who will be speaking. The speech must reflect that person's belief, as well as the tone and cadence of how he or she would actually express them. The writer must become familiar with words and terms the speaker uses or would use, as well as words and phrases the speaker would definitely *not* use.

Apart from the fact that its content should be of substance and value to the audience, a most important point speechwriters must remember is that the speech cannot sound as if it were the work of someone other than the speaker—and certainly not that it was the work of a professional writer.

A wonderful line attributed to Winston Churchill has him replying to a woman who wrote to him following one of his speeches. The woman criticized him for ending a sentence with a preposition.

"Madam," the prime minister is said to have written back, "this is the sort of nonsense up with which I will not put."

It is highly unlikely the person delivering the speech is known for using grammar in its most perfect form. It should be written the way the person would say it if he or she were delivering it without the benefit of preparation or assistance—and without "academic" flourishes.

The Role of the Speechwriter

A question often asked about speechwriters is: *why are they necessary?* If the speaker is important enough to be in the position of delivering a speech on a subject about which he or she is knowledgeable, perhaps even an expert, then why does someone else need to write it?

There are several answers to that, the first being that the speechwriter or PR person has been hired to write the speech and is being paid. The second and more serious reason is that the PR person or speechwriter is especially skilled in organizing and laying out a presentation that encompasses the major message points the speaker must be certain to note. People who are experts on a particular subject may not also be inherently well organized or literate.

The third reason is that the speaker presumably does something of note that makes him or her someone the public wants to hear deliver a speech—runs a company, explores space, manages investments, invents string, saves the earth, etc.—and has neither the time nor expertise to prepare a presentation with sound bites worthy of being picked up and quoted by members of the press.

Another frequently asked question is why hasn't society moved beyond the antiquated form of making and listening to speeches?

With an emphasis on fast-paced entertainment, streaming video, and the "information superhighway" at everyone's fingertips, the public still indulges a scene that appears not to have evolved even a step since Socrates lectured the freshman class, except, of course, for the PowerPoint.

The most logical explanation is that when a speaker is delivering a presentation in person, the majority of civilized people sit courteously listening, not having conversations, making phone calls, eating or napping as they might in a pre-taped or online presentation. The speaker thus has a degree of control. The traditional question-and-answer period allows a connection to be created between the presenter and the group.

A live presentation promotes the involvement of speaker and audience members who know that a live program, like a great stage play, only happens once as they witness it, even if the script is used again and again.

But the main reason the system perpetuates itself is that clients and company executives want it to continue. It provides a vehicle to be managed in the building, maintaining, or changing individual or company reputations. Even in these enlightened times, it is the job of PR people to accommodate their clients' requests.

In actuality, a notable person delivering a speech is an event, and events are among the great weapons in the PR arsenal—providing opportunities to re-channel concise, punchy sound bites into press releases and letters to important constituent groups, as well as post on the organization's web site.

So it is both the *content* of the speech and the very fact that the speech will be/is being/was delivered that provides material for merchandising and marketing for the PR professional.

The typical speech is between 20 and 45 minutes, followed by a brief period where the audience members comment or ask questions of the speaker. In panel discussions, each panelist has from five to 15 minutes to deliver his or her prepared remarks.

The job of the speechwriter is to fashion the most important elements of the speaker's message or story into a very focused and organized presentation of the desired length.

An outline is essential to make certain that all the necessary points are covered and in a logical, proper order. This outline should be developed by both the speaker and the writer or by the writer after sufficient consultation with the speaker. It must be what the speaker thinks he or she *should* say.

Once the outline is approved, the writer should develop a draft and present it to the speaker, typewritten and *at least* double-spaced for easy reading and editing.

It is crucial that the writer capture the speaker's voice and personality for obvious reasons—first, of course, so the speech will *sound* like something the speaker would say and, second, because it is also a factor in accurately gauging the length of the speech in terms of words and pages.

A person whose speaking style is moderate and even—that is, neither rushed nor lazy—might take about one minute to read a page of text that is typed, double-spaced, on a standard sheet of paper—about 250 words per page. Someone speaking in a slower, more reflective manner might take a minute and a half to two minutes to read the same page, while a more aggressive speaker with a hurried style might take less than a minute.

This means that the same 15-page speech could be presented in ten minutes (or less), 15 to 17 minutes, or even 30 minutes, depending on the speaker—an important matter to a writer who needs to cover a specific amount of information in a specific, allotted time. The issue becomes more significant when a speech is being recorded and "running over" a couple of minutes (or coming up short) can be a problem.

The writer needs to listen to the speaker talk as much to gauge the pattern, rhythm, or cadence of the speaker's voice as to understand the information being presented. Tape record the speaker and become comfortable with the style of his or her voice.

The length of sentences is important to writers. Most people in normal conversations speak in sentence fragments or trail off without always completing a thought. Listeners understand what is inferred or implied. But speakers present their thoughts in complete, carefully structured sentences. The writer needs to blend these factors, being familiar enough with the speaker's style *and* comfort level as to how long (or parenthetically) a sentence or thought can be expressed before the speaker might begin to stumble over words or phrases.

This is one reason most speechwriters stick to short sentences, which delivered correctly also allow the speaker to sound more emphatic.

Most speechwriters also like to be quoted (or to at least think of what they say as being quotable). Since relatively few people can remember, much less correctly repeat, a quote that is 350 words long—

roughly the typewritten equivalent of a page and a half of text—it's better to be brief.

As when speaking with interviewers, a speaker and speechwriter should think in terms of sound bites, short, punchy, quotable lines that offer a touch of color as well as content.

Delivering a speech should not be a generic exercise:

- What does the speaker want to say?
- What is the audience expecting to hear?

The speechwriter's challenge is not to disappoint those on either side.

The speechwriter is *first* a writer. Many of the most successful comedy writers were true writers who had no ambition to perform what they wrote. Many others were frustrated performers who put much of themselves into their writing, which made it difficult for others to present their work. Speechwriters must have no such confusion as to whose voice the audience will be hearing. The following points will help writers craft speeches that best reflect their speakers:

- The speech must first fit the speaker and reflect what the speaker thinks, feels, believes, represents, and knows—and be presented in the speaker's style.
- The standard rules of writing apply, content should be researched and presented in a logical order that can be easily followed by the audience.
- The writer should observe the usual protocol—a greeting or welcome and an acknowledgement of the host organization, moderator and/or master of ceremonies, and any appropriate dignitaries or honored guests present.
- Numbers always punch-up a presentation whether they represent good news or bad. Include statistics, dollar figures, growth/decline percentages, etc.
- Most people, whether they admit it or not, like to know if other people agree or disagree with their opinions. Citing what percentages of people agree—whether strongly or slightly—or disagree with the speaker's premise or support

his or her position is a way of guiding an audience toward consideration or discussion of the subject.

- As a general rule, the actual presentation should be kept relatively short—a 15 to 20 minute presentation of a thesis or establishing statement, challenge, proof of thesis, and summary points, if appropriate, with recommendations or call to action and conclusion.
- Quote experts who agree or disagree with the speaker's position, but avoid quoting the same experts the audience has heard quoted again and again.
- Have the speaker read through the speech several times—aloud—to be certain the words and phrases flow easily, "sound right" and "work" comfortably within the speaker's normal range and style.
- If the speaker chooses to read the speech, remind him or her to look up every few sentences to maintain a sense of connection to the audience.
- Have speakers who prefer to memorize the speech keep the printed copy within viewing range. It will serve as a guide and help speakers remember to include the best sound bites and present the information in its proper order.

Using the Speech to Generate PR Opportunities

To generate media coverage of a speech for public relations purposes, concise, punchy sound bites, a colorful title, a hook, and a theme are useful. Of course the speech should be written with the audience in mind, but be mindful of the fact that a major *reason* for the speech being written and delivered is public relations, and the opportunity to generate awareness, promote visibility, and influence the public regarding the subject.

The subject should be important to an identifiable target audience, not only to the speaker and a small special interest group. Almost any subject can be positioned within the context of something topical or newsworthy, whether the speaker's subject is healthcare, finance, technology, transportation, entertainment, education, sports, crime, sociology, food, or environmental issues. Virtually anything that is the speaker's cause, issue, product, or concern can be related to a news story of the day, making it relevant to the news media, and as such, deserving of press coverage.

And while it is important in any case that facts are checked and the context of a speech is well researched, it is essential if the speech receives media attention. Taking the information to a larger audience increases the likelihood that if any errors of fact exist in the speech, someone will spot them and possibly seek to create the type of attention the speaker would prefer not to have.

Speechwriting Misconceptions and Missteps

There are three popular myths regarding speeches and speechwriting:

1. The speech must include an opening (icebreaker) joke and at least another joke or two in the body of text.
2. A speech must include quotes from Mark Twain, Abraham Lincoln, John F. Kennedy, or Woody Allen.
3. The speech must be accompanied by a PowerPoint presentation.

Most audiences respond courteously to what is commonly termed "the obligatory opening joke," but increasingly regard it as patronizing, condescending, and irrelevant. Further, people who are normally uncomfortable in the role of public speaker under the best of circumstances can appear even more pained when forced to stand before a group and adopt the pose of standup comic. In addition, as the subject then turns serious, the idea that an audience would be relaxed because of having shared a joke seems incongruous.

There are thousands of experts and millions of quotes, yet in overwhelming numbers, speechwriters seem to call upon the wit and wisdom of the same few individuals to add a touch of celebrated power, dignity, and sizzle to their speeches.

Quoting Lincoln to subtly associate the speaker with the dignity, strength, and character of Lincoln is a leap. Give the audience a break by quoting someone they might not have heard quoted twice this week or skip the quotes and stay with the substance of the message.

Now imagine Socrates or Plato addressing the eager assembled crowd with remarks reduced to key, bulleted sentence fragments or phrases on a PowerPoint presentation. It might be slick to some people who require the presence of a large screen at every event, but it's not necessary. Focus on substance, not props.

Visuals are appropriate when they add something to the speech besides proof the speaker has a laptop computer.

PowerPoint presentations have become as obligatory as the speaker's opening joke, merely a sampling of typed lines that the speaker reads aloud that condescendingly suggest the audience is incapable of focusing on what is being said unless the key words are projected alongside his or her head. Further, the presence of PowerPoint actually draws attention away from the speaker. Few human figures on a stage or platform can compete with a big screen.

If visuals truly add to the information or presentation, then absolutely bring them on. But if the speaker is saying the words "33 percent growth" as a PowerPoint image appears with the words "33 percent growth" on a large screen, the message should be to leave the laptop at home.

Some marketers insist that everyone responds better to visuals than to just the spoken word and this is especially true of members of the younger generations. The argument is that generations brought up on television, Nintendo, Game Boy, and the Internet are less literary and have shorter attention spans, so PowerPoint, videos, and laser presentations are what they expect from a speech, rather than just someone talking.

There may be some truth to that—perhaps a *lot* of truth. But consider some of the major moments in a person's life: being welcomed by a teacher on the first day of school and hearing what comes next; the graduation speech where a classmate shares his or her sense of what is and what can be; the moment when someone says you've got the job or we should be together or our family is about to grow.

These are snapshots of words spoken without PowerPoint or slides and everyone remembers forever what was said. If the message is there and the speaker presents it well, any visual elements are frosting on the cake, but they are not the cake—and a really good cake can be enjoyed without frosting, but wonderful frosting will not make up for a boring or tasteless cake.

An interesting, well-paced speech that offers information, is easy to understand, and clips right along is a credit to the speaker and the speechwriter. If visuals are absolutely needed to hold the audience's attention, then something in the speech is definitely lacking.

Some speakers feel obliged to involve the audience in the speech by asking a series of questions, requesting a show of hands or a verbal response from first the women, then the men, etc.—all devices to warm up a crowd and win an audience's approval.

Other speakers find such engaging tactics less than engaging, believing it produces an atmosphere more like a TV game show than a serious presentation event.

Finally, the question must be addressed as to whether or not it is appropriate for a speaker to *read* a speech. For decades, the short answer has always been *no*.

The material in the speech is supposed to be the speaker's own—a reflection of his or her knowledge, insight, and expertise. To stand, looking at the pages as if seeing the information for the first time (which is actually sometimes the case) diminishes the power of the speaker and the impact of the speech and at the same time suggests a certain lack of respect for the audience.

Some people insist that a speaker who reads a speech that is supposed to represent his or her own words, vision, opinions, and story looks like a fraud. They even expand that sentiment to people who need speechwriters to give them the words to express what they supposedly already know.

As a general rule, a speech plays better when it is not read word-for-word with eyes fixed on the page as if it were a letter from Mom.

The other long-time general rule was that the speech should be memorized and recited as if by an actor delivering his or her lines. The feeling is that even the most engaging of speakers, armed with excellent material, come across as less knowledgeable—even boring—if he or she simply reads from a stack of papers.

There are people who regard public speaking as a form of performance art, noting that the most successful political figures through the years were usually those who could excite a crowd with stirring orations, often coached and rehearsed, as a performer would be for a theatrical production. The speaker, however, is *not* an entertainer, but a corporate CEO, an executive director of a nonprofit organization, an expert on finance, law, or social issues, etc. Is it appropriate to turn such people into performers so their presentations will be considered more interesting or entertaining to their audiences? Or should the *message* carry the day—a speech so well constructed with solid content and something of value to the audience that the speaker's inability to be mistaken for a performer is forgiven?

As with most issues, the vote invariably comes in mixed. One side insists that the message will never be heard if the presentation is dull and flat. The other side, having been fighting the style versus substance battle for a long time, argues that *what* is said is more important than *how* it is said.

The public relations expert's position should be, as it has been with some consistency on the matter of style versus substance issues, that it does not have to be a choice of one or the other.

Few people would argue that some folks are simply not very exciting speakers, whether they read their presentations, commit them to memory, or set them to music. Other speakers clearly love to perform, can be funny, and excited about their work, but leave the audience with nothing much of value at the end of the day.

While audiences always say it was the information that they came for, they really do expect—and want—to be entertained when sitting through a speech.

Prepare the speaker with a coaching session (even if he or she has done this before) and rehearse the speech—out loud—noting the importance of gestures and body language.

Discuss how the speaker should dress for the speech, in clothes that do not draw the audience's attention away from the presentation.

This would rule out coats, suits, or dresses that were originally designed for Seabiscuit or to be displayed on a pole outside a stadium.

Emphasize the importance of projecting a relaxed, confident stance.

Then, tell the speaker to go ahead and read the speech.

Reading a speech is not something to avoid. Being uninteresting is something to avoid.

World leaders *almost always read* the most important speeches of their careers; teachers read aloud from the classics; clergymen read from scripture; parents read to their children.

In every example, if the material is solid and the delivery is thoughtful and sincere, the listeners hang on the speaker's every word—words, incidentally, that were written by someone else. On the other hand, people who commit speeches to memory often stand and recite them as if repeating back a school assignment, quite oblivious to what the words mean.

Some excellent speakers are confident and familiar with their material and can deliver the same speech in the same way over and over again. But for those people who feel more confident reading a speech, no blanket prohibition is necessary.

Look up and out into the audience often and depart occasionally from the text to include anecdotes that will keep the presentation from seeming "canned" and maintain a connection with the audience.

Reading a speech that includes numbers, whether stated in dollars, percentages, or other statistical breakouts, is also totally appropriate in the interests of accuracy, as well as credibility. That is, a speaker who consults a written page before providing statistical information appears to be checking the figures in an era where many speakers are accused of making up facts and figures to support their arguments and hoping no one will ever check.

An exception to the permission-to-read-the-speech rule is when the remarks of the speaker are supposed to be heartfelt, reflective, and personal. When a company's CEO appears before a camera and reads from a printed page, "I am innocent and am sure that when the facts are out, that will be proven," or some such phrase, both the CEO's honesty and intelligence become suspect. Of course, the public statement delivered must be the same as the printed version that was

---

EXIBIT 14.1: SIX THINGS
TO REMEMBER WHEN WRITING
AND DELIVERING SPEECHES

1. Write in the speaker's voice.
2. Remember that a well-constructed speech, when it's read aloud, can sometimes sound like a well-constructed speech. A speechwriter will recognize immediately that is not a compliment.
3. A speech should never *sound* as if it is being read. Writing for the page is very different from the way most people actually speak. This is true whether the speaker is the president or a bright young comedian.
4. A speech should sound as if it is part of a conversation the speaker is having with the audience. In conversation, even acknowledged masters of language rarely adhere firmly to rules of grammar.
5. Speakers should speak with feeling, with emotion, with heart.
6. Audiences come to listen to what a speaker has to say, but they really want to know about things that interest *them*. Know they audience, what it cares about and be sure to address that in the speech.

---

distributed, but heartfelt remarks should not *appear* to have been written by someone else, even if that is the case.

Which comes back to the case for having a speechwriter. Recall that the main reasons are lack of time, a need to focus message points succinctly, and the ability to present information in sound bite form.

Some people are extremely knowledgeable on a particular subject, but have problems speaking in front of a group. They become nervous, have difficulty expressing themselves, lose their train of thought, digress, and fail to cover all they intended to cover, sometimes earning the disapproval of an otherwise admiring audience. This is where the help of a speechwriter can be invaluable.

Speech is an excellent vehicle for generating public relations activity, but as with a press release, it should be positioned and merchandised with other activities as part of a plan.

SUMMARY

- A speech is a substantive end in itself, but it is also a vehicle to market—an instrument that extends and promotes a message.
- Some people criticize a speech because they simply dislike the speaker or feel the speech did not deliver what they wanted to hear.
- *Where* a speech is delivered can be as significant as *what* is being said. A strong venue or a particularly prestigious audience or conference at a highly recognized institution is a story hook itself.
- Know the makeup of the audience, such as the percentage of CEOs, other executives, managers, and decision makers attending, what they expect from the event, what issues to note or avoid, and what message will send the audience away satisfied.
- Writing a speech to be delivered by someone else requires the writer to reflect the speaker's beliefs, tone, cadence, and expressions, become familiar with terms the speaker uses, would use, or would *not* use, and make certain that the content of the speech provides substance and value to the audience.
- To attract media coverage, a speech should be punchy, include sound bites, have a good or timely hook, and information that is useful. To a particular segment of the public.

15

Crisis Management and PR

For many years the insurance industry had a great slogan, *"It's better to have insurance and not need it than to need insurance and not have it."*

Crisis management, an area of public relations that has emerged as a specialty practice within many PR agencies and consulting firms, is much the same. As with insurance, companies and organizations are learning that it is better to have a crisis management plan and not need it than to need a crisis management plan and not have it.

Preparing for Disaster

"Crisis" is a relative term that can suggest a variety of individual or corporate problems, from a merger gone wrong or major financial difficulties to product recalls, executive malfeasance, a publicized lawsuit, or a stock price in freefall. Several of the largest companies unexpectedly filing bankruptcy or being taken over by less successful companies a fraction of their size can be a crisis to many observers and investors, but to others, a mere sign of how things are.

A charge of racial or sexual or age discrimination, price gouging, or unfair business practices—even if proved to be wholly unjustified—can damage the reputations of everyone associated with an organization.

Pickets, demonstrators, a card on a supermarket bulletin board, a posting on an Internet site, or the most absurd or outrageous rumor can trigger a crisis.

People no longer stop using products they don't like, they sue the companies that manufacture the products. And the cases make headlines. Some examples:

- A woman puts a cup of hot coffee between her legs as she drives away from a restaurant. The coffee spills. She suffers burns on her legs and sues the restaurant.
- Another woman checks into a motel and asks someone in the parking lot she assumes to be a motel employee to help her carry items to her room. He is not an employee. He follows the woman to her room and allegedly attacks her. She sues the motel chain.
- Sufferers of a variety of diseases sue tobacco companies for manufacturing and marketing cigarettes they purchased that caused them to contract the diseases.
- People gain weight and file lawsuits against the fast food chains that sold them the food they ate.
- A movie studio is sued because a person is injured after attempting to recreate a stunt he saw performed in a film.

In Chapter 13 (Ethics) it was noted that if the rules that govern behavior in society have not changed, then it is society itself that has changed—or at least the times have. In terms of crisis management this means that in times of relaxed standards (1) more activity occurs than would occur under more controlled circumstances; (2) more activity increases the odds of something negative occurring; and (3) prevailing conditions encourage confrontation between companies or organizations and the media; companies and their competitors or rivals; companies and their shareholders, regulators, and customers as well as more aggressive negative activity in general.

Consider the soaring number of medical malpractice lawsuits, the huge number of highly publicized class action lawsuits against a variety of companies and the government, the shamelessly aggressive corporate takeover tactics and "greenmail." The term "takeover artist" is commonly used to refer to predator-investors as if they were symphony conductors.

Earlier books on *crisis marketing* and *image marketing* were prompted in part by the fact that for decades certain industries, professions, and institutions were believed to be above the fray—members of the medical profession, the clergy, the military, accountants, lawyers, and virtuous former cabinet officers never expected to be candidates for crisis management. All that's changed.

From the notorious domestic diva being indicted and accused of possible securities law violations to the giant airline that moved to protect executives' lucrative compensation packages in the same week it asked union members to accept cuts in pay and benefits to a litany of charges directed at the Catholic Church, no person or organization is immune to crisis.

Among the reasons no one is safe is that:

- Society has become more litigious.
- Standards of civility have diminished significantly.
- Many people have learned that a shorter route to success is at the expense of someone else through a lawsuit—or the filing and quick settlement of a lawsuit.
- A virtual industry now exists wherein companies will take on any corporation, issue, or cause and will sue, harass, or otherwise publicize a subject for the sole purpose of attracting the attention of the public, with further objectives not always obvious.

Ineffective Approaches to Crisis Management

To this point pretty much all aspects of public relations covered in this book—and most other books on PR—have accentuated the positive and anticipated a happy ending. But the very terms "crisis" and "crisis management" imply something gone very wrong.

While it is true that many bad situations give rise to opportunities that might otherwise not be available, trying to put a positive spin on a crisis is a very risky strategy. It can be interpreted as being out of touch with the reality of the situation and its potential impact on specific constituent groups or the larger public.

Worse still are two other approaches. First is the standard lawyer's approach, which is to say nothing then issue a "no comment" statement on the crisis if and when it receives public attention. The second bad strategy is the "do nothing and hope it blows over" approach, which unfortunately has succeeded in enough instances that management is often prepared take the risk and hope it works again.

What is *most* wrong with the "no comment" strategy—which recognizes the potential legal implications of the problem and almost any response to it—is that outside of the legal system is a public that has perhaps invested a great deal of its time, money, and loyalty in the company or organization and now wants to be reassured that its support was justified.

Employees are often caught in a crossfire during a crisis, wanting to be loyal to their employers, but lacking sufficient information to defend it. Brokers need to be able to advise their clients to be patient and not rush to sell the company's stock—a frenzy to do so at the hint of a crisis could compound the company's problem.

Whether it is a publicly traded company or a privately held business, an association, institution, or nonprofit organization, consider how much in the way of resources might have been devoted to building and sustaining a good reputation that is first threatened by a connection to a crisis and is compounded by a lack of explanation.

To be fair, lawyers have a job to do and may believe they are protecting the organization by not offering comments that could become problems later. But lawyers must look at the larger picture and appreciate how damage to an image or reputation could *compound* short-term problems and be enormously damaging over the longer term. On the other hand, by acting quickly and being responsive to perceived public interest, the company or organization's reputation could be enhanced and the benefits of doing so could be useful later on.

The longer a company or organization delays its response, the more time critics, rivals, competitors, and adversaries have to take advantage of the situation at the company's expense.

The "do nothing and hope it blows over" approach is the ultimate abuse of a positive mental attitude. No one *wants* problems or to have to deal with problems, but to do so is part of the job, taking responsibility for what happens and setting mistakes right. To simply hope that the public will never learn of something that occurred and might somehow be damaging is to put a skeleton in the closet that might still be discovered at a later date and reflect even worse on the company.

One of the most famous scandals in recent American history was said to be not about what was actually done, but about attempts to cover up what was done, creating a suggestion of guilt that might well exceed anything associated with the act itself. There might have been an explanation or mitigation for the problem, but a cover-up is itself the intentional withholding of information from people who, rightly or wrongly, believe they have a right to know and may be slow to forgive someone who arbitrarily overrides their perceived right.

For this reason the first rules of crisis management, often stated in different ways, comes down to: *Acknowledge the problem, deal with it, and move on.*

Creating a Plan for an Uneven Playing Field

The list of cases that made the headlines noted above creates a bleak picture. Public relations is supposed to be an effective way of creating awareness and influencing decision-makers. When used effectively as part of a negative agenda—a campaign attack or to discredit a rival or competitor—alas, the process can be just as powerful, albeit destructive.

In the American presidential election campaign of 1988, one of the major candidates told his supporters "we've got to define our opponent," which he did in an often-repeated series of characterizations that misrepresented both the opponents' record and position on several major issues.

The candidate under attack kept protesting that his record and positions were not as they were being reported and spent the entire campaign on the defensive, attempting to clarify his positions, correct the record, and in the process appeared to be either confusing voters or changing his mind.

Several years later, in another campaign, another candidate appeared constantly angry and ill-tempered, as he shouted at his rival, "Stop lying about my record!" The rival continued to repeat the distortions, all the while shaking his head as if pitying the pathetic candidate who, as Jack Nicholson bellowed in one of his most famous movie lines, couldn't *"handle the truth!"*

In both cases the candidates under attack failed to run a "crisis" strategy. They ran as if their opponents were playing fair, which attackers rarely are.

The unfortunate truth is that, while various theories can be put forward about such crises as the bursting of the technology bubble, the collapse of both the dot-com market, and the implosion of the savings and loan industry more than a decade earlier, the usual "crises" that businesses experience are not inevitable aspects of doing business, but are the results of deliberate acts. Again, as noted in the chapter on ethics, most every major individual and corporate scandal that precipitated a crisis and shook the markets and mores of the early 21st century—Enron, WorldCom, ImClone, AOL Time Warner, the Catholic Church, and the rest—was the result of an overt action that someone intentionally set in motion.

The big crises were, as they often seem to be, about greed, power, mismanagement, and the attempt to avoid discovery. But thousands of smaller crises occur each year—the misunderstood comment or gesture in the workplace that becomes the lawsuit and news story, the failure to provide enough handicapped access locations that prompts the photo-op protest, the letter to the editor from the disgruntled employee, the accident on the premises that triggered rumors of inadequate safety and security measures . . . and on and on.

A crisis doesn't need to be a scandal and the CEO need not be Jack Welch or Martha Stewart to catch the media's attention. Knowing this, and planning for the possibility that opportunistic characters might have the company or organization in its sights, is an indication of good management of an account or a company.

The Three Stages of Crisis Management

The three main stages of crisis management are *before, during,* and *after* a crisis occurs. Certain types of possible crises should be expected if the company or organization is a bank, an airline, a power company, or other public utility. Obviously it is not possible to anticipate and plan for everything that could occur, so the initial plan is general in nature.

Before the First Indications of a Crisis

It is strongly advised to stay connected to the public that makes up the company's or organization's key constituencies. Know what is important to customers, prospects, investors, regulators, employees, and media. To do this:

- Listen to the voice of the market.
- Create a reservoir of goodwill that can be tapped if or when times get tough.
- Let customers know someone is available to discuss their concerns. Though the vast majority of customers never contact companies or organizations, they still would like to know that if they wanted to call someone is there to listen to their comments.
- Convey that the customers' opinions matter.
- Establish and maintain communications, such as newsletters or bulletins.

- Let the public know the company or organization's mission and what its contributions are to its industry and community.
- Be responsive to inquiries and complaints from both admirers and critics. It may not be possible to please everyone, but it is worth the effort to try.
- Invite comments at all times, welcome inquiries, and pay attention to what people say. Such comments might reveal the first hint of a problem taking shape.
- Survey the public for attitudes and awareness.
- Do not wait for the public to bring problems to the attention of management—go looking for them.
- Do not assume that because nothing negative has filtered back to the management offices that there are no problems brewing. Ask employees and sales reps who are out and in touch with members of the public if there are any potential trouble spots.
- Think positively. Stuff happens, but be confident that doing good things for the public will bring benefits.
- Build trust and be honest. Honor guarantees and thank people for their business and support. Many companies and organizations do not—and people notice.
- Be "out there" telling the company's story and collecting information. To create awareness of an issue or product or company, tell people about it—do not wait to be discovered.

At the First Indication of a Crisis

When a crisis becomes apparent:

- Designate one person to be the spokesperson for the company or organization during the crisis. The CEO, the lawyer, or PR rep might all have good points to make, but if at any time any comments seem inconsistent or contradictory, that could be a problem.
- Tell the public your side of the story first. By being "out front" quickly the company has an opportunity to define the story and control its course up to a point. By coming in late—after the media or someone else (such as a competitor,

rival, or critic) has told the world the organization has a crisis on its hands—the only position is a responsive one where others lead the discussion and agenda.

- Present the company or organization in a larger context than the crisis, providing the public and the media with information about the history and positive contributions the company has made—particularly with regard to cause-related matters such as community service, job creation, and support for local institutions and programs.

- Keep people within the organization informed. Employees (and even former employees) at all levels, investors, vendors, and other stakeholders in the organization have an interest in what is going on. Don't make them pay to read it in the newspaper. They can be a positive force and a valuable base of support during a crisis, and they deserve to know what's happening first.

- Keep the team together. Sending express mail, e-mails, and web site postings to the company or organization's core constituent groups (everyone on the mailing list and then some) creates a sense of pride, avoids promoting a negatively charged work atmosphere, and maintains productivity.

- Be honest and responsive. Accept and return calls. Even if the company is at fault in the crisis, acknowledging that, taking responsibility for it, pledging to correct the problem, promising to monitor so there will be no reoccurrence—and apologizing to customers, supporters, shareholders, employees, and anyone else who was let down or disadvantaged and making restitution—will likely win the respect of the public, which tends to be very forgiving and willing to work with people who *do the right thing*. This is not the perfect response in all cases, but it will likely find greater acceptance with the public than hiding behind legal maneuvers and technicalities and looking for someone else to blame.

After a Crisis

When it appears as if the worst of the crisis has passed, repeat all the steps outlined above. By maintaining a public profile, being visible, accessible, involved in industry and community matters, *and not being known only for having experienced a crisis,* the company or organization has the best chance of regaining any ground lost during the crisis and winning respect from its industry and community.

Other Benefits of Crisis Management

For many companies that become caught up in some type of problem or crisis, the experience is their first time in the news, meeting the media and coming to the attention of the public. That's too bad because then the public's first impression of the company will be related to a negative event. With proper planning and effort, the public might have had a favorable opinion of the company and judged its problems very differently.

How the company or organization handles its crisis—hopefully with directness, honesty, and integrity—will determine how the company is regarded after the crisis.

Crisis management is not always simple or easy. To most of the public (and the media) bad news is more interesting than good news, so a company in trouble is interesting. The more colorfully the facts can be represented during the crisis, the *more* interesting the story will seem, but at whose expense?

A word of warning: crisis management can be very effective when bad things happen to good companies. But if the company at the center of the crisis is *not* a good company, then crisis management will be a short-term cosmetics approach to a problem that needs more than a public relations program.

Being out early with a concise explanation of the problem and decisive comments on how the crisis will be addressed is the least complicated, most efficient way of dealing with a crisis, salvaging a good reputation, keeping the respect of the public, and getting back to business.

SUMMARY

- Crisis management is necessary when something negative occurs–a confrontation between companies or organizations and the media; companies and their competitors or rivals; companies and their stakeholders or customers; or negative activity in general.
- Society has become more litigious; standards of civility have declined; more people seek to profit from lawsuits; a virtual industry now exists with people taking on corporations, issues, and causes–suing, harassing, and publicizing subjects solely to attract attention in order to further objectives not that are always obvious.
- The longer an organization waits to respond to a crisis, the more time critics and adversaries have to take advantage of the situation.
- The three main stages of crisis management are *before, during,* and *after* a crisis occurs.
- Listen to the voice of the market; create a reservoir of goodwill; establish and maintain communications; be responsive; be honest; tell your side of the story first; present the organization in a larger context than the crisis, providing the public and the media with information about positive contributions the company has made.

16

Measuring the Effectiveness of Public Relations

$\mathbf{M}$ore than a century ago, Philadelphia department store magnate John Wanamaker reportedly said, "I am certain that half of the money I spend on advertising is wasted. The trouble is, I don't know which half." Some advertisers believe that despite the passage of time and advances in knowledge and technology, not much has changed. There are also certain phrases heard often enough in public relations meetings that each might qualify as a mantra of the profession . . .

How can we tell if it's working?
How long before we see results?
What's our return on investment?

The answer to all these questions is *research,* more specifically, the type of research that focuses on measuring effectiveness. And it is a highly underutilized process.

The Role of Research

Katie Delahaye Paine, CEO of KDPaine & Partners, a Durham, New Hampshire-based measurement resource organization, notes, "I've come to the conclusion that we communicators are great at communicating but we're really lousy listeners. Take this statistic, for example: Most companies spend 98 percent of their PR budgets communicating and only 2 percent on research that 'listens' to their constituencies. . . . "

Ms. Paine's firm is one of several whose specific niche is providing tools to measure the effectiveness of marketing and PR programs. Among the range of products and services available are *The Measurement Standard,* a monthly newsletter featuring the current information, news, and tips on measurement, evaluation and analysis; the *One Minute Benchmarking Bulletin,* a bulletin that updates marketers and managers on the developments in the measurement industry in a minute or less; and the *Do-It-Yourself Dashboard,* a customized kit that teaches managers to conduct their own measurement programs in days. "The Measurement Mall" is a service that provides a range of alternatives from analysis to reporting tools, books and benchmarking data.

EXHIBIT 16.1:
PUBLIC RELATIONS SYSTEM OVERVIEW

Include these steps as part of the communications process:

1. Set objectives.
2. Pick a benchmark.
3. Conduct a tactical media analysis.
4. Compare results against objectives.
5. Evaluate and improve the system.

In 2003, Dr. Walter K. Lindenmann, a respected authority on effectiveness measurement, noted in a publication of the Institute for Public Relations at the University of Florida in Gainesville,

> In the short-term, PR measurement and evaluation involves assessing the success or failure of specific PR programs, strategies, activities or tactics by measuring the outputs, outtakes and/or outcomes of those programs against a predetermined set of objectives. In the long-term, PR measurement and evaluation involve assessing the success or failure of much broader PR efforts that have as their aim seeking to improve and enhance the relationships that organizations maintain with key constituents.
>
> More specifically, PR measurement is a way of giving a result a precise dimension, generally by comparison to some standard or baseline and usually is done in a quantifiable or numerical manner. That is, when we measure outputs, outtakes and outcomes, we usually come up with a precise measure—a number, for example, 1,000 brochures distributed . . . 60,000 hits on a web site . . . 50 percent message recall . . . an 80 percent increase in awareness levels, etc. PR evaluation determines the value or importance of a PR program or effort, usually through appraisal or comparison with a predetermined set of organization goals and objectives. PR evaluation is somewhat more subjective in nature, or softer, than PR measurement, involving a greater amount of interpretation and judgment calls.

Exhibit 16.2: PR Evaluation—Outputs

Short Term Results

- Number of press releases disseminated or persons attending an event
- Number of news stories printed or aired (clips, tapes)
- Content analysis of media coverage
    - —# of company references
    - —Length of coverage
        - ~ converting to ad equivalency
    - —How positive the references or coverage
- Adherence to budget and timeline

Exhibit 16.3: PR Evaluation—Outcomes

Long Term Changes in Awareness, Attitude, and Behavior

- Intermediate term
    - —Message received, attention received, understanding, retention
        - ~ # of requests for information from 800# or web site
        - ~ # of product trials
        - ~ pre & post benchmark survey results:
            - increased awareness levels
            - more favorable attitudes
- Long term
    - —Changes in sales, votes, contributions, stock price, etc.

Guidelines for measuring effectiveness are posted on the Institute for Public Relations web site (www.instituteforpr .com).

Terms such as *output, outcome, and outtakes* when used in research have become buzzwords of sorts, but they do describe very significant distinctions, identifying how specific tactics undertaken differ from the results of those tactics in numerical terms versus their impact. Such a process, which involves considerable "numbers crunching" and analysis, is in contrast to the perception of public relations held by many people that the profession is all about writing press releases and seeking publicity. It is that and much more.

Public relations efforts over the years have been measured in a variety of ways. Some obvious methods of gauging if a PR program is working include:

- Sales increase noticeably.
- Onsite traffic increases noticeably.
- There are more visitors than normal to the web site.
- Telephone inquiries and orders increase.
- Media interest increases.
- Management stops asking if the PR program is working.

The Problems with PR Research and Measurement

Unlike advertising, where the cost of a page or an increment of broadcast time is based on the size of the audience the ad will reach, PR programs have historically been, if not actually *difficult* to measure, at least somewhat complex in terms of quantified results under normal circumstances—"normal circumstances" meaning that a response to a PR program does not always register immediately or in a predictable time frame.

In *The Publicity Handbook,* David R. Yale quotes Gary Blake of The Communications Workshop as saying, "I don't think you can say 'this press release yields that amount of business.' That's asking too much. Publicity sets the scene and indirectly leads to new business."

The word "indirectly" is the operative term here because sometimes the smallest bit of publicity can *very directly* be responsible for a major spike in business.

For example:

- When President John F. Kennedy told an interviewer that he liked to relax and unwind by reading one of Ian Fleming's James Bond novels, the 007 franchise rocketed from modest paperback sales to a multi-billion-dollar book/film/merchandise empire that was still soaring more than four decades later.
- Radio personality Howard Stern casually mentioning on his program that he likes a book has been known to advance it several hundred notches upward in a single day on the amazon.com list of best sellers.
- In his nationally syndicated newspaper column, humorist Dave Barry listed the telephone number of the largest association of telemarketers in the United States and suggested that his readers might call the association to express their opinions on telemarketing. The group's lines were jammed and overloaded for days as tens of thousands of people took Barry's cue.

In all three instances, it should be noted that the intention was not to "publicize" the respective subjects. President Kennedy, Howard Stern, and Dave Barry were not trying to promote the interests of the entities on which they had created such an impact. Yet, that impact is no less dramatic—and measurable—in terms of book sales, rankings and the number of phone calls measured.

The organization e21 developed the table in Exhibit 16.4 to summarize typical PR evaluation tools in use today.

EXHIBIT 16.4

Measuremnt Tool	Description
Client Feedback	The most common measurement tool that PR firms employ is client feedback. While not an objective measure, it does include all factors that are meaningful to the client's interpretation of good PR service, such as industry knowledge, staff rapport, writing ability, response time, strategic council, and publicity results.
Number of articles and News Mentions	Clip counting is the most popular "objective" measure of performance for publicity programs. This method of evaluation provides a quick economical, and tangible measure of publicity results.
Advertising Value Equivalent	Clip counting can be supplemented with an estimation of the total advertising value of news articles. For example, at e21 we use a program that applies published ad rates and applies it to the size of the news articles generated for a period of time. The value of the advertising equivalent of PR can be used to provide a return on investment (ROI) for PR. While this technique doesn't tell a very rich or complete story, it does deliver a very clean ROI number.

Content and Competitive Analysis	Clip counting can also be supplemented with additional criteria such as impressions (estimates of how many people saw the publicity), key messages delivered, and how the publicity compares to that of competitors. Other performance criteria include long versus short mentions, total column inches, articles in top-tier media, and articles by subject, in addition to other criteria. These techniques add a time consuming ($$$) component to clip counting, but also a very valuable qualitative aspect to quantitative analysis.
Inquiries and Web Hints	In the past, inquiries from magazines through so-called "bingo cards" in B2B trade magazines were one of the top measurement tools for both advertising and publicity. Now, the prominence of Web sites in the sales cycle of most products has introduced Web traffic as a potential measurement. And today, e-mail and inquiry capture on Web sites required for literature and other downloads provides a method for measurement.
Sales	It is difficult to evaluate the impact of PR on sales because so many variables are at work, but it's not impossible. With many firms employing sophisticated inquiry tracking through customer relationship management (CRM), it is

Awareness and Opinion Research

now becoming more common for companies to identify the inquiry source for all sales. Some companies even interview their customers for insights into where they entered the sales cycle and what impacted their purchasing decisions. Market research surveys of target audiences are the best way to measure whether your marketing communications program is influencing awareness, attitude, opinions and actions. Only audience surveys can determine whether impressions, key messages, competitive actions, and market positioning have made a difference in the customer's mind. While it is the most costly measurement tool, and doesn't easily isolate the impact of PR from other variables such as advertising, market research does target the ends, not the means, of your communications programs.*

*The above information is copyrighted by e21 corp.com and is used by permission.

All of the techniques in Exhibit 16.4 focus on the traditional outputs of PR, namely publicity, and do not measure other objectives such as strategic development and execution, company and product positioning, and marketing guidance. While most PR programs pursue multiple objectives and execute a variety of programs beyond publicity (special events, users groups, industry standards groups, etc.), it is never wise to lose focus on the principal ways target audiences obtain information and form opinions.

On any given day, companies and organizations direct their public relations representatives to send messages that will move the needle, generate a response, create an impact. Sometimes measuring and recording the response is easy, sometimes not.

But it shouldn't seem like rocket science. If an ad for a one-day sale appears in a newspaper and the store is packed on the day of the sale, the ad did its job, right? That would appear to be the case.

But in public relations case studies, newspapers rarely publish stories about one-day sales. Newspapers might publish a story about a terrific store that has just opened, become a new favorite of young socialites or is still doing well after 100 years at the same location. People who see the story might check out the store the next day or a week later or at some future date. But how does the retailer know if the newspaper story was the reason shoppers visited the store or if they just happened to be in the neighborhood or came in to get change and decided to buy something?

Retailers have been wrestling with this question for decades. In fact, there was little need for the wrestling match to have gone on so long because there actually *are*—and have been—methods of measuring the effectiveness of PR programs but, for many in business, they remain well under the heading of "well-kept secrets."

Effectiveness measurement methods are forms of research and therein lies part of the problem. Companies and organizations of all sizes and types are often reluctant to allocate funding or authorize even the most basic market research because (1) they don't want to spend the money to learn what they think they are already supposed to know, and (2) they don't want anyone to know that there are things about their businesses that they don't already know.

With measurement effectiveness studies, the situation is even worse. Not wanting to spend the money is listed as the number one reason companies don't do it, but not far behind is surely the unspoken reason: no one wants to admit they had to pay to have someone tell them whether or not their public relations program was effective.

In the words of one research professional, "Is it any wonder that, in the world of big business, with jobs, budgets and egos on the line, PR measurement is sometimes less useful than a loud voice, a strong personality and a fat clip book?"

Reading the Tea Leaves— and the Reports

Most people are accustomed to reading polls and surveys that are somehow skewed, incompletely reported, or misrepresented. How often when one's opinion does not match the results of the poll do the questions resonate: Who's doing this polling and who are they talking to in order to get that answer?

Clearly there will always be managers who only want to receive information that supports their own opinions, theories, and the programs they have already approved. For everyone else, there's research.

Just as research and rating services can now report within hours if a new TV show has found an audience or if the President's State of the Union speech changed people's minds, the measurement and evaluation of marketing and public relations programs can be managed quickly, accurately and efficiently. Market research can tell marketers where the bar is set in order to determine if the objective should be to rise to that level, exceed it or redefine the standard.

The Importance of Defining Objectives

The resources are available to adequately address the questions of whether or not the PR program is effective. The company's or organization's management, however, must be absolutely clear about what the program is to accomplish before it should try to assess whether or not it was successful.

EXHIBIT 16.5: TACTICAL MEDIA ANALYSIS

- Quantitative
  —Share of voice
  —Media name, date
  —Reporter
  —Spokesperson quoted
  —Favorability of mention
  —Extent/Prominence of
   mention
  —Key message appearance

- Qualitative
  —Tone
  —Message
   communication
   context
  —Positioning on issues

A marketing executive noted, "It is easy for a public relations or marketing manager to fail to meet clients' expectations if they don't know what those expectations are."

Is the aim of the public relations program:

- To generate greater awareness of the subject?
- To stimulate requests for information?
- To increase market share?
- To help increase sales?
- To attract more members, supporters, subscribers or volunteers?
- To build goodwill within a community?
- To change public perceptions regarding the subject?
- To get votes?

Repeated exposures create awareness and familiarity. The result is that the brand becomes better known and it is commonly accepted in marketing that a better-known brand is perceived by most people to be a *better* brand. Whether such familiarity results in consumers being immune to the brand image or absorbing its message unconsciously is something marketers need to know.

If the product flies off the shelf the morning after a major sponsored TV event or coinciding with the appearance of a favorable mention in the media, it is reasonable to conclude there is a connection. Apart from such a signal occurrence, the best way to measure the effectiveness of a program is to go out and ask people if it's working through the tested, reliable methods of professional market research.

Clipping and Taping and Technology

While many people declared the Internet the final word on access and communication perhaps a bit prematurely, there is no question that it represents a huge advancement in research. For example, a clipping and taping service has long been essential in tracking the effectiveness of public relations efforts in generating exposure and monitoring changes in opinion, sentiment, and support. A press release or other announcement sent to a wire service, which then disseminates the material to perhaps several thousand subscribers and media outlets, will likely result in coverage that would go unnoticed without such a service. Analysis of the coverage is a separate function of market research.

For decades this process involved painstaking and costly scanning, viewing, and reading newspapers and magazines and watching thousands of hours of television news and features. Stacks of pages were photocopied and circulated to interested parties. The Internet, with its tens of millions of pages and files and hundreds of search engines, completely revolutionized the process. Searches that took weeks are completed in seconds or minutes. While the intelligence and analysis that defines and drives research still depends on the skill, training, and judgment of professionals, the "grunt work" that provides them with masses of data has been reduced, literally, to the push of a button.

Internal Communications

Chapter 8 considered the role of an organization's employees as a factor in public relations. Not only is it in the organization's best

EXHIBIT 16.6: INTERNAL RESEARCH TOOLS

- Communications Audit
  —survey employees on satisfaction with communications tools and information flow
- Network Analysis
  —traces one message through an organization
- Duty Study
  —employees record daily communication in diary
- Observational Study
  —trained observers record employee commications
  activities
- Cross-Sectional Interviews
  —ask employees about communications interactions

EXHIBIT 16.7: INTERNAL OUTPUT OBJECTIVES

How Success is Measured

- Show respect in communications
- Produce certain materials over set time frame
- Recognize employee successes
- Establish two-way communications
- Schedule interpersonal communications

EXHINIT 16.8:
INTERNAL *OUTCOME/IMPACT* OBJECTIVES

How Success is Measured

- Increase knowledge
- Adopt behaviors
- Keep them informed
- Enhance favorable attitudes
- Obtain feedback
- Create partnerships

interests to create and maintain positive relations with employees from a legal, ethical, economic, business standpoint, but employees at every level—management executives, field staff, support staff, labor force—represent the organization's public face, its image and reputation, to shareholders, suppliers and the rest of the outside world.

It is important not only that an employee relations program be in place, but that those charged with implementing such a program be aware as to whether or not it is achieving its objectives. It is not enough to simply fund employee communications and *assume* if no one criticizes or attacks the effort that it must be a success. As with the external public, those inside the organization should not take loyalty or support as a given among constituents just because a relationship or connection exists.

Measuring Failure

When a public relations program is a success, its managers should want to know not only their return on investment, but any related information that would better position them in presenting future programs.

Critics of market research, usually tight-fisted when it comes to taking the pulse of the market, are even harder on measuring a program's effectiveness, insisting that if it is successful, success should be obvious, and if it is unsuccessful, that such failure will be readily noticed as well. While that point is valid, it is also simplistic and fails to note that, while success or failure is the final line of the story, the true value of research is to provide information that is *not* obvious— in other words, discovering *why* the results were as they were.

For example, a major, well-publicized event has a disappointing turnout. A typical first reaction is to suggest the event was, in some or many ways, lacking in sufficient appeal and its producers and promoters misjudged the level of interest in the subject. Or the advertising failed to do its job. Or there might be other explanations that attribute blame to specific individuals who overlooked some details or otherwise under-performed.

Or the program could have been well-conceived, well-presented, and all aspects of the plan executed flawlessly. If that was the case, why wasn't the event successful? Consider these possibilities:

- The public transit system went on strike earlier that day.
- An unpredicted storm developed.
- Another event scheduled for the same day siphoned off nearly half the crowd that would have most likely attended the subject event.
- A negative news alert that same day caused many people to reconsider leaving their homes.
- All of the above occurred at once.

With so much at stake, it should be important to know *why* a seemingly well-crafted effort failed as much as to know *that* it failed. For example:

- A senator announced his candidacy for president of the United States on a date that a terrorist set off a bomb in on Oklahoma City.
- A water-retaining wall collapsed, flooding tunnels and underground spaces that ran beneath a major city's downtown business area.
- A rumor of lower than expected earnings of a major technology company circulated early one morning, sending tech stocks into a steep decline at the same time another technology company was beginning its initial public offering of stock.
- A pop singer's new album was released with much fanfare on a day the local district attorney issued an arrest warrant that charged him with unlawful acts.
- On September 11, 2001, virtually everything scheduled in America was rescheduled as all air traffic was suspended and a national state of emergency was declared.

Not all such disruptive situations are likely to be as extreme as the examples offered. Yet, *things happen,* and if they affect the success of an event, a major sale or grand opening, a corporation's initial public offering, or any other planned activity, it should be important to people responsible for that activity to understand the impact of unforeseen occurrences.

Measurement research should not be viewed as an added cost for acquiring nonessential information; it should be regarded as a last step in a program to analyze its results and a first step in effectively preparing and planning future efforts.

SUMMARY

- Public relations programs are difficult to measure, as a response to a PR program does not always register immediately or in a predictable time frame.
- Every day companies and organizations direct their public relations representatives to put out messages that generate a response and create an impact.
- Market research tells marketers where the bar is set in order to determine if the objective should be to rise to that level, exceed it or redefine the standard.
- Some managers will want only to receive information that supports their opinions, theories and the programs they have already approved. Market research will provide the real story.
- Specialty firms within the research field focus specifically on providing tools to measure the effectiveness of marketing and PR programs.
- The brand that enjoys greater visibility becomes better known and a *better-known* brand is perceived by most people to be a *better* brand.

References

Charles Goodrum and Helen Dalrymple, *Advertising in America: The First 200 Years* (New York: Harry N. Abrams, Inc. Publishers, 1990).

Walter K. Lindenmann, "Guidelines and Standards for Measuring the Effectiveness of PR Programs and Activities" (Gainesville, FL: The Institute for Public Relations, the University of Florida, 2003).

David Yale, *The Publicity Handbook* (Chicago: McGraw-Hill/Contemporary, 1991).

PART II

Public Relations Portfolio

A CEO delivered a speech to the National Press Club and everyone in government paid close attention. The organization of which he is the CEO is AARP, which has more than 35 million members. But there's more to it than clout. There is a vision, a cause, and a smart marketing plan that included that speech.

A press release for a homebuilder was carefully prepared and sent to media where it was thought it would be well received and had the best chance of being picked up and presented to the right demographic segment of the public . . . and picked up it was, several times.

Employees are a company or organization's public too. Internal communications work for keeping employees better informed, but what about helping them do their jobs better?

The challenge was to create awareness, get the attention of the media and the public during the crowded, hectic holiday season. Where do you start? With 350 tubas, of course!

A management firm, a crisis consultant, a bakery, a builder, an elegant hotel, AARP, the Official Airline Guide, . . . Everyone has a story to tell and everyone does it a little differently—sometimes a lot differently.

The Public Relations Portfolio provides examples of large organizations, small businesses and several in-between—what they did, how they did it, and how it all worked out.

Public Relations in Product Turnaround and a New Product Introduction: OAG*

Having published the world famous "Pocket Flight Guide" for more than 30 years, OAG has always been synonymous with travel solutions. As the leading provider of independent flight information in its 75 years of business, OAG was the first resource ever to put flight schedules and data in one central location.

Yet with the emergence of the Internet and online booking sites, coupled with the lack of proactive media relations efforts, the popularity of the OAG name had begun to diminish over the last few years. New management, which took over the company in 2001, expressed a strong commitment to introducing several industry-leading products. But in order to effectively market those products, OAG needed to reintroduce its brand to business travelers and the airline industry, while reinstating the same levels of respect and trust garnered over the past 75 years.

Public relations agency Slack Barshinger took on OAG's communication challenge with passion, beginning with a solid foundation of research and planning. Weeks of group brainstorming and an all-day media training session helped the team to develop concrete messages and a plan to disseminate its story to key consumer and trade publications, associations, and business leaders. Simultaneously, the PR team hit the phones and e-mail, making personalized outreach to industry writers, introducing themselves while offering OAG and its data as a resource to the media.

To reintroduce OAG, Slack Barshinger coordinated a profile of Bill Andres, the new senior vice president and head of OAG Americas, in an exclusive interview with *Crain's Business Chicago*. The article, which incited a snowball of media interest, positioned OAG as a leading Chicago business and put the OAG brand in front of business travelers.

The agency team built additional momentum when OAG attended the National Business Travelers Association Trade Show. As a

* Information courtesy of Slack Barshinger, Chicago, Illinois

key sponsor, OAG was already generating a lot of attention. But the company, with help from its agency, managed to secure coveted time with the top trade publications in the industry. Meeting with *Business Traveler*, *Business Travel News* and *Business Traveler Executive*, OAG secured relationships with the top trade reporters in the industry. OAG representatives also garnered interviews, and coverage, from *The New York Times*, *Wall Street Journal*, and a ¾ page corporate profile in *USA Today*—the top three periodicals for OAG customers.

In August, OAG released its "State of the Industry" report. Providing an overview of how things had changed in the past year, OAG compiled detailed data for both global and domestic travel, beginning with an exclusive in *The New York Times*. OAG partnered with world-famous airline analyst, Henry Harteveldt from Forrester Research, to provide statistics and analysis, including positive trends, relating to the travel industry. The release was carefully timed to not interfere with the inevitable coverage in September, and instead provided factual data that proved invaluable to reporters at CNN and MSNBC.

With excitement building around the "new" OAG, the company launched the "Executive Flight Guide," the successor to the "OAG Pocket Flight Guide." This next generation flight information guide included membership to the OAG club, an online resource with high-tech travel solutions available exclusively to OAG subscribers. Slack Barshinger helped to promote the guide and club by sending personalized letters to CEOs of Fortune 500 companies, along with a complimentary guide. Key media also received a sample book, a free online trial of the OAG club, a personalized letter and the opportunity to interview Eddie Bell, Chairman of OAG.

Since it began working with the agency, OAG has been mentioned or featured in more than 500 articles and television programs, generating an ad value equivalency equal to ten times its public relations investment.

Interest in OAG is higher than it's been in years, with as many as a dozen media requests a week. OAG has been featured in *Newsweek*, referenced on Martha Stewart Living, cited on CBS Evening News, is a regular item in *New York Times* writer Joe Sharkey's aviation column, and is quoted almost weekly in *USA Today*. Senior management from OAG has also been courted for speaking engagements at key industry tradeshows.

For OAG, public relations helped to cost-effectively rebuild a brand and position it strategically in the minds of the right audience. By building a solid foundation of media contacts, OAG was able to begin to influence and educate potential customers, using the third party credibility the media lends to a story. Public relations helped OAG to expand its reach and increase its visibility as part of an overall marketing communications program.

Communicating a Vision through Speeches, Ads, and Other Vehicles: AARP*

Introduction

AARP has a mission: to be a force for positive change that will make society stronger and healthier and life more fulfilling for all persons 50-plus years of age. The organization focuses its collective energy on providing information, serving as an advocate, using the purchasing power of its membership, identifying opportunities to help members volunteer and give back to their communities, and by offering opportunities for enrichment and personal fulfillment.

William D. Novelli is the Executive Director and CEO of AARP, the nonprofit membership organization founded in 1958 as the American Association of Retired Persons. Its name was changed to reflect the fact that about half of its more than 35 million members, age 50 and older, are not retired, but still active in the workplace. They are all concerned, however, with the products and services available to them—particularly the services, as they find themselves at or near retirement and worried about insurance, healthcare and the myriad of other issues the government routinely threatens to eliminate or reduce.

Early on, the organizers of AARP recognized there is strength in

* Information courtesy of AARP

numbers. A few people standing together to make a point—whether it is about rights and entitlements or recognition and being treated well—was more effective than one person alone. And if the size of that group should be 35 million and growing, it is reasonable to expect that governments and industries will listen to their concerns.

Still, life can often be an uphill struggle and numbers alone won't make positive change happen. It takes research, a vision and planning.

In November of 2002, Mr. Novelli summarized the concerns of his members and reality for others facing the same issues in a speech to the National Press Club in Washington, DC, one of the most coveted venues, whose own members are among the most influential media figures in the United States. The speech received broad coverage at the time it was delivered. Copies were made available to the media and it was posted on the organization's web site. Its content delineated points that would become the essential focus of AARP's message, the importance of protecting programs that provide assistance to a growing—and aging—American population.

2011 in America: A New Vision

William D. Novelli
AARP Executive Director and CEO
National Press Club Newsmaker Luncheon
Washington, DC
November 19, 2002

In Washington, a vision is often measured in two or four year election cycles. But today I want to ask you to join me in taking what Teddy Roosevelt called, "The long look ahead." While 2004 is an important year for obvious reasons, there is an even more critical date looming just over the horizon.

It's the year 2011, the year when the first wave of America's 76 million baby boomers turns 65. This will be the beginning of one of the most profound changes in American history. It will exert enormous pressure on our nation's social structure. Some of the pressures may not wait until 2011 to boil over.

In 21st century America, more people are living longer and living better than ever before. As Richard Hobbs, of the American Institute of Architects, wrote recently, "The impact of the aging population on markets, employers, and culture cannot be overstated. Just as the baby boom flooded maternity wards, ignited school construction, and made 'youth' the cultural icon of the 1950s, '60s, and '70s, the 'senior boom' of this century will shape the 2010s, '20s, and '30s."

In addition to the graying of America, there is another major demographic change occurring simultaneously. It is what Richard Rodriguez and others have called the "browning" of America. Whether your forebears came here on the Mayflower, or nearly a century ago, as mine did, or last month, the American melting pot has become the American mosaic.

We live today in a nation where Asian kids eat pizza, where Mexican kids can tell you what they think of you in Yiddish, where Polish kids eat empanadas, and Arabic kids ice skate. And so do their parents. Hispanic Americans are the fastest growing minority group in the country, and we welcome more Asians and Africans every day.

These demographic shifts are triggering other changes in our society that foretell a new vision of 2011 in America . . . changes in health, work, retirement, community and family life. Consider, for example, that:

- Our health-care delivery is based on providing acute care, while more and more people are living with chronic conditions. Over 40 million people are uninsured. Our society is aging, but our new doctors are not studying geriatric medicine. While the cost of health care goes up, the quality of care is going down.

- People are being asked to take more personal responsibility for their own health care. Yet the expense of health care makes it less affordable for many people. Out-of-pocket spending on prescription drugs and long-term care represent the greatest health-related financial risk for older Americans.

- The workplace has changed from back work to brain work. This enables people to work later in life, but requires them to learn new skills and work in new ways. Our workforce, like our society, is also aging. More boomers want to work beyond traditional retirement age, but many employers are still reluctant to hire after 40, train after 50, and retain after 60.

How we prepare for retirement is changing, too. People can no longer balance their retirement needs on the traditional three-legged stool of Social Security, pensions and savings. Today, we need four pillars—Social Security, combined pensions and savings, earnings from work and health-care coverage—for retirement security.

Employers who once offered employees defined-benefit pension plans have shifted the responsibility for retirement security to their employees, with defined-contribution plans such as 401(k)s. Many employers don't offer pension plans at all, and retiree health insurance is becoming a thing of the past.

- The American view of retirement is changing. I come from a family of steel workers in Pittsburgh, and when my parents' generation retired, they did it the old-fashioned way. They really retired. I remember my uncle Andy. He came home from the mill one day, put down his lunch pail, sat down on the porch and said, "That's it. I'm retired." And he was.

  Except for an afternoon walk to the Italian club, his new domain was that front porch. But boomers and older Americans today tend to see retirement not as termination, but as transition-to a life that may include work, education, civic engagement, and of course, being ardent consumers.

  Yet the boomers' exuberant expectations don't match their behaviors in preparing to live an active, productive, and well-financed life as they get older:
- Studies show that boomers are not saving nearly enough to finance the lifestyle they envision in so-called retirement. At the same time, as many employers cut back or eliminate retiree health care and downsize older employees, those 55–64 are one of the largest groups of uninsured.
- Too many boomers and older people live sedentary life styles. Poor physical fitness is a better predictor of death

than any other risk factor, including smoking, high blood pressure and heart disease. And obesity is threatening many of the gains in health over the last 20 years.

- More middle-aged people are struggling to raise their children and take care of their parents. This sandwich generation is being chewed on at both ends.
- As we live longer, people have more opportunity to give back to society through meaningful volunteer work and other civic involvement. Yet, we're slow to adapt our social structures to encourage such community service. So, then, where do we stand at this point only nine years from 2011?
- Boomers have not prepared adequately for their long futures.
- Companies are rapidly shifting risk and responsibilities to workers and retirees.
- Government programs are not working as well as they should, and many need to be modernized, better financed and more engaging to the public.
- We have a health-care system that is designed to pay bills, but doesn't promote health and wellness.
- We have a growing older population that by and large is vital and active and possesses great intellectual wealth. But we have not structured a social model to optimize their continued involvement.

Clearly, America has to change and change substantially, before the baby boomers begin turning 65 in 2011. To recall an ancient proverb, "Where there is no vision, the people perish." That's a 2000 year old soundbite that provides an important lesson for today.

A New Vision

We need a new vision of 2011 and beyond, framed by productive, active engagement and high quality of life throughout the human lifespan. We need to change the partnership among government, the people, and private institutions to help our citizens cope with the realities of life in the 21st century.

Let me sketch out a vision, one that applies not just to older America, but to all generations and all segments of our society.

To begin, there is a clear need to motivate individuals to take more personal responsibility for their own well being. But we must also recognize that strengthening our universal institutions-Social Security, Medicare, voting, community service, and education-is more important than ever. These are the foundations to build upon.

First, we need to rethink work and retirement together. In the old model, people paid into Social Security and received a guaranteed income when they retired. Employees enrolled in a pension plan with their company, and many people had a savings account at their local bank. Preparing for retirement was fairly passive and predictable, with a role for government, business and the individual—Social Security, company pension and savings.

Today, retirement planning calls for active engagement. Defined contribution plans such as 401(k)s require employees to make their own savings and investment decisions. So, for practical purposes, corporate pensions and personal savings have become one.

People have far more personal savings options and investment opportunities. These additional choices should encourage more people to save, but they also mean that people need more help to be able to do that.

Should government guide individuals toward wise savings and investment choices? How well can it regulate investment information? What is the corporation's responsibility, which may have an interest in employees investing in company stock or in their own financial products?

Just how much choice . . . and protection should employees have? We've seen some recent horror stories in all this. And how can consumer groups and others help people navigate these difficult waters? We need to get this right, for the good of the individual and of society.

As I said, many boomers see continued earnings from work as part of their so-called retirement future, and retirement is becoming an integration of education, work, and leisure. But, for this to become real, individuals must be willing and able to learn and adapt.

Likewise, for employers to get the most out of an aging workforce, they must refine such strategies as flexible work schedules, telecommuting, training and education, phased retirement, and "bridge jobs" that offer new experiences and work-life flexibility.

Government must also support a new vision of continued earnings from work in retirement. We outlawed most forms of age discrimination in employment in 1967, but the EEOC reports that age discrimination complaints are increasing as the workforce grows older. Change is happening, but not always for the better.

Social Security is the only portion of retirement income that is guaranteed, and remains the foundation—in many cases, the only source—of retirement income, as well as providing disability and survivor benefits for all ages.

Although Social Security can pay full benefits until 2042, now is an important time to work on long-term solutions. We should think about measures that improve overall retirement savings and security, especially at a time when Americans face greater risk for all their other sources of retirement income.

We need to recognize Social Security's role in the retirement income framework and strengthen it for future generations. We must also figure out how to help people achieve greater savings in addition to Social Security. We are all aware that making Social Security solvent for the long term requires difficult choices. The longer we put it off, the tougher the choices.

We must also tackle the big issues of health, health care, and health insurance. Older America is generally healthier than previous generations, but as people advance in age, they spend more time, energy, and money on their health-caring for it and paying for it.

The American health-care system is a mess-and not just for individuals. Employers and government also struggle with its costs and complexities. In many ways, our health care is the best in the world . . . for those who can afford it. But it is fragmented, and as many have said, not really a system at all.

In order to set it right, we need to think about the role of health care in an aging society—not just health care for older people, but for a society in which people are living longer than ever before.

First, we need to make sure our kids get a healthy start in life and maintain healthy habits. My wife, Fran, and I have three young grandchildren. They're getting a healthy start in life. For them, and all children, health maintenance must be life long. And we need to continue support for medical research, certainly including government and pharmaceutical industry R & D.

We also have to deal with utilization—that is, how and how often people use health care. We can reduce over-utilization with better health education, with more preventive programs, with more focus on the effects of aging and how to counter them, and a greater role for non-physician professionals, such as nurse practitioners.

And finally, we have to accept the economic facts. Health care is expensive . . . for individuals, for government, and for business. We all have to share in its costs. But we cannot sustain current levels of cost increases. We spend more on health care than any other nation in the world. Yet, we are the only industrialized country that hasn't figured out how to make health care available to all our citizens.

Creating a better system of health care for an aging America forces us to challenge conventional wisdom. For example, think of doctors making house calls, which are considered outdated and inefficient in 21st century medicine.

But with today's technology, what if we moved at least some medical practice out of expensive offices and into the patient's home? Some practitioners are finding that it is effective, less costly, more personal, and helps keep people out of nursing homes.

The same is true for coverage of more home service, which is cheaper than nursing homes and usually more satisfactory. And we might also consider greater use of—and reasonable compensation for—consultations with physicians on the phone and by e-mail to save time and money.

These aren't total solutions, but this is the kind of thinking we need to construct a real system of quality, compassionate and cost-effective health care for our aging society.

As part of this, Medicare reform is urgently needed, including a prescription-drug benefit that is affordable, voluntary and accessible to all. This is high on our agenda and the agendas of the White House and Congress, and it should be.

Will we have the political will and courage to structurally reform our health care system before 2011 . . . or before we have a melt down, whichever comes first? There are many influential policy makers, business leaders and others ready to try. At AARP, we're ready to be part of it.

Another element of a new vision of active engagement requires that we change the way we think about older people. Contrary to popular belief, not all older people suffer from disabilities, they don't all live in nursing homes or with their adult children, most will not get Alzheimer's disease, they're not all rich and they're not all poor.

If you want to see a great picture of aging, take a look at the cover of the current issue of our *AARP Modern Maturity* magazine. A lot of the negative stereotypes will change as boomers move into their older years, because they just won't tolerate it.

And things will change because the sheer size of this demographic wave is making mid-life and older people the key consumer segment of the next decade. In coming decades, the U.S., with our steadily growing population, will remain the center of the world economy.

Age does not equal disability. About 80 percent of Americans 65 and over have no limitations to their daily activities and are capable of fully contributing to society. We offer support to the remaining 20 percent who are limited—as we should. But what do we offer to the majority who want to contribute and stay engaged?

How do we capture, as our founder Ethel Percy Andrus put it, "the accumulated experience, the knowledge, wisdom, and skills of all older adults"? How do we capitalize on the increased longevity of our population, which Theodore Roszak calls "the true wealth of nations"?

Our research tells us that older people want to volunteer even more than they already are . . . and that many of them want to work with children. So, we're developing a new partnership with Big Brothers/Big Sisters to give them that opportunity.

This is just one example. But the point is, we need new ideas and structures to get the best from all our citizens at any age. This requires an awakening . . . an understanding of American social and demographic change. We're now close enough to see what's coming, and we must create a future of active engagement to address the new realities of 2011 and beyond.

Two hundred years ago, if a farmer were asked what could be done to improve his life, he might have said, "Give me more horses."

He would not have thought of a tractor or a combine. Today, when we ask, "How do we address the needs of an aging society," the answer is not to put up more nursing homes or build a better wheel chair.

We need to think about changing the environment we live in and how we interact with it. At the MIT AgeLab, they are doing just that. They're creating homes, workplaces, clothes and lifestyle strategies for the actively aging.

In one example: they are working on a biosuit, modeled after sleek Olympic track suits that will improve circulation, control temperature, protect fragile areas like the knees and hips during falls and simulate the effects of leg and muscle groups helping people to stand and walk. As one researcher put it, "I think they'd certainly like it more than the standard aluminum walker, which is an insult to engineering."

At AARP, we intend to be part of the new vision. We have three great goals:

- To be one of the most successful organizations in America for positive social change. In other words, to make a real and lasting contribution to this great nation.
- To help our members have choices, reach their goals and dreams, and make the most of life after 50.
- And to be a world leader in global aging.

Our information services, federal and state advocacy, the purchasing power of our membership, our expanding volunteer opportunities and growing prospects for member enrichment are aimed at helping Americans of all generations to be healthy, to age with dignity and purpose and to participate actively in society.

No one can do it alone. We need a national sense of urgency. 2011 is not far off—only four election cycles away. Considering how slowly our public policy machinery grinds, it is almost tomorrow. And 2011 will be the beginning of a new era, not a one-time event.

On today's date, November 19, in 1863, President Abraham Lincoln traveled about 70 miles north of here to deliver a two-minute speech. In his Gettysburg address, Lincoln captured the essence of the war: the symbolic birth, death, and rebirth of the nation. He spoke of the principles of our democracy and rededicated efforts to "the unfinished work . . . the great task remaining before us . . . a new birth of freedom."

We, too, have a "great task before us" as we prepare for 2011. It is the creation of a society where everyone lives and ages with independence and dignity . . . where aging brings us that "new birth of freedom."

This is not a partisan idea . . . not a liberal or conservative agenda. It's not an idea just for the old or the young. It will require everyone-government, business, non-profits and individuals—to accept new responsibilities. Active, productive engagement is a vision we can all achieve and share . . . a new vision for 2011 in America.

AARP is a strong voice but to remain strong it must retain and continue to attract new members. Some critics could interpret a significant decline in its membership as a sign of diminishing influence. Over the year that followed the speech that articulated a vision, an advertising campaign was launched to emphasize the need for a powerful organization to keep the pressure on lawmakers. Its message continued to stress, "AARP—The power to make it better."

The AARP
Strategic Plan

LEADING
POSITIVE
SOCIAL
CHANGE

DELIVERING
VALUE TO
MEMBERS

AARP

AUGUST 2002

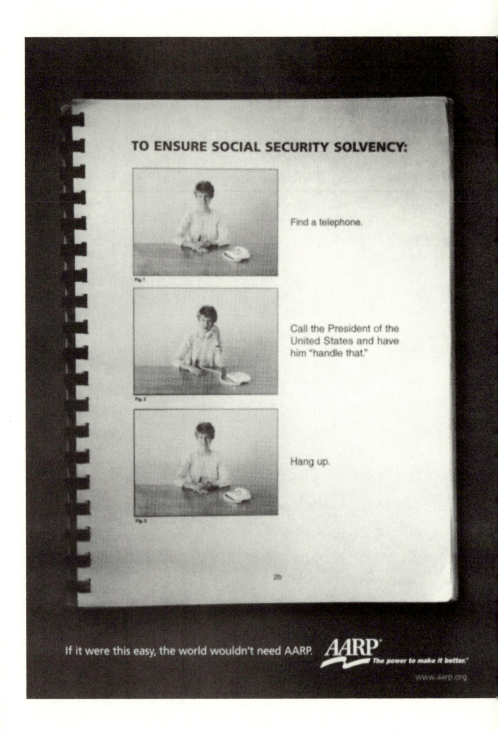

Developing an International Communications Strategy: Matha MacDonald

Matha MacDonald is a Chicago-based consulting firm specializing in helping companies execute strategies and achieve improved business through more engaged employees.

With "Reinventing Internal Communications" the firm developed a communications strategy that addressed employee communication skills and a schematic for implementing the program to maximum effectiveness.

How management communicates with employees and employees communicate with one another—individually and departmentally—is central to a successful employee relations program.

The presentation is an example of how maximizing employee communications can result in greater efficiency and cost effectiveness.

Strategic Organization: Matha MacDonald

MATHA MACDONALD

REINVENTING INTERNAL COMMUNICATIONS
TO GET BUSINESS RESULTS

- The company is launching a new advertising and marketing thrust to build customer loyalty that requires higher levels of customer service and specific employee behaviors. How do you engage employees to deliver the "defining moments" of your brand?

- Your company's oldest, unionized plant is changing manufacturing processes. Since the change began, quality and productivity have plummeted. How do you engage employees to support the change and turn around performance?

- Your company needs to reduce inventory, which requires cross-functional planning and measurement against total delivered cost and customer satisfaction. How do you rally employees to make decisions based on the company and customer instead of departmental goals?

- CEOs are now obliged to sign off on financials. How will management ensure that employees at every level of your organization are willing to bring "bad news" to the top?

More than ever, business leaders recognize how effective internal communications can affect business issues like these. As a result, greater expectations are placed on Communications functions, and many of them are delivering. Once looked upon only as a staff service function, yesterday's "spin masters" are reinventing themselves into high-performance functions that partner in decision-making and strategy execution.

To deliver the goods in this new role, Communication functions have to rethink everything they do: their very reason for being in terms of *mission*, *organization* and *staffing*.

MISSION: DEFINING YOUR CONTRIBUTION

Companies are looking to Communications functions to help manage real business challenges—market strategy, quality improvement, supply chain integration and corporate governance, to name a few. Departments that focus on such results "get a seat at the table" and receive resources to get the job done. The alternative: watch other functions do the necessary work and get the influence, resources and rewards.

That's why establishing the right department mission is vital. In setting direction, the first question a function must answer is "How do we want to contribute?" or, "Where will we put a stake in the ground?" The choices made in answering these questions will affect everything the department does. Two well-known and respected Internal Communications functions articulated their contributions as follows:

Figure 1:

Department One	Department Two
• Protects, enhances, preserves and promotes the brand (and the business) to all audiences. • Develops, implements and manages communication strategies that align management and support the direction that the business is heading. • Bridges the gap between the company's long-term vision and the current situation by developing and implementing strategies that audiences can understand. • Provides the organization customer-focused coaching and consulting. • Maintains an ear to various customers, and works with the organization to ensure it is meeting the needs of its audiences. • Promotes a shared responsibility for achieving results.	• Aligns the organization around key business goals so that all employees understand the direction the company is heading and see how they fit in. This includes engaging management and motivating employees. • Helps the organization understand the importance of communicating the same message to all audiences. • Coaches management on the principles of simple, concise, consistent communications to all audiences. • Helps identify areas of vulnerability – and provides strategic counseling to help the organization respond appropriately.

There are a number of similarities between the two approaches. Both departments provide fundamental communication services to their organizations, which are not specifically articulated here. Both indicate a role as **coach to management** and **instrument of alignment**. Both support the concept that the Communications department acts as **management's eyes and ears** to the world. Both departments also identify their role as **management's interpreter**.

While there are many similarities, there also is an important distinction. Department One has set an aggressive role as participant in **managing the company**. It clearly states that the department "protects, enhances, preserves and promotes the brand (and business) to all audiences." Its mission has a **strong connection to business results** such as improving customer satisfaction and reducing operating costs.

Department Two defines itself more as an instrument of management—a department that executes management's will after the goals are set. This department's results are communications oriented, measured in understanding and message consistency.

In defining a mission, a Communications department faces an important decision: *Long term, how aggressive do you want to be in participating in the management decision-making process? Do you want to actively participate in and influence critical business decisions; or, do you want to execute the communications around decisions after they are made?* How the department answers has implications on its results orientation, role in the company, organization, staffing and the level of risk and reward it takes on. **Figure 2** illustrates the three primary paths to which a department's mission can lead: strategic influence, strategic communications or communications execution.

Figure 2:

	"A" Strategic Influence	"B" Strategic Communications	"C" Communications Execution
Mission	Drive business results/ influence business decisions	Support decision-making/ convey knowledge, information and motivation	Service requests
Results Orientation	Financial and operating metrics	Communication metrics	Tasks, service recognition metrics
Organizational Structure	Organized around results	Organized around communication disciplines	Organized around clients and channels
Staff Requirements	Senior business people	Communication experts	Communication skills
Risks and Rewards	High	Medium	Low

These options are not mutually exclusive. In fact, Communications departments must have a leg in each camp to get the job done. Nonetheless, how leadership envisions the department's role, even if it is an aspiration, will determine its staffing decisions, training and department structure. (Conversely, if the decision is not made deliberately, events will dictate the answer *to* the department.)

Today, companies are calling on their Communications functions to act in the "A" dimension, as a strategic influence, more often, while also acting in the other two dimensions. A Communications function can operate in this dimension at various levels of the organization and position itself to influence decisions of greater import. To do that, however, the department must organize and staff itself to make operating in the various dimensions possible.

©Matha MacDonald LLC, 2003

ORGANIZATION: THE SCHEMATICS OF SUCCESS
YOUR WISH IS OUR COMMAND: COMMUNICATIONS ORGANIZED AS A SERVICE FUNCTION ("C")

Departments operating in the "C" dimension **act as service bureaus for their organizations, and are set up around clients and communications channels.** When a function is organized to execute communications, department employees focus on specific jobs. In this model, communicators manage specific channels (such as the company newsletter), and are on call to do specific jobs for executives or departments.

Departments operating only in this dimension can use it as a platform to move into more advanced areas. These responsibilities can be used to develop new relationships within the company and to grow the department's influence by providing solutions instead of simple services. For example: A sister department calls Communications for a video, and Communications offers a different solution: a face-to-face meeting tour, which will have a greater impact on the sister department's objectives.

Organizing a service Communications function typically requires an ability to apply specific communication skill sets to specific communication problems, and making those skills readily available to the rest of the organization. Individuals within the department usually work for various parts of the organization. In other words, people call and Communications serves their needs.

Communications skills are very important to departments organized to serve channels (i.e., publications editor or senior speech writer) and clients. These skills include strong writing, editing, listening, channel knowledge, presentation skills and the like. These departments measure success against service metrics that focus on the number of engagements (speeches written, publications distributed), services provided and client (executive) satisfaction. The risk level in this area is commensurate with skill levels. For example, strong writers usually deliver good writing, so if people are skilled, the risk is relatively low.

While the "C" function enables some information sharing, the scope and breadth of this dimension's reach is limited, at best. This model does not facilitate systematic top-down communications from leadership to employees, nor does it permit opportunities for employee feedback or cross-functional communications. In this dimension, Communication departments are not organized to affect significant organizational change or real business results. These departments are organized around tactical activity and are typically couched in the human resources, marketing or legal functions.

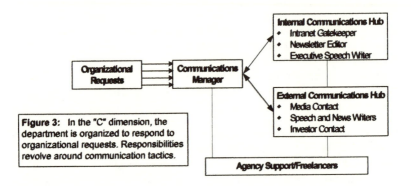

Figure 3: In the "C" dimension, the department is organized to respond to organizational requests. Responsibilities revolve around communication tactics.

CONSULT THE EXPERTS: DEPARTMENTS ORGANIZED FOR STRATEGIC COMMUNICATIONS ("B")

In the "B" dimension, **Communications acts as a focused function to do the job of communications in the organization.** This department might provide services, but the focus is on doing its job, not the job of others. If an executive needs a speech, the department will write it *if it serves the communications needs of the organization.* This concept is not so foreign when other functions are considered. For instance, the accounting department's job is to track financial information and provide it to management in an understandable and usable format. They might help another department with a budget in a pinch, but they are not going to do it as a matter of course, even though the task involves numbers.

The "B" Communications function sets broad objectives beyond "client service" or executive support. Historically, this job involved taking management's larger, strategic messages and delivering them to employees. The job takes on the additional responsibility of facilitating upward communications to management. "B" departments often are considered the "eyes and ears" for management, requiring a much more focused and strategic approach to channel management and communications infrastructure.

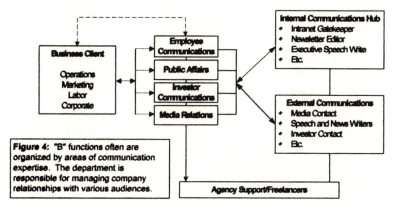

Figure 4: "B" functions often are organized by areas of communication expertise. The department is responsible for managing company relationships with various audiences.

Strategic Communications functions often are structured around communications disciplines, such as internal communications, public affairs, investor relations and others. They are staffed with experienced communications professionals, all reporting up through a hierarchy to a functional head, who may be on the executive team because leadership believes communications is important. Communications expertise and experience in this dimension are essential. These departments use communications metrics such as employee awareness and understanding of strategies, internal reputation management, intranet usage, movement in communications scores in an employee survey and other communications-centered measures.

Departments operating in the "B" dimension add credibility and depth to the Communications function. These departments take on greater risk as functional experts and, therefore, have greater autonomy and carry greater clout within the organization. This approach builds upon the "C" function, but still is not necessarily set up to give Communications a seat at the decision-making table.

GET IN ON THE ACTION: COMMUNICATIONS ORGANIZED TO BE A STRATEGIC INFLUENCE ("A")

A new dimension of communications is emerging that extends strategic communications expertise deeper into the realm of management decision-making and strategy execution. In the "A" dimension, **Communications works to help run the business, not just report on it.** Sometimes, there is confusion about how the "A" and "B" options differ. While "B" does the job of communications in the organization, the "A" Communications department distinguishes itself in three ways: Everything it does is focused on driving the actions the company needs to take vs. simply creating a set of words; it speaks the language of business, not the language of communications; and it strives to create an environment where information flows freely up, down and across the organization so that employees can make decisions that continually improve performance. A real-life situation may provide a more practical understanding of the differences between the "A" and "B" dimensions.

As part of its long-term strategy, a manufacturing company was considering building a large offshore facility to reduce its dependence on unionized domestic plants. Management believed that the facility would provide negotiating advantage. Leaders of the Communications function participated in the management meetings that developed and debated strategy, and could have served two roles in this process:

IN THE "B" DIMENSION, they would have taken management's decision to build the offshore plant and communicated it to internal and external audiences as best they could. Their primary goal in participating in the strategy meetings would have been to gain a deep understanding of the decisions to aid communications efforts.	**IN THE "A" DIMENSION,** they would have actively participated in management's decision whether to build the offshore plant using departmental knowledge of what the organization's unionized employees would or would not accept, and what a focused, successful cross-functional initiative might accomplish in winning support (or union acquiescence) for management's strategy.

In this particular example, the Communications department acted **IN THE "A" DIMENSION**. Communications participated in the decision and, based largely on their input, the company decided to build a smaller facility that was less threatening to the unions and represented employees. It also launched a multi-year, focused business effort to build greater understanding among represented employees of the business issues and strategic necessities for the long-term viability of the company.

In this case, the decision-making was at very high levels and in a critical situation. There are many decisions with various levels of risk in which Communications departments can participate to help run the business, while also building credibility to earn an invitation to help answer the critical questions surrounding decisions:

- Given employee relations, do we negotiate higher medical co-pays in the next contract?

- Will employees support a new supply chain system so we get the expected returns?

- As we design the new advertising and marketing campaign, can we be sure employees will deliver on the promise?

- Can we improve our quality and productivity in manufacturing by getting more out of our employees?

- Can we eliminate forced overtime to reduce absenteeism?

- Will a downsizing really net the savings we expect?

- Can we get the synergies we expect from this acquisition?

- Before we commit financial goals to the Street, are we confident we're getting the full performance story from our organization?

These types of issues are often considered the purview of line management, and rightfully so. In the strategic influence dimension of communications, however, the Communications function acts as a line function responsible for line results. As such, Communications is evaluated on those results, not executive inputs. The risks associated with this approach are higher, but so are the rewards.

Communicators operating in the "A" dimension require a greater degree of business experience than in the other dimensions. They combine business experience with communications expertise. This is necessary to determine what the function can accomplish from a business sense, not just a communications expertise.

In dimension "A," much of the channel infrastructure is intact. So are many of the traditional communications functions such as media relations. These functions serve as tools for the department, which generally are used by communicators providing support to other departments or organizations. The greatest difference in structure emerges as Communications staff becomes assigned to specific issues (such as those listed above).

As they relate to these kinds of issues, communicators are removed from traditional silos and responsibilities and, instead, assigned to business metrics and objectives. For example, a Communications staff member might be assigned to the team that is trying to "capture the full value of an acquisition," or to the cost reduction team that is assigned the responsibility of finding $20 million in savings, or to the function that is trying to improve manufacturing quality or to drive the business strategy into the organization. This approach forces new and aggressive thinking among the Communications staff. It also changes the relationship they have with line management, as collaborators and business partners.

PLANNING FOR RESULTS

The most effective communications start with a connection to an organization's business objectives. In the "A" dimension, the yearly Communications department objectives closely mirror what the company as a whole is attempting to achieve. If a Communications department plans against financial metrics and ties communications to business goals, communicators and management will ensure their work adds value in a measurable way. This "planning for results" approach requires the Communications team to think and plan differently. Here are some general rules of thumb to get a team on the right track:

- **Start with the company's business objectives:** Understand the company's primary business objectives: *Is the company trying to reduce variable costs? Does the company need to reduce inventory lead times? Does the company need to lower absenteeism across its manufacturing facilities? Etc.*

- **Identify the results your department can affect:** Some business objectives are outside the influence of Communications, but not many. After understanding the company's goals, dig deep into each objective and identify if the result requires employees to think about or behave differently in their jobs. If so, Communications can affect the result.

- **Attack issues and their behavioral root causes:** Business results stem from employee action, and employees behave in a certain way because of their beliefs shaped by past experiences. In order to address issues in an organization, Communications must get to the "root cause," or the experiences that drive employee behavior. Changing the employees' experiences will change their behavior.

- **Provide clarity, information and inspiration:** Communications can play a significant role in aligning employees to execute the company's strategy and achieve its objectives. In starting the effort, the Communications function must cut through the clutter to clarify what it is the company really wants employees to do. The department must meet employees' needs for information that is critical for them to do their jobs. Finally, yet most importantly, Communications must give employees a reason to care (inspire them to action).

In Dimension "A," the metrics by which Communications initiative owners are measured do not differ from the financial and operating metrics with which line management is charged. The staff certainly uses communications metrics to determine communications strategy and to ensure quality of implementation, but communications improvement does not equal success: Only bottom-line results matter.

Reinventing your Communications function into a high-performance business team requires that your staff operate in all three dimensions. When organized together, the high-performance Communications department might be structured along these lines:

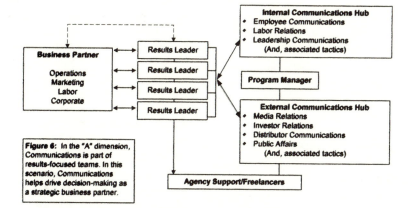

Figure 6: In the "A" dimension, Communications is part of results-focused teams. In this scenario, Communications helps drive decision-making as a strategic business partner.

STAFFING FOR SUCCESS: EIGHT SPECIAL INGREDIENTS

If today's high performance Communications teams are to contribute directly to the bottom line, they must function in ways outside the purview of traditional communications: influencing and aligning management's decision making; partnering with other functions to help the company meet its objectives; winning employee support, commitment and action for the business strategy; and driving cross-functional/cross-divisional work (to name a few examples). Placing the right people in the right positions is critical to the successful reinvention of a Communications function.

As a department organizes to meet the pressing, chameleon-like requirements of today's business environment, it must focus attention on staffing. Of course, Communication team members need to have strong verbal and written skills: those competencies are greens fees. However, as the department expands its reach and builds its capabilities to act in all three dimensions, these core competencies—a combination of emotional and rational traits—become increasingly critical to its success:

Business acumen is critical to winning the respect and trust of the organization. If communicators do not have a good understanding of how the company works, their ability to counsel top management and provide value in the decision-making process is severely limited. To function in the "A" dimension of communications, department employees must focus on the business first.

Bias for action is at the heart of strategic influence. Achieving results requires action. Communicators with a bias for action seize opportunities to make a difference in the company's performance. Without a bias for action, communicators often end up falling into the trap of "reporting."

Passion for the job and the business is a must. Period. If communicators are not energized by the business and passionate about the company's success, it will be very difficult for them to ignite those feelings in others.

Comfort around higher management and willingness to stand alone are key to the success of "A" dimension communicators. Companies' decision-makers usually are high-level managers and executives. If communicators are to provide strategic counsel and earn a seat at the decision-making table, they must have an ability to work one-on-one with leaders and feel comfortable enough to push back when leaders' ideas do not make sense.

Interpersonal savvy enables communicators to build trust and respect with the audiences they are addressing: front-line employees, business unit leaders, middle management or senior management. The ability to understand the different realities of each of these groups, how to champion their perspectives and diffuse high-tension situations is essential to success, as most business results are reached through compromise among varying viewpoints.

Common sense generally is not identified in a job description, but as the cliché goes, common sense is not as common as you'd think. It's critical for this function. Communicators who provide strategic influence must be able to look through the clutter of the workplace and their own biases in order to see the truth in a situation and the various realities affecting people. They must be able to quickly identify what will work at the earliest possible stage, separating fact from fancy, to provide management with effective counsel and influence their thinking at critical times. Life experience is more important than formal training in this regard.

Positive attitude is realistic optimism. It is not "cheerleading" or "sugar coating" information. When leaders are faced with a tough challenge, they know all too well what can go wrong. To them, finding solutions is much more valuable than issue identification. Communicators must see the opportunity in things more than the barriers, and have a bias toward taking action to make things happen. Communicators must be energized by tough challenges and committed to finding solutions.

Dealing with ambiguity is essential in today's rapidly changing business environment: as the saying goes, *those who do not change are left behind.* Dealing with ambiguity includes flexibility, ability to shift gears comfortably, risk taking and effectively coping with change. Industry and Wall Street dynamics will affect company goals and strategies. As the company changes direction, so must its communications approach.

THE ROAD TO REINVENTION:
CREATING PARTNERSHIPS FOR CHANGE

Communications functions across corporate America are working to reinvent themselves to deliver what the organization needs to be successful. To be sure, this kind of change is not a cliff event, but a gradual process that could take two to three years to accomplish—especially if a Communications function has always played exclusively in the "C" dimension.

To complete the transformation to a multidimensional approach, Communications must earn the trust of the organization, and build relationships with the people responsible for achieving key business objectives—in operations, product development or sales, for example. Start small with one department or objective, and demonstrate the possibilities. If a line manager isn't getting what he needs from employees to hit his numbers, show him how communications can help. *(See "Planning for Results" sidebar.)*

Once the organization sees that communications can affect bottom-line results, it will clear the way for more opportunities—leveraging communications to new levels.

> Bob Matha, Morgan Marzec and Macy Boehm of Matha MacDonald LLC authored this White Paper on Internal Communications. Matha MacDonald is a consulting firm that specializes in helping companies execute strategy and deliver business results through engaged employees.

Creating the Big Event: Palmer House Hilton*

The Christmas season is a magical time for many people and many reasons. It is a time of religious celebration and renewal, of children and sleigh bells, snowmen and Santa. It is the major selling season of the year.

For public relations people Christmas is a time to do something special—something really different. And the competition is intense because *everyone* is trying to a greater extent than usual to offer something special and different.

Many retailers devote more creativity and more of the year's budgets to their Christmas windows and displays than to all the remaining months of the year combined, hoping for the photograph in the newspaper, the minute of local television and the Christmas memory that lasts.

Sometimes traditions are born and live on year after year, such as the live performances of *The Nutcracker* or Dickens' *A Christmas Carol*, the animated figures in Santa's workshop, the giant tree in Rockefeller Center, the Sing-along performances of Handel's *Messiah*, or the Rockettes' Christmas Show at Radio City Music Hall.

In Chicago, the Palmer House Hilton was more than 100 years old and was still regarded as one of the world's great and elegant hotels. But in 1999, with new hotels going up all around it and holiday travelers' attention focused on the "hot" Gold Coast area a mile north of the Palmer House, would elegance be enough to draw visitors and guests?

Gary Seibert, Vice President of Hilton Midwest, knew the hotel was a special place and sent a memo to the Palmer House Director of Public Relations, Ken Price, asking, "What can we do in terms of PR to showcase our spectacular holiday lobby décor? We really should share the spirit of the season with our local community. I want us to do something that is truly out of the ordinary!"

Ken Price had spent more than a quarter of a century with the Palmer House and shared Seibert's appreciation for its sense of style,

* Information courtesy of The Palmer House Hilton

elegance and spirit. It was a grand place, but not stodgy—the site of countless high-spirited events. It was something in that tradition that was needed—something big, grand and dramatic, nut fun.

The big idea: a tuba! (Hundreds of tubas to be more precise.)

First performed at Rockefeller Center in New York in 1974, *Merry TubaChristmas—A Concert of Christmas Music*, had been the brainchild of an Indiana music professor. The large gleaming instruments, played by some 350 musicians ranging in age from 10 to 80, brought the most beautiful music of the season to one of the most beautiful sites for the concert event's Chicago debut.

The musicians assembled in the Palmer House lobby under the beautiful and stately tree, and began to play the music of Christmas as local and network TV crews recorded the event alongside the photographers and reporters from major newspapers.

The event was a huge success—as it was again in 2000, 2001 and 2002, widely covered by all local print media as well as by local and network TV.

"It has been a beloved and much anticipated holiday classic," said Ken Price. "Visually it is a stunner!"

A media advisory was issued 48 hours prior to the event and another on the day of the concert. Media was assisted by the hotel's PR staff in recording the event from several of the 18 balconies that overlooked the lobby, the tree, the Palmer House Hilton's holiday décor . . . and 350 gleaming tubas.

It was a live concert that became a holiday tradition through the years, a part of Christmastime in Chicago at the Palmer House Hilton.

News Releases

State & Monroe • Chicago, 60603
(312) 726-7500

Release Date:

For Further Information Contact: Ken Price   Public Relations Department 312/621-7326

TubaChristmas At a Glance!

➢ **350 Gleaming Tubas!**

➢ **350 Tuba Players**

➢ **Swelling the 'swellegant Palmer House Hilton Lobby!**

➢ **Performing a Concert of Christmas Music arranged solely for the Tuba**

➢ **A dedication to those who gave their lives in New York on September 11th and to the men and women who defend with their lives, the honors and freedoms of our great nation.**

➢ **Noon – Thursday, December 20, 2001**

➢ **The Palmer House Hilton Lobby**
   17 E. Monroe

Media Advisory

State & Monroe • Chicago, 60603
(312) 726-7500

Release Date: **IMMEDIATE**

For Further Information Contact: Ken Price Public Relations Department 312/621-7326

TOTALLY TOO MUCH!

350 TUBBY TUBAS TO TOOT TIMELY TERRIFIC TUNES IN THE PALMER HOUSE HILTON LOBBY!

WHO: 350 - **count 'em** - tuba players ranging from 10 to 80 years of age!

WHAT: Performing *"Merry TubaChristmas - A Concert of Christmas Music,"* orchestrated solely for the Tuba in honor of famed musician Arthur Bell.

WHERE: Around the two story Christmas Tree in the **Palmer House Hilton Lobby** at 17 East Monroe Street, Chicago, IL.

WHEN: **Noon, Thursday, December 20th.**

WHY: First performed in 1974 at New York's Rockefeller Center, TubaChristmas has become an annual - albeit unusual - Christmas concert because of its unorthodox instrumentation make-up. Created by Indiana Music Professor Harvey Phillips, known as the "Paganini of the Tuba," as a salute to the aforementioned Bell who was born on Christmas Day, 1902, and the late composer Alec Wilder, first arranger of TubaChristmas, who died on Christmas Eve, 1980.

This year, the entire program will be dedicated to those who gave their lives in New York on September 11th, and to support our uniformed service men and women who defend with their lives, the honors and freedoms of our great nation.

ADDITIONAL INFORMATION:

Filling the vast expanse of the **Palmer House Hilton Lobby** in its full Holiday regalia resplendent with its soaring Christmas tree, 350 gleaming Tubas and their players will create outstanding, incredible visuals. Superb vantage points for TV cameras and still photographers from one of the 18 balconies overlooking the lobby.

YOU ARE CORDIALLY INVITED TO COVER TUBACHRISTMAS !

###

Tuba-charged blowout

Rich Mateyko of Elk Grove Village does his part in an eardrum-bursting concert of 4/
tuba players playing Christmas music in the Palmer House Hilton on Thursday.

Repeat the sounding joy

About 400 tuba players, some with tuba's musical cousins,
sousaphone and euphonium, host their Merry TubaChristmas
concert Thursday in the Loop's Palmer House Hilton Hotel.

Press Releases and the Feature Articles They Generate: Town & Country Homes

"What was old is new again in outdoor living space."
That was the headline on the press release, but by the time head-line writers at three newspapers had their way, that would change to:

> *Tradition makes a comeback.*
> *Front porches making comeback in builder's homes*
> *Front porches make a comeback.*

The press release itself, however, enjoyed a warmer welcome, being used as the body text for stories that appeared in several different local newspapers (three of which are included here). This is exactly the result public relations people hope to achieve: Develop a good story written for a newspaper in the style of a good journalist, create a target list of newspapers that would be interested in such a story, send it out in press release form, precede it or follow-up with a phone call to the editor, see the story in print.

Some editors and reporters insist on an exclusive, but many other papers, years earlier resigned to publishing mostly wire service stories, will accept a story sent to them, fully aware other papers are receiving the same material. That's the purpose of the press release—to bring a story to the media's attention.

PRESS RELEASE FROM SCHINDLER
COMMUNICATIONS FOR TOWN & COUNTRY HOMES*

Contact: Judi Schindler
Jim Nathan
464-9660
August 20, 1999

WHAT WAS OLD IS NEW AGAIN IN OUTDOOR LIVING SPACE

Special to Copley Windfall of Homes:
Backyards are great for barbecues, sun bathing and privacy, but another outdoor living space is adding a new/old dimension to suburban living and recreating the ambiance of small town America.

Having virtually disappeared from the typical new home in the 1950s, the front porch is making a huge comeback, according to Steve Sandelin, vice president of product development for Town & Country Homes, which features full covered porches in two of its single-family communities—Centennial Crossing in Vernon Hills and Cornerstone Lakes in West Chicago.

"Unlike the backyard, the front porch is visible to passers-by— which encourages neighborly chats and builds a sense of community," says Sandelin.

Porches were displaced by modern conveniences and a changing lifestyle.

"The front porch used to serve a number of important functions for the American family," says Sandelin. "It was the next best thing to air conditioning before air conditioning became inexpensive enough to use in homes.

"Families would gather on the porch after dinner to cool off— sometimes sleeping there in bed rolls when the temperature really soared. The porch also shaded the home's first-floor front rooms, keeping them cooler as well."

* Information courtesy of Schindler Communications

Television was another factor that spelled the demise of the front porch, says Sandelin.

"Sitting outside and exchanging pleasantries with neighbors was once a major form of family entertainment," he says. "But it couldn't compete with Milton Berle and 'I Love Lucy.'"

Porches, which began to reappear in the '80s, got a major boost with the growing popularity of neo-traditional communities that recreate the look of turn-of-the-century small towns. The movement was launched in the 1980s with Florida's "Seaside" and received widespread attention in the mid-1990s when Walt Disney Company introduced "Celebration" near Orlando.

In addition to porches, the hallmarks of a neo-traditional community include traditional architecture, linear streets, back alleys, rear (or recessed) garages and an abundance of sidewalks and pocket parks—which encourage walking and visiting with neighbors along the way.

"We believe people have a natural longing to return to this small-town lifestyle," says Sandelin. "It's a reaction to the impersonal, fast paced, high-tech life we lead and the loss of the extended family with all its natural support mechanisms."

At Cornerstone Lakes and Centennial Crossing, the porches are not just decorative architectural detailing but have been designed to be functional spaces. "Homeowners are putting out furniture and flower pots. They're basically furnishing them as an additional room . . . one that just happens to be outdoors. They sit out at night and talk with their neighbors," reports Sandelin.

Most homes at the two communities feature a variety of porch elevations, ranging from covered entries to full-width front porches. To allow for furniture, porches with railings are at least 6-feet deep, while "open" porches with columns are 5-feet deep. Some elevations at Centennial Crossing feature verandas and virtual outdoor covered "living rooms" that are as large as 19 feet by 16 feet.

One major improvement in the modern porch is that it is built on a poured concrete slab rather than framed and enclosed in open lattice.

"The slab is a little more expensive, but it eliminates the maintenance associated with wood decking and lattice, as well as the problems of pets and wild animals getting under the porch—a common occurrence in vintage homes," Sandelin says.

The homes at Centennial Crossing, priced from $315,000 to $365,000, offer three, four and five-bedroom plans ranging in size from 2,402 to 3,703 square feet. All have 2, 2½ or 3 baths and include two-car garage and partial basement.

At Cornerstone Lakes, the homes are priced from $188,000 to $218,000 and range in size from 1,671 to 2,500 square feet with three or four bedrooms and 2½ baths. Partial basements and oversized two-car garages are included.

In both communities, every home offers a choice of three, four or five exterior elevations, at least one of which has a covered porch large enough for furniture.

For additional information and drive out instructions, call (847)478-8451 for Centennial Crossing and (630)587-8946 for Cornerstone Lakes.

-more-

Established in 1958, Town and Country Homes currently has 10 communities in the Chicagoland area. The Westchester-based company also has home building operations in Minneapolis and Florida.

Town & Country recently won 12 1998 Key Awards from the Greater Chicagoland Home Builders Association for architecture, interior design and community design. It was the first company to receive the National Housing Quality Award, presented by the National Association of Home Builders and *Professional Builder* magazine. Town & Country also received the National Award for Construction Excellence from Home Owner's Warranty Corp., and recently was named Residential Contractor of the Year by the Residential Construction Employers Council.

Tradition makes a comeback

B 86

The front porch is back.

Having virtually disappeared from the typical new suburban home in the 1950s, the front porch is making a big comeback, according to Steve Sandelin, vice president of product development for Town & Country Homes, which features full covered porches for all models in two of its single-family communities, Centennial Crossing in Vernon Hills and Cornerstone Lakes in West Chicago.

Porches were displaced by modern conveniences and a changing lifestyle.

"The front porch used to serve a number important functions for the American family," says Sandelin. "It was the next best thing to air conditioning before air conditioning became inexpensive enough to use in homes.

"Families would gather on the porch after dinner to cool off — sometimes sleeping there in bed rolls when the temperature really soared. The porch also shaded the home's first-floor front rooms, keeping them cooler as well."

Television was another factor that spelled the demise of the front porch, says Sandelin.

This week's feature

Porches

"Sitting outside and chatting with passers-by was once major form of family entertainment," he says. "It was a wa to keep stay in touch with your neighbors and develop a sens of community. Unfortunately, it couldn't compete with Mil ton Berle and 'I Love Lucy.' "

Porches, which began to reappear in the '80s, got a majc boost with the growing popularity of neotraditional commu nities that recreate the look of turn-of-the-century smal towns. The movement was launched in the 1980s with Flori da's "Seaside" and received widespread attention in the mid 1990s when Walt Disney Co. introduced "Celebration" nea Orlando.

In addition to porches, the hallmarks of a neo-traditiona community include traditional architecture, linear streets back alleys, rear (or recessed) garages and an abundance c sidewalks and pocket parks, which encourage walking wit neighborly chats along the way.

"We believe people have a natural longin to return to this small-town lifestyle," say Sandelin. "It's a reaction to the impersona fast paced, high-tech life we lead and the los

Continued on page 15

TOP: Front porches have returned at many developments, including Centennial Crossing at Vernon Hills.

Porches from page 3 B86

of the extended family with all its natural support mechanisms."

At Cornerstone Lakes and Centennial Crossing, the porches are not just architectural detail but have been designed to be functional spaces. "Homeowners are putting out furniture and flower pots. They're basically furnishing them as an additional room — one that just happens to be outdoors. They sit out at night and talk with their neighbors," reports Sandelin.

Most homes at the two communities feature a variety of porch elevations, ranging from covered entries to full-width front porches. To allow for furniture, porches with railings are at least 6-feet deep, while porches with columns are 5-feet deep. Some elevations at Centennial Crossing feature verandas and full covered outdoor "living rooms."

One major improvement in the modern porch is that it is built on a poured concrete slab rather than framed and enclosed in open lattice.

"The slab is a little more expensive, but it eliminates the maintenance associated with wood decking and lattice, as well as the problems of pets and wild animals getting under the porch — a common occurrence in vintage homes," Sandelin says.

The homes at Centennial Crossing, priced from $290,000 and $365,000, offer three, four and five-bedroom plans ranging in size from 2,402 to 3,703 square feet. All have 2, 2½, or 3 baths and include two-car garage and partial basement.

At Cornerstone Lakes, the homes are priced from $188,000 and $218,000 and range in size from 1,671 to 2,500 square feet with three or four bedrooms and 2½ baths. Basements and oversized two-car garages are included.

In both communities, every home offers a choice of three, four or five exterior elevations, at least one of which has a covered porch large enough for furniture.

For more information and drive out instructions, call (847) 478-8451 for Centennial Crossing and (630) 587-8946 for Cornerstone Lakes.

Front porches make comeback in urban North America

HERALD NEWS SERVICE

Photo provided

The front porch is back.

Having virtually disappeared from the typical new suburban home in the 1950s, the front porch is making a big comeback.

Steve Sandelin, vice president of product development for Town and Country Homes, said covered porches for all models are standard in two single-family communities — Centennial Crossing in Vernon Hills and Cornerstone Lakes in West Chicago.

"The front porch used to serve a number of important functions for the American family," said Sandelin. "It was the next best thing to air conditioning before air conditioning became inexpensive enough to use in homes.

Families would gather on the porch after dinner to cool off, sometimes sleeping there in bed rolls when the temperature really soared. The porch also shaded the home's first floor front rooms, keeping them cooler as well."

Television was a factor to spell the demise of the front porch, Sandelin said.

"Sitting outside and chatting with passers-by was once a major form of family entertainment," he said. "It was a way to keep in touch with your neighbors and develop a sense of community. Unfortunately, it could not compete with Milton Berle and I Love Lucy."

Porches began to reappear in the 1980s.

They got a major boost with the growing popularity of neo-traditional communities that recreate the look of turn-of-the-century small towns. The movement was launched in the 1980s with Florida's "Seaside" and received widespread attention in the mid 1990s when Walt Disney Company introduced "Celebration" near Orlando.

In addition to porches, hallmarks of neo-traditional communities included 19th century Victorian architecture, linear streets, back alleys, rear or recessed garages and an abundance of sidewalks and pocket parks to encourage walking with neighborly chats along the way.

"We believe people have a natural longing to return to this small-town lifestyle," Sandelin said.

"It is a reaction to the impersonal, fast paced, high-tech life we lead and the loss of the extended family with all its natural support mechanisms," he added.

At his company's two communities, Sandelin said porches are functional as well as architectural additions. "Home owners are putting out furniture and flower pots. They are basically furnishing them as an additional room, one that just happens to be outdoors. They sit out at night and talk with their neighbors," he said.

To allow for furniture, porches with railings are at least six-feet deep while porches with columns are five-feet deep.

One major improvement in the modern porch is that it can be built on a poured concrete slab, rather than framed and enclosed in open lattice, Sandelin said.

"The slab is a little more expensive but it eliminates the maintenance associated with wood decking and lattice as well as the problems of pets and wild animals getting under the porch, a common occurrence in vintage homes," he said.

His company's homes are priced from $188,000 to $365,000 and include 1,671 to 3,703 square feet of living space.

They include basement, two-car garages and, of course, porches.

For information, call (847) 478-8451 or (630) 587-8046.

This porch even has a white picket fence. Many new homes today include front porches as a standard feature in the exterior design.

Front porches making comeback in builder's homes

The front porch is back.

Having virtually disappeared from the typical new suburban home in the 1950s, the front porch is making a big comeback, according to Steve Sandelin, vice president of product development for Town & Country Homes, which features full covered porches for all models in two of its single-family communities: Centennial Crossing in Vernon Hills and Cornerstone Lakes in West Chicago.

Porches were previously displaced by modern conveniences and a changing lifestyle.

"The front porch used to serve a number important functions for the American family," says Sandelin. "It was the next best thing to air conditioning before air conditioning became inexpensive enough to use in homes.

"Families would gather on the porch after dinner to cool off, sometimes sleeping there in bed rolls when the temperature really soared. The porch also shaded the home's first-floor front rooms, keeping them cooler as well."

Television was another factor that spelled the demise of the front porch, says Sandelin.

them as an additional room ... one that just happens to be outdoors. They sit out at night and talk with their neighbors," said Sandelin.

Most homes at the two communities feature a variety of porch elevations, ranging from covered entries to full-width front porches. To allow for furniture, porches with railings are at least six feet deep, while porches with columns are five feet deep. Some elevations at Centennial Crossing feature verandahs and full covered outdoor "living rooms."

One major improvement in the modern porch is that it is built on a poured concrete slab rather than framed and enclosed in open lattice.

"The slab is a little more expensive, but it eliminates the maintenance associated with wood decking and lattice, as well as the problems of pets and wild animals getting under the porch — a common occurrence in vintage homes," Sandelin says.

The homes at Centennial Crossing, priced from $290,000 and $365,000, offer three, four and five-bedroom plans ranging in size from 2,402 to 3,703 square feet. All have 2, 2-1/2 or 3 baths and include two-car garage and partial basement.

Pitch Letters

*Public relations professionals know it's never "easy"
but a well-crafted pitch aimed toward well-chosen media can bring results that make it **look** easy.*

Krusinski Construction*

"THE PITCH"

From: Judi Schindler, Schindler Communications
To: Terri Colby, Chicago Tribune
Subject: "Krusinski's Mistake" (Krusinski Construction)

When Krusinski Construction Company was founded 30 years ago, doing business was fairly simple.

"We'd 'run and gun,' making decisions as we went along," says Joseph R. Krusinski, founder and president.

Some 25 years later, the company had grown to 50 employees and $50 million in revenues, but decisions were still being made on the fly.

One day Krusinski brought in a training consultant. In preparation for the training, the consultant interviewed Krusinski's executives and managers to get a sense of the company's vision.

"That's when we found out that we had 50 different people with 50 different ideas about where the company was going. While we had a shared value system, everyone was operating on his own perceptions. We needed a written plan with clear-cut objectives everyone could embrace."

To correct the situation, Krusinski hired an outside facilitator who met with the company's 12 key managers to create written mission and vision statements as well as a long-term strategic plan.

From there, employees were divided into one or more action teams charged with planning and implementation. Over the past five

---

* Information courtesy of Schindler Communications

years the teams have developed a number of initiatives that have kept Krusinski Construction Company focused on its goals. These include:

- The company's first formal, departmentalized budget.
- A client-satisfaction program.
- A marketing/ incentive program in which every employee participates.
- A cost-justification program.
- A training and development program.
- An open-book management system, which allows all employees to review revenues and expenses every quarter.

The 12 key managers continue to meet on a monthly basis. The facilitator returns once a quarter and at year-end to make sure the company is meeting its objectives.

Five years later, Krusinski says everyone is operating on the same page.

"Now, when decisions are made, it is because they further our long-range goals. Also, with everyone participating in the planning process, there is greater understanding of why decisions are made."

I believe your readers would benefit from reading about Joe Krusinski's mistake and how he corrected it. I will call in a few days to discuss this story further.

————

MY BIGGEST MISTAKE

Tribune photo by Ovie Carter

'We did not have a set of established processes'

Name: Joseph R. Krusinski
Company: Krusinski Construction Co.
Founded: 1973
Number of employees: 60

When our firm was smaller, for our first 20 years or so, the principals handled most client contact, and we worked so closely with our small group of construction superintendents and project managers that we were always aware of what they were doing.

As our business expanded and we began to add staff, our grip on the details began to slip. Nonetheless, we resisted the need to abandon our freewheeling old ways. Before long, problems began to emerge.

Our biggest mistake was that internally we did not have a set of established goals, processes and clear lines of responsibility. So with each new job we were forced to reinvent the wheel. We were constantly involved in meetings to do that, which reduced our productivity and hampered our continued ability to grow.

In operations, for example, our dealings with subcontractors and suppliers suffered from a similar problem—each of our people did things a bit differently, so the subcontractors and suppliers we dealt with didn't know what was really expected of them. Instead, we were periodically confronted with misunderstandings and delays that detracted from our efficiency.

The second problem, clearly related, was that we lacked a consistent approach to customer service. A case in point is that we lacked a standardized approach to familiarizing clients with their new buildings. They need to understand the systems, the maintenance requirements, all the warranties, etc., but at times we did a less-than-flawless job of communicating that information to a client.

Moreover, we had never developed a good way to measure client satisfaction or communicate with clients on that subject. As managers, we could see that we weren't achieving the levels of repeat business or of client referrals that our firm had previously enjoyed.

Eventually, we realized that the old ways just weren't working. To address the problem, we hired an outside facilitator, who met with the company's 12 key managers to create written mission and vision statements, as well as a long-term strategic plan.

Next, we divided our staff into action teams charged with de-

PLEASE SEE **MISTAKE,** PAGE 4

Continental Air Transport*

"THE PITCH"

May 14, 2001

Francine Knowles, Financial Dept.
Chicago Sun-Times
401 N. Wabash
Chicago, IL 60611

Dear Francine,

Continental Air Transport may be the most unusual "21st Century Company" you've covered.

The company, which operates the Airport Express van service to and from the airports, was founded in the 19th Century, reinvented itself in the 20th Century and is once again undergoing a major transformation in the 21st Century.

Continental traces its history to 1853, when the railroad was king and Chicago was its hub. At the time, each rail company had its own station, and one enterprising Chicagoan, Frank Parmelee, founded a company to provide horse-drawn transport between stations.

The first major change in operation came in 1947 when the company began serving Chicago's airports and changed its name from Parmelee Transportation to Continental Air Transport. A second was in the 1980s, when the company stopped using buses to transport passengers in favor of smaller vans, which facilitated faster, more frequent service. The Airport Express name reflects that change.

Today the company is in the process of a third major shift. Since its inception, Airport Express has relied primarily on business and convention visitors to this city. Now, with a newly expanded service calling for door-to-door pickups and returns in a growing number of Chicago neighborhoods, the company is focusing on the travel needs of local residents.

* Information courtesy of Schindler Communications

Since 1987, Continental has been headed by John C. McCarthy, president, on behalf of a group of outside investors. An interview with McCarthy would provide insights into:

- why the company is shifting its emphasis to Chicago-based passengers;
- how it plans to roll out this service;
- how the Internet and other technological innovations are improving operations.

I'll call in a few days to further discuss how one company has managed change across three centuries.

Best regards,

Judi Schindler

———

A 21ST CENTURY COMPANY

Continental Air Transport

B30

By Francine Knowles

John C. McCarthy says adapting as the L was extended to O'Hare Airport helped Continental Air Transport stay in business when major changes took place in the hotel industry.

President: John C. McCarthy, 51
2000 revenues: $15 million
Employees: 275

Georgette Klinger Salon and the Signature Room*

"THE PITCH"

Contact: Judi Schindler
            Robyn Velasquez
            (312) 464-9660
            January 16, 2001

GIVE VALENTINE AN 'AFFAIR TO REMEMBER'

For Immediate Release

Any woman who has shed a tear over the 1957 classic movie starring Cary Grant and Deborah Kerr will be thrilled with the opportunity to recreate the couple's romantic reunion.

The Georgette Klinger Salon at Water Tower Place and the Signature Room on the 95th floor of the John Hancock Center are jointly offering a $460 "Affair to Remember," Chicago style.

While the film hinges on an aborted meeting between Grant and Kerr at the Empire State Building, in the Chicago version, the couple completes its romantic encounter on the top of a tall building. Furthermore, the female half gets prepped for the occasion with the assistance of a highly trained staff.

The package features a Deluxe Full Day of Beauty for her at Georgette Klinger, a $310 value, plus a $150 gift certificate for the Signature Room, directly across the street.

Known for the world's best skin care, Georgette Klinger is including its Essential Nine-Step Facial, a body massage, manicure, pedicure, scalp treatment, blow dry, makeup lesson and spa lunch.

At the Signature Room, the couple will have a panoramic view of Chicago at night along with the opportunity to select from such classic cuisine entrees as roasted lobster tail, vanilla scented duck breast and roasted rack of lamb.

Certificates for An Affair to Remember may be purchased by calling Robyn Velasquez, Schindler Communications Inc. at 312.464.9660.

---

* Information courtesy of Schindler Communications

Museums　■　Festivals　■　Day trips　■　Outings

on the go

Not quite spring: The WinterGreen Festival continues through March 18 and includes an exhibit of art by Gerda I at the Chicago Botanic Garden, 1000 Lake Cook Road, Glencoe. $7 non-member parking fee only. 847-835-5̸

Acts of love

22 different ways to make this Valentine's Day special

There may be no day of the week that's less romantic than Wednesday. It's too far in to successfully blend into a long weekend and not late enough to justify taking off early for a romantic getaway. Unfortunately, this year, Valentine's Day falls on that weird middle day, and you'll just have to deal with it.

But not without help. Here are some suggestions from the Tribune staff to help make to the most ordinary day of the week into one of the most romantic days of the year.

Kiss, kiss, kiss

■　Re-create the magic of "An Affair to Remember" by arranging to meet your sweetie in the observation area of the John Hancock Center at sunset. Have drinks in the Signature Room (which could be very crowded; if you plan to dine, reservations are a must), then slip away for a naughty night away. Check hotels and spas for Valentine's Day specials like "Romance for All Seasons" at The Four Seasons and the "Affair to Remember" package at the Georgette Klinger Salon at Water Tower Place. Or go home and snuggle up while watching the video of that classic film.

■　Reserve a copy of the tasty, Tai-

wanese movie "Eat, Drink, Man, Woman" at your local video store and order a Taiwanese takeout feast to pick up on the way home. We favor Mei-Shung at 5511 N. Broadway (773-728-5778 or www.mei-shung.com), where the ultra-rich shrimp with walnuts (a supposed aphrodisiac, incidentally) is a major turn-on.

■　Go to the Paper Source — they have stores in Evanston and Chicago

— and get some beautiful, artisan-made paper and a heart stamp and make a valentine the way you did in 6th grade. Put it in one of their brightly colored envelopes and seal it with a heart sticker. Place the valentine on the breakfast-in-bed tray next to a carafe of freshly ground coffee, a perfect rose and an apple pancake

SEE VALENTINE'S, PAGE 60

"An Affair to Remember" fans may want to congregate at sunset at the top of the John Hancock Center.

Media Calendar: Turano Bakery

Stone Tunnel Oven Introduction*

The Turano Baking Company, one of Chicago's oldest and most recognized commercial bakeries, installed a unique piece of equipment called a stone tunnel oven. This new, state-of-the-art machine allows Turano to produce a greater volume of bread as well as many more varieties. The new machine is housed in a new addition to the Turano facility.

Turano wanted to take advantage of being the first bakery in the Midwest to have the stone tunnel oven and communicate to customers what the new oven would mean to them.

The process of making bread using this oven in the company's new facility provides a strong visual and became the backbone of a plan to attract local television coverage.

With some explanation of the process necessary, the broadcast options were limited due to the prospective time allotment on local news, but the company's agency, DiMeo & Co., identified and contacted the powerful local "super station" WGN-TV, regarding the possibility of the company and oven featured in a segment of its highly-rated weekday morning news program.

After considerable negotiation regarding scheduling, WGN booked Turano for a lengthy morning segment which allowed company executives to discuss the machine in detail and show it in operation—as well as highlight the finished product.

The resulting segment ran more than six minutes on morning television—live from the company's facility—and highlighted the oven and the plant.

The placement was part of a larger awareness campaign in which focusing on the new oven coverage allowed for specific details about Turano and benefits of its products to be communicated while, at the same time it put a "face" on the company as Giancarlo Turano served as spokesperson:

* Information courtesy of DiMeo & Company

Promotional Calendar—2003*

January / February / March

Public Relations

Stone Tunnel Introduction to industry media

- Host ribbon cutting event/photo op for media, politicians, etc.
- Demo machine for visiting media, etc.
- Trade Promotions TBD

April / May / June

Public Relations

Turano Corporate Feature

- Use existing info & create new historical background/historical corporate feature for local and national consumer business media

Stone Tunnel Products

- Once oven is operational, create in-depth look at the old-world products it creates plus look at additional new products it can make with unique recipes

July / August / September

Public Relations

Recipe Contest

- Promote national search through consumer media for unique/ themed meals, highlighting the use of Turano products

October / November / December

Public Relations

Turano Pastry

- Focus on Holiday theme as hook to increase exposure of Turano pastries

* Information courtesy of DiMeo & Company

Media Alert/Calendar: Columbus Foods Product Line Introduction

Product Line Promotion*

Columbus Foods, a 70-year-old manufacturer and seller of a wide variety of cooking oils and other related products, wanted to raise its overall brand profile and promote its product offerings to a wider audience.

While the products do not generally lend themselves to broadcast coverage, one of the early public relations goals became finding a way to present the company and its products on television. It was determined that the company's line of soap-making oils and additives would be an appropriate vehicle for TV promotion.

A soap making authority (and one of Columbus' largest customers) was contacted by the company's agency, DiMeo & Co, provided with media training, and booked to deliver an in-studio soap-making demonstration with the local ABC-TV affiliate.

Columbus Foods product containers were placed all around the studio within camera range and the spokesperson (as trained) made frequent references to Columbus's products throughout the segment.

Information about Columbus Foods' was also posted on the TV station's web site a week before—and for several weeks after—the program was broadcast.

The effort resulted in a substantial increase in telephone inquires from potential customers, as well as new consumer positioning for a company that was previously known only for its cooking oils.

2002–'03 Public Relations Planning Calendar*

Fall/Winter—*"Soap"*
Products like those manufactured by Columbus Foods are not normally suited to widespread broadcast media exposure. However, if we include Columbus' products in a larger context—as key ingredients

* Information courtesy of DiMeo & Company

MEDIA ALERT * MEDIA ALERT * MEDIA ALERT

NEW YEAR = NEW CAREER
MAKE SOAP AT HOME!

Imagine being able to easily make high-quality, "gourmet" soap right from your very own home!

With a few simple steps, and some interesting ingredients, anyone can make spa-worthy soaps – great for gift giving or staying true to that New Year's resolution by starting a home-based business.

Mike Lawson, Master Soap Maker at Columbus Foods in Chicago, has been making soap and developing soap recipes for more than 10 years.

Mike regularly teaches private and small-group soap making classes and has perfected a brief, visual demonstration that shows how, with a few simple steps, anyone can make great soap right at home.

The demonstration:
- Mike will touch on all the equipment needed (a few simple stainless steel pots, a scale, some containers to hold measured oils, a spatula, and that's about it).
- Next, Mike covers the order of mixing and melting the various elements. (Note – Mike also discusses the safety precautions necessary when making soap at home).
- The next step is adding those items that make the soap truly personal (lavender, coconut oil, rose petals, etc.).
- Mike will pour the final mixture into the desired molds to take shape.
- While the actual soap will take two weeks to "cure," Mike will have examples of the finished bars of soap – ready to use.

FOR MORE INFORMATION, OR TO SCHEDULE A SEGMENT
PLEASE CONTACT
CHRIS JANSON at 312-923-1010

* Information courtesy of DiMeo & Company

for other things—we stand a far better chance of gaining valuable television coverage.

An expert can be trained to present soap making as a gift idea on local television. Columbus Foods oils would be heavily featured (and potentially displayed). Any soap-making recipes would recommend Columbus Foods oils to maintain quality. The use of any other oil might result in an inferior product.

Local television producers have been contacted simply to gauge interest in the above concept. One producer has already expressed initial interest in pursuing the segment.

Winter/Spring—*"Anniversary/History"*
Company milestones, especially local companies, are traditionally strong media hooks. Columbus Foods executive bios and company history will be detailed in the context of their packaging design changes and 70th Anniversary celebration. A story can be written focusing on the "born and bred" Chicago company that continues to evolve and remain a leader in its industry.

Spring/Summer—*"Health"*
By including Columbus Foods' products in larger contexts, we stand a far better chance of gaining desired exposure.

Cooking ideas as well as the healthy aspects of Columbus Foods' products will be packaged and pitched to local media in the context of getting in shape for summer and eating right.

Summer/Fall—*"Industry Authority"*
Creating the perception among the media that Columbus Foods is the authority in their industry provides a solid base for current and future promotion. Develop cooking oil fact sheets and position Columbus Foods as an industry authority on all related issues. Discuss cooperative arrangements with cooking demonstrations at food markets, area chefs, restaurants, grocery stores, etc. for additional, regular exposure.

Code of Public Relations Professionalism: Cole Webber (Pembroke Resources) *

Responsible and responsive interaction with the media has always been at the core of any professional public relations and marketing communications discipline. In significant ways, our work begins with media relations, thus it can and should be said that journalists come first. If we are to serve our clients effectively, our clients necessarily understand this.

Yet in an increasingly promotional world moving at Internet speed, with more new and newly public companies than ever before, with many 'old economy' businesses in rapid transition, the overall media marketplace has grown not only more fragmented, it is overburdened and often subject to barrages of inconsequential, inappropriate and irrelevant news pitches and materials. The result: much noise, nonsense and clutter in the inboxes of many annoyed reporters and editors.

This Code of Media Relations Conduct is not meant to remedy problems only likely to intensify. Instead, it is to make sure that the media relations professionals at Cole & Weber (and Pembroke Resources) represent themselves and our clients with the utmost professionalism in any and all contacts with the media, per the following guidelines:

1. First, always understand what is pertinent, useful and interesting to the readers/listeners/viewers of a particular publication or broadcast.
2. Equally important, know a given publication/broadcast inside and out. Know what sections or segments are right for our clients' news, information, perspectives, etc.
3. Become knowledgeable about what a reporter covers before you approach her/him with a certain story. The reporter you happen to know at a given publication may not be the right one for a particular story idea. Determine who covers what.

* Information courtesy of The Murray Communications Group

4. Stay current with editorial changes. As in any business, editorial people come and go. Don't embarrass yourself, our
   clients or the agency by sending your story pitch to someone
   who doesn't work there anymore.

5. Similarly, don't 'blast' news releases to a lengthy media list
   unless you are sure every name on this list is valid and potentially in1erested in your story. Reporters complain increasingly about receiving this type of 'Spam mail.' It is no way to
   win friends and influence people.

6. Know and respect deadlines.

7. Know exactly how and when to approach a specific story—
   How (phone, mail, e-mail, fax, all of the above?)—When
   (which days, what time of day?).

8. Be concise in delivering story ideas. Reporters think in
   terms of writing a 'nut graph' (summary paragraph). So
   should we.

9. Only conduct 'call-downs' on releases that have demonstra-
   ble value to the reporter you will be calling. If you can't answer the question, "Of what potential interest/use is my news
   to this reporter's readers/listeners?," put down the phone.

10. Don't over-persist. Even if you believe your story idea is the
    right fit, you may not be able to sell it for various and
    sometimes unknown reasons. Know when to give it up,
    take it elsewhere, live to pitch another day.

11. Be consistent in delivering 'news you can use.' One good item
    deserves another, and another, etc. Work smart and hard to
    build your credibility as a reliable resource.

12. Being a 'reliable resource' for useful news and opinion leads
    to relationship building with various reporters. Be sure to in-
    volve our clients in these relationships. Ultimately, it's our
    clients' stories that matter.

13. Understand that professional media relations is a process.
    Know the process. Use it to build useful relationships for our
    clients and the agency. Become a proven part of the process.

    —G.E. Murray

Communicating in a Crisis

GERALD E. MURRAY AND
DANIEL J. REID

You might not know if, when, or what type of crisis is likely to affect your business, but you can still be prepared.

Gerald E. Murray is a vice president at the Financial Relations Board, Inc. Over the past two decades he has served as a corporate and crisis communications consultant to dozens of companies. He also serves as the editor of two newsletters, Crisis Management Reporter and Investor Relations News.

Daniel J. Reid is a senior partner and national director at the Financial Relations Board, Inc. During his 15-year career at FRB and other major public relations agencies, he has counseled clients on marketing strategy, crisis communications, investor relations, media relations and training, and public affairs.

No means of business communication is capable of converting poor performance into convincing leadership, turning bad judgment into wisdom, or portraying falsehood as truth. But in the face of industrial disasters, product problems, and management snafus, you can mitigate the shortcomings of people and processes with honest communication that confines speculation, demonstrates compassion, and puts people before short-term profit.

In a world of huge corporate structures, global markets, and complex technologies, it is difficult enough for the professional manager to render his or her organization intelligible, much less appealing. This is especially true when one considers the diverse audiences that senior executives might face at once: consumers, shareholders, media, employees, community leaders, vendors, and governments. In a crisis situation, these factors exacerbate the already uncomfortable reality of change.

Yet change is a curious phenomenon—often at once both a problem and an opportunity. It also is essential to the world of communication: without change, we don't have much to communicate or interpret. Conversely, change—especially rapid and drastic change—is not easy to communicate.

This is particularly the case with so-called "crisis communications"—communications relative to a specific but largely unanticipated product failure, personnel or union problem, or aberration of process. Very often these situations and incidents become headlines—be it a major oil spill, cowardly product tampering, divisive labor action, casualty-causing industrial accident, or embarrassing corporate scandal due to lack of management oversight.

Public relations disasters—both small and large—are increasingly common. They affect virtually all industries and have the potential to damage some of the largest and best-known names in business. Johnson & Johnson, Exxon, Pepsi-Cola, McDonald's, Union Carbide, Morton Thiokol, Budweiser, Audi, Johns Manville, Baker & McKenzie, Baring Bros., Sumitomo, Astra, Royal Dutch Shell, Perrier, and most airlines, to mention but a few marquee names, have all been subject to major crises in recent years. Most of these occurred without warning, and certainly none of them could have been anticipated precisely. But all created havoc.

What are some of the aspects of crises? Where do they come from and how do they affect their victims? What are the primary characteristics of a crisis? How do companies respond to them? And how might one prepare for the possibility of a crisis encounter?

LIVING IN A CRISIS ENVIRONMENT

Nearly everyone has heard of the now-classic cases—the tragedy at Bhopal; the Tylenol tampering cases; the Exxon *Valdez* oil spill; the *Challenger* space shuttle disaster—but these are only the most spectacular examples. On an annual basis, local, state, and federal authorities receive in excess of 2,000 threats or complaints regarding product tamperings, arson, and extortion. All which must drive businesspeople to ask in disbelief, "What's going on out there? What's gone so wrong?"

For one, it is becoming abundantly clear that we live in a "crisis environment." The explanations are numerous and complex. The world in which we conduct business offers increasingly intense competition. We know we must do things better and faster if we are to survive. There seems to be no end in sight to the trend toward mergers and acquisitions and with that, the threat of eliminated jobs. In order to develop companies that are lean and mean, we are cutting costs left and right. We do it to survive. And that struggle for survival can become a downward spiral, as we often leave in our wake weaker competitors, many of whom find themselves in "crisis" struggling against us.

Then, too, a cultural value system has emerged which declares that everyone in our society must at all times be protected. No risk is acceptable, no matter anyone's socioeconomic status in society or one's "rank" in business. If an accident occurs, blame must be assigned. And with blame comes responsibility. And with responsibility comes liability. And may Chapter 11 help you if you happen to be the defendant with the deepest pockets.

THE NAMES OF THE GAMES

Most top executives appreciate the concept of planning for a crisis. But they seldom enthusiastically authorize a plan or participate in its develop-

ment until they are forced to. For example, virtually all building standards relative to earthquakes were established after an earthquake. By then, of course, it was too late for crisis planning. Absent preparedness, responses become predictable.

First, anyone confronting a crisis attempts to stonewall while trying to decide what to do. Then corporate managers will muddle a bit; in other words, management now understands the threat to the company but is still unprepared to speak with clarity in public. Next, the company stumbles, saying or doing something misleading or callous or silly. And finally, the company seeks to repair itself. But at what cost?

Just going to work during a crisis, and for a long time afterward, can be torturous. Companies can consume their corporate resources at an unprecedented rate. They can make mistakes in terms of both strategies and people. Misjudgments are common in terms of organizational outlook. For the corporate executives who must deal with the crisis, there is potentially stress, fatigue, exhaustion, career derailment, even death.

SEEDS OF CRISIS

Not every crisis explodes in your unexpecting face. Many smolder over time, and in some ways, these are more difficult to reconcile than an accident or specific incident. So how do you know if there is a crisis building within your organization? A crisis may be imminent if three conditions exist at the same time:

- Something is going in a direction other than the direction that was planned;
- The result of this change in direction will affect people in a dramatic fashion; and
- The situation has the potential to become highly visible through the media or otherwise to important audiences.

What produces conditions that can lead to a corporate crisis? There are three basic carriers of the disease:

- Products or processes—The automobile that accelerates without help from its driver, or the chemical plant that runs away from its operators, for example.
- Corporate issues—The lawsuit that arises from a dispute you underestimated, the takeover attempt you didn't seek or expect,

the boycott from the special interest group you failed to flatter.

- People—The worker who assaults or stalks a fellow worker, the product tamperer, the embezzler, the employees forming a picket line in front of your plant.

Thus, the manifestations of a crisis are almost endless. And for as many crises as are possible, no two are ever the same. Consider the "crisis alpha-bet" confronting businesses in the 1990s, in the sidebar below.

CHARACTERISTICS OF A CRISIS

Still, most crises do share a number of characteristics, or at least several of them:

1. **Surprise.** When a crazed gunman started shooting in a fast-food restaurant in San Ysidro, California, when the space shuttle blew up, when

THE CRISIS ALPHABET

Abortion	Death—employee	Inconsistency	Product tampering
Accidents	Death—key executive	Indictments	Proxy contests
Acquisitions	Demographic changes	Insider trading,	Public testimony
Activist action	Depositions	information	Quote in context
Acts of God	Deregulation	International	Quote out of context
Adverse government	Discrimination	competition	Rationalization
action	Disparagement	International issues	Reclamation
AIDS	Divestiture	Irradiation	Rumors
Aircraft crashes	Downsizing	Irritated reporters	Sabotage
Aircraft safety	Drug and alcohol	Judicial conduct	Scandal
Airport safety	abuse	Labor problems	Security leaks
Airport security	Embezzlement	Landfill siting	Seepage
Ambush interviews	Employee injury	Lawsuit	Sexual addiction
Analyst presentations	EPA hearings	Layoffs	Sexual harassment
Annual meetings	Equipment malfunction	Leaks (news and	Shifts in values
Anonymous accusers	Exposure as a source	otherwise)	"60 Minutes"
Asbestos	Extortion	Leveraged buy-outs	Special interest group
Bad debts	Falling reputation	Liquidation	attacks
Bankruptcy	False accusations	Lying	Strikes
Bribes	Falsification	Mergers	Takeovers
Chapter 11	Federal investigations	New product	Tax shifts
Chapter 7	Fiberglass	introductions	Technology transfer
Chemical abuse	Fire	New product failures	Television interviews
Chemical dependency	Foreclosure	"Nightline"	Terrorism
Chemical spills	Government intervention	No comment	Traffic
Civil unrest	Government spending	Noise	Transplants
Competitive	cuts	Nuclear emissions	Transportation
misinformation	Grand jury investigations	Odor emissions	accidents
Contamination	Grassroots demonstra-	OSHA	"20/20"
Corporate governance	tions	Plant closing	Uncontrolled exposure
Cost overruns	Hazardous materials	Political problems,	Unethical behavior
Counter-espionage	accidents	enemies	Vandalism
Crashes	Hostage takeovers	Premature disclosure	Visual pollution
Customer misuse	Image distortion	Price fixing	Whistle blowers
Death—customer	Inaccessibility	Product recalls	Zealots

seven unrelated people in Chicago died taking a pain capsule. McDonald's, NASA, and Johnson & Johnson were thunderstruck.

2. Insufficient Information. After the shock, there is a frantic search for information. Who was the gunman? What malfunctioned with the *Challenger* tragedy? Who tampered with Tylenol? Is one person primarily responsible, or are there cohorts? If a rocket explodes, which manufacturer or regulator or inspector was negligent? If a food or drug product was poisoned, could it have been an inside job?

3. Escalating Flow of Events. After the shock, and during the first search for answers, events move on, escalate, adding new elements of surprise or uncertainty previously unknown, and raising more questions.

4. Loss of Control. There typically comes a point when the loss of control appears complete. Each hour brings new revelations of the worst kind. Nothing to do but hide.

5. Intense External Scrutiny. But hiding won't do, because there is now intense scrutiny from the outside. The media are at the door. And it's hard to lose any good reporter once he or she gets hold of a story.

6. Siege Mentality Sets In. Sometimes you get the sense that a crisis is only going to go away if you tough it out. Play ostrich. "No comment, because we don't have all the facts yet." "Don't call me, I'll call you."

7. Panic. This is a natural reaction that can either precede or follow the natural siege mentality. "What if we are asked this?" "Suppose we don't know that?" Or worse, "Suppose we do know and it ain't good?"

8. Short-term Focus. This is a serious sin. Instead of asking, "Who will take the fall," or "How can we survive the day?" the company should focus on the long-term solution. One of the classic strategies in this regard was Johnson & Johnson's tough but successful decision to sweep $100 million worth of Tylenol product off the store shelves of America in one day in order to save the brand name for the future.

ARGUMENTS AGAINST COMMUNICATING

A critical situation may last only a few days, or it can be protracted and go on for months, even

> *Focusing exclusively on responses to news media is a sure-fire way to distract you from solving the problem.*

years (consider Bhopal). What often occurs is that management comes up with apparently well-reasoned but truly self-defeating rationalizations for not communicating. In other words, management's instinctive response to a crisis is sometimes to offer little or no comment.

"We need to assemble all the facts," executives will say. "We want to avoid panic," they declare. "We have no trained spokesperson," they reason. "There are legal implications that must be explored at length with counsel," they argue. "We must protect our corporate image," they maintain. "We don't know how to 'solve' the crisis, so we might as well keep a low profile," they think. "After all, there are sensitive matters involved here, a lot of them proprietary, and the public has no need or right to know."

But for every one of these apparently sensible reasons for not communicating, there is one overriding factor that dictates that companies must communicate: the need to control its corporate destiny. If a company does not communicate in a period of crisis, it has basically surrendered control. Nature abhors a vacuum. Someone else will tell the story. The company becomes the bystander—and then can easily become the target.

If you and your company do communicate, you will begin at least to gain a level of control over the problem. Who but you should inform important decision makers? Who but your company should be addressing those affected by the critical incident? Would you rather have some government watchdog or consumer advocate be on television every night denouncing you for business irresponsibility? Who else but the company involved in the crisis should take the initiative and respond to media inquiry, or better yet, in some cases, call the media first and be out in front of the story?

Only by taking the lead and stating its case can a company in crisis control the escalation factor. Only by assuming the offensive can a company or institution get up off the floor.

KEY PRINCIPLES OF CRISIS COMMUNICATION

Failure to follow these principles is likely to lead to loss of control when the crisis hits, which will surely lead to even more disaster.

1. Define the real problem. In both the short and long term. Is it a life-threatening situation or simply a corporate embarrassment? Is it a matter of saving a billion-dollar brand or just saving face? If you have a Bhopal or Tylenol-tampering crisis on your hands, the problem is not that you are going to have to appear in Ted Koppel's interview dungeon tonight—it ultimately doesn't matter what the media does unless you let it matter. Focusing exclusively on responses to news media is a sure-fire way to distract you from solving the problem. Instead, do and say everything in a manner that focuses on whatever your operational and communications goals happen to be and resist talking about anything else. In short, don't be defensive.

In the final analysis, no matter how many thousands of questions the media might pose, they basically all boil down to these three: (1) What's the story—what happened? (2) Who is to blame? (3) How will it be corrected (or paid for)?

If you can deal with those questions—and you don't have to give away the store to do so—you can deal with the media and, thus, just about anyone else.

2. Centralize and control the flow of information coming in and going out. In other words, develop a single media reception point, and respond with a single voice. In the hours and days following the nuclear-leak incident at Three Mile Island, as many as three different press conferences were conducted simultaneously. Representatives of the utility, the Nuclear Regulatory Commission, and the designers of the power plant and its equipment were all trying to tell the story. The result: the media and public's confusion and perception that no one was in charge and that a major disaster had occurred.

Understand your physical vulnerabilities and liabilities.

3. Identify and isolate a crisis team. Put the emphasis on "team." Depend on no one individual completely. Isolate the crisis team from daily business concerns. All focus should be on the crisis—not the price of tea in China. The team should be developed with an eye toward functions—communications, operations, legal, finance, safety, depending upon the exact situation.

4. Contain the problem. Recognize the value of short-term sacrifice. Clear the shelves, if that's what it takes to preserve and protect the good name and reputation of a company or institution. And that should really be the overall communication goal: preserve and protect, as did the makers of Tylenol.

5. Resist the combative instinct. It's natural and easy to ask, "Why me, why us?" That only gets in the way. While you may be sorely tempted to strike back at what you consider unfair treatment, don't. If you lose control of yourself, you lose control of the situation.

6. Understand the media. This is almost elementary, but it is amazing how fundamentally unprepared some crisis reactions are, scrambling after-the-fact for media lists and dialing information for media numbers. Have all the basics ready all the time, including a basic press kit describing your company or institutions. You should have that type of material prepared anyway for the course of normal business. Also, understand that local media do not treat stories in the same fashion as national reporters. Radio and television people have different perspectives and needs than print reporters. Know who has a deadline and when. In that regard, daily newspapers and TV and radio differ from weekly and monthly news magazines. Have your spokespeople trained so that they know how to treat each kind of reporter or editor. Have spokesperson training include interview sessions

so your people can make, study, and refine simulated responses.

7. Remember all your constituents. Internally, you have to be concerned about all employees and their families: staff and line, operations, supervisors, unions, plant managers, divisional, regional, corporate management, and the board of directors or trustees. Externally, be sure to consider your many publics: the customer; shareholders; media; local authorities such as police, fire, medical; community leaders and residents; also distributors, suppliers, and shippers; the financial community; technical experts; and so on. In short, it's essential to identify and develop allies—sooner rather than later.

8. Plan for the worst case. Nothing is as important as this: Have a plan for disaster. Develop guidelines for crisis now. Assign responsibility for decision making and communicating with the media—now.

GUIDELINES FOR CREATING THE CRISIS MANAGEMENT PLAN

Recognizing that no two crises are the same, here are some core guidelines to follow in establishing a plan that will help see your company through its, time of crisis:

1. Start with a top-down look at your corporate philosophy and policies. What is the company's position on disclosure, concern for public safety, honesty, etc.? Is there a corporate mission or values statement? If so, how will it guide your actions and communications during a crisis?

2. Establish your resources. Know where and how to get the information you need to confront a crisis. Keep your eyes on potentially troublesome industry developments. Understand your physical vulnerabilities and liabilities.

3. Set a plan for internal communications. Define roles and responsibilities. Be sure you are able to reach your key constituents, especially employees first—don't let them read bad news about the company in the morning press without first hearing from the company.

4. Create a crisis team and update and periodically train it. In crisis, organize management for complete control. That means using your best people in their respective roles.

5. Be ready to respond quickly and thought-

If you lose control of yourself, you lose control of the situation.

fully. The first actions a company takes are often the most important.

6. Be prepared to confront crisis in an honest and direct manner. Look only at the facts. Avoid "crisis-typical" emotions—such as evasiveness and "siege mentality." The corporate voice should be clear, credible, and, most of all, compassionate.

7. Develop a plan for media response. Know your key media contacts. Establish and maintain good media relations before any crisis occurs. Have basic press material prepared and ready for distribution.

8. Have an effective public relations plan in place before a crisis strikes. Public opinion can and will play an important role during a crisis.

9. Expect the unexpected. Have a back-up spokesperson waiting in the wings. Develop a list of emergency numbers so key contacts can be made at any time or place. Also, have available a list of outside resources and experts you might need to call upon—public relations, advertising, legal, technical, governmental, etc.

10. Make your plan broad and flexible. It cannot and should not be all things to all people. Respond to the situation and not the plan.

11. Each crisis holds opportunity. Seek out ways to project credibility and gain respect. Develop a mindset that helps you turn crisis into advantage.

PREPARING FOR PROBLEMS

In the crisis-prone environment so many companies exist in today, it is not so much a matter of whether a critical situation will occur, but rather when and how hard it might descend. So it only makes sense to conduct a basic program of preparedness.

One approach to crisis communications focuses on the proactive, which is to say identifying potential crises, preempting them where and when possible, and preparing a system to minimize the public relations impact on an organization when a crisis occurs.

In general, effective crisis communications planning includes four distinct tasks:

1. Preventative liability inventory;
2. Comprehensive planning, including development of a response plan;
3. Crisis simulation training; and
4. "Pre-emptive" relations.

Virtually every kind of crisis is foreseeable and can therefore be anticipated. A "liability inventory" identifies potential trouble spots and outlines contingency plans for dealing with them before a crisis erupts.

The Liability Inventory. The key to developing a successful liability inventory is creating a candid environment in which communications and public affairs professionals and operations executives can understand the importance of identifying potential trouble spots early and cooperate to design contingency plans.

Close, confidential relationships between public relations professionals and operations managers are more the exception than the rule. Some operations managers are skeptical of public relations-types prying into their perceived vulnerabilities. Consequently, they let their worst concerns go unspoken, so the communications specialist gets an incomplete liability inventory.

One way to overcome this problem is to set up a small task force to conduct the liability inventory. The task force should include a senior operations manager, senior communications/public affairs officer, staff members from legal, marketing, and health and safety functions. Through a series of meetings and structured interviews with operations managers (and others as appropriate), the task force can compile the inventory of potential vulnerabilities.

The liabilities inventory should involve all aspects of an organization's operations—be it services and product development, sales, engineering, manufacturing, quality control, marketing, transportation, research, safety, and so on. In almost every crisis, someone in some functional area saw the warning signs long before senior management had an inkling of potential trouble.

Unless operations managers are involved in

Periodically train your crisis team.

each step of the planning process, they are less enthusiastic about the preparation and, ultimately, less reliable supporters of the communications function in a crisis situation.

The Contingency Plan. The contingency plan describes in detail what the communications response will be for each of the potential trouble spots identified in the inventory. It is the "Response Manual" or "Red Book" that every key manager and the corporate spokesperson should rely upon in a crisis.

The response manual must be comprehensive, but not necessarily encyclopedic. It should contain step-by-step instructions for the communications professional or local representative during a crisis. It designates spokespersons and lists phone numbers (office, home, car, pager), home addresses, and other vital information for each manager who might be involved in a given crisis. The book should be customized for each operation, plant, facility, etc. with names and addresses of local media, emergency officials, and community leaders. In short, the response manual should establish a logical and comprehensive system to manage crisis communications, and is also the foundation for the next step—crisis simulation.

Crisis Simulation. A response manual is of little value if it just sits in executive offices collecting dust and getting out of date. Management should be well versed in applying the lessons of the manual to actual crises.

It makes sense to organize a series of crisis simulations. These simulations should simulate potential crises as identified in the liability inventory—a product recall, plant explosion, or health threat, for example. The day-long sessions include role playing, "real-time" assessment of information that develops in a crisis, simulated interviews, press conferences, briefings for families of injured workers, etc. It should be as life-like as possible.

Experience also strongly recommends regular

follow-up to the simulation training—usually semi-annual meetings. These sessions can include updates on emerging issues, status reports on ongoing community relations efforts, and perhaps an outside speaker to relate experiences on handling recent crises. In this regard, a recent trend is training sessions shared by two or more companies with similar liabilities. This first occurred with two consumer products firms with significant vulnerabilities and crisis experience—Pepsi-Cola and Johnson & Johnson.

Another important aspect of follow-up is in-depth media training. The simulation introduces participants to the media and goes over the basics of working with the press in a crisis. The media training sessions allow for more detailed work on television and print interview techniques.

The Pre-emption Factor. No matter how well designed or professionally executed, crisis communications plans work best when the company or institution in question has "equity"—the support of customers, the faith of employees, the community's trust—steadily cultivated long before a crisis occurs. Johnson & Johnson's Tylenol experience illustrates the point. So does McDonald's experience after the San Ysidro massacre, about which one columnist wrote, "how sad for such a terrible thing to happen to such a quality company."

There are several "pre-emptive" steps that can help build bridges to the audiences that will be most directly involved in a crisis situation. Obvi-

Train your spokespeople so that they know how to treat each kind of reporter or editor.

ously, in a physical disaster, emergency organizations—police, fire, ambulance, and rescue services—will be involved. You should know who is who in these organizations before you need them, and what their expectations are for success.

Further, a long-term structured program that involves both charitable and educational support for these organizations can go a long way toward building the close working relationship that is essential in a crisis situation. Whether on local, regional, national, or international levels, being known and appreciated as a good corporate citizen pays many different kinds of dividends.

The key concept in all these situations is, of course, preparedness as a state-of-mind and a management necessity. Considering the stakes involved, placing readiness among the most important corporate priorities is not only the "right" course of action, it's the wise one. ●

1997 HANDBOOK OF BUSINESS STRATEGY

TROUBLE IS HIS BUSINESS

Crisis work has transformed the public-relations industry—and turned G. E. Murray into the man for bad

by ROBERT SHAROFF

BHOPAL, TYLENOL, SALMONELLA—THE NAMES define a certain kind of modern corporate nightmare. One can deal with quarterly earnings that aren't up to snuff, with greenmailers and bloodthirsty arbs—that's life, just the way they said it would be all those years ago at Kellogg. But what about the flawed widget, the cracked employee, the deranged decision made 30 years ago by some long-gone regime before PCBs were being blamed for everything but the common cold? What then, when all about you are losing their heads, your stock price is wavering, Pam Zekman is camped in the reception area, and millions of people—your former customers—are starting to have doubts about whether you can be trusted?

Enter that late-eighties phenomenon, the Spin Doctor. Yes, there is in-house public relations—but those guys aren't trained to do anything but write speeches and type up releases about earnings statements. What you need is a professional fire fighter, someone who's used to working under extreme pressure and is an expert at damage control.

In Chicago, that means G. E. Murray. "We tend to live in a crisis environment today," he says matter-of-factly. "There are a number of factors at work that tend to make people run faster with less control. They start taking risks they normally wouldn't take. It's called survival. And that's when the trouble begins."

Murray, 44, has been the general manager of the Chicago office of Porter Novelli, a division of the New York-based Omnicom PR Network, since 1988. He has also worked for Golin/Harris and Burson-Marsteller over the years. Wherever he's been, he's worked on the front lines. In addition to the three companies mentioned above, Murray has been involved in sorting out everything from the PCB prob-

lem in Waukegan Harbor back in the mid-seventies to the recent takeover battle at Carson Pirie Scott.

Murray is a genial papa-bear sort of guy and it's easy to see why it would be comforting to have him around as a combination father-confessor and corporate exorcist. He's optimistic—"I think you always have your day in court"—but frank and just a wee bit stern.

"You can't always be a yes man in this business," he says. "A lot of the time you have to tell people they can't say something that's misleading or conceal a certain portion of the truth. They have to consider their responsibility to the community."

The cornered CEO is an animal Murray has spent a lot of time observing. "When a crisis happens, most CEOs are gripped with panic, fear, self-doubt, and a feeling of 'Why me?' They're so close to the fire—they're losing their jobs, their companies, their reputations—that they have a hard time seeing the situation clearly," he says.

And here he cites some Union Carbide executives with their own notions about putting the best light on Bhopal. "They wanted to get into an argument about the body count. I told them, Look, when you're talking 1,600 or 2,000, it doesn't matter any more. If there's more than one or two, don't argue about it."

While crises differ in severity, all of them have what Murray says is a normal life cycle. "In general, you've got the explosion, the fireball, the dousing, the sigh of relief when it seems to be over, and then another little spark or flare-up," he says.

Understandably, Murray usually gets involved during the fireball stage—that period when the crisis is at its peak. "They generally bring me in to apply cold compresses to their foreheads," he quips.

During those early moments, three things have to be determined and then relayed to the media: what happened, who's to blame, and who's going to take care of it. The only problem, Murray says, is that the answers are often elusive, particularly when it comes to blame. "There's somebody in jail right now for the Tylenol poisonings, but the feeling among the cops is that he's not the actual guy. In the Jewel salmonella case, they dismantled that plant and never found the source of the virus."

Even when blame has been determined, Murray argues against "throwing a body out in the street" to pacify the public. "When you're in the fireball of the crisis," he says, "that sort of display just makes everything worse. Look at what happened last summer with the *Exxon Valdez.* They threw the captain to the wolves very early on in an effort to get Exxon off the hook but somehow Exxon kept getting back on the hook. It didn't solve anything."

Whenever possible, Murray says—that is, when the guy gives off the right level of warm, fuzzy concern and sympathy—the CEO should handle the major *mea culpas.* "The Jewel crisis didn't begin to go away until the chairman of the company went on TV and apologized to the community."

Unfortunately, says Murray, some companies can expect to suffer lasting damage from a crisis—no matter what the circumstances—just because of the nature of their business. "At Bhopal, the plant was 25 percent owned by the Indian government and they were mainly responsible for the screw-up but it didn't matter. Union Carbide is a chemical company and people don't look on chemical companies in a friendly way," he says. In contrast, Jewel and Johnson & Johnson—the makers of Tylenol—basically were perceived as being unfairly victimized. "Johnson & Johnson are the people who give you Band-Aids, and Jewel is your neighborhood grocery

store. They seem more human, somehow."

In some ways, Murray has to operate between a rock and a hard place—his client on the one hand and the media on the other. "When you consider the circumstances, the media coverage of crisis situations is usually at least OK. A lot of the time I have trouble getting the facts straight and I'm on the inside. It's a lot harder when you're on the outside." Still, there are times when he's ready to cry foul. "The broadcast people are the hardest to deal with because they usually don't have the time or ability to do these stories properly. Terry Savage is probably better than most of them but an in-depth story for her is five paragraphs. That doesn't begin to get to the bottom of the issue."

Murray says his own feelings about a case are rarely a problem. "The only case I've refused to work on was when Burson was doing something with Oral Roberts. I just told them that I felt queasy about television evangelists," he says. Asked if there's anyone else he'd refuse, sight unseen, he mentions the National Rifle Association.

"I work mainly for large corporations— like Sears and General Mills—and while you might not love all of them, it's not usually a case of approving or disapproving of what they do."

Murray says that crisis work—which a decade ago was just about unheard of—has transformed the public-relations industry. "The Tylenol case was probably the main event. Since then, most of the big agencies have started advertising that they know how to do crisis. I think as time goes on, it will come to represent a much bigger part of the business."

One reason so many firms have jumped on the crisis bandwagon is that it's profitable. According to Murray, clients can expect to pay a double premium in a crisis situation. "Very rarely does anyone debate the price going in," he says. "Afterward, it's a different story—so you have to get it in writing right away."

And even though crisis work is, in Murray's words, "a pain in the ass," it has bestowed on the public-relations field something it's rarely had in the past—glamour. "It's hard-hitting, headline-grabbing stuff," says Murray. "I get a phone call and immediately have to drop what I'm doing, round up my best people, and start making plans. I usually tell my staff, 'Fasten your seat belts; we're going in.'" ~

Robert Sharoff is a Chicago-area business writer.

> "There are a number of factors that tend to make people run faster with less control," says Murray. And that's when disasters happen.

The
Investor Relations Group

Craft an impactful corporate image; conduct
more effective investor communications

Close your
valuation
gap and
ease your
assets
to capital

EXPERIENCED INVESTOR
RELATIONS MANAGEMENT
CONSULTING AND SERVICE
SUPPORTING AND
POSITIONING CLIENTS
IN CAPITAL MARKETS
WORLDWIDE

Enhance
market
liquidity
and
stifle
vlatility

Sharpen your market intelligence;
serment and target investors

Strategic Management: Smock-Sterling

Profile: Industry Authorities*

Smock-Sterling Strategic Management Consultants, a fifteen-year-old Chicago-based management-consulting firm, has two main areas of business: consumer-related business clients and law firms. Smock-Sterling had a desire to increase its visibility specifically among potential law firm clients.

Within the relatively narrow niche of law firm management consulting, competition is fierce and the few large consulting firms tend to have a lock on media exposure—being quoted regularly—and generally being held up as industry authorities for important trade articles.

Smock-Sterling, with a long and distinguished client list and legitimate claim to industry authority, wanted to be considered for these same commentary opportunities, as well as other chances to display their abilities and way of thinking to law firm decision makers through the materials they read on a regular basis.

DiMeo & Company, the firm's agency, embarked on a comprehensive plan to get the name and credentials of Smock-Sterling in front of legal media as well as industry influencers (law firm associations, etc.).

Through broadcast e-mail, press releases and significant media relations, information about Smock-Sterling was sent to a highly targeted list.

The media results involved inclusion in several industry-related articles, as well as several reprints of existing Smock-Sterling white papers. The business results included an increase in potential client inquiries and general image elevation of the law firm practice segment of Smock-Sterling Strategic Management Consulting.

* Information courtesy of DiMeo & Company

Smock-Sterling*

Strategic Management Consultants

Why Are They Different?

Smock-Sterling Strategic Management Consultants offers clients a wide array of professional services to meet their particular needs. To that end, they differ significantly from their competitors in the field of law firm consulting.

One of the key differences between Smock-Sterling SMC and their competition is the use of a unique, strategic planning tool they call FOCUS. With FOCUS, Smock-Sterling SMC can clearly and succinctly get to the root of a particular firm's needs and begin the process of making change.

FOCUS enables firm management teams and/ or strategy task forces to apply leading edge strategy development principles and techniques to their own issues. The resulting strategies are aggressive, yet pragmatic. The FOCUS methodology yields a one-page strategic plan for a firm that all those participating in the process can agree upon. It is flexible and allows for very broad or narrowly focused participation.

Beyond the tangible approach of FOCUS, Smock-Sterling SMC prides itself on a number of other elements that help differentiate them from other law firm consultants.

First, Smock-Sterling SMC consultants were management consultants first, who later developed expertise in the law firm environment. So, the processes or plans advised are generally applicable to the larger corporate world, yet fine-tuned for the business of law.

Second, the breadth of Smock-Sterling SMC's regular client experience, dealing with a substantial non-law firm clientele, allows timely, cutting-edge practices and procedures to be crossed over and implemented within the law industry.

Finally, Smock-Sterling avoids law firm "dogma." Since they are not veterans of any law firm or legal practice, the consultants at

---

* Information courtesy of DiMeo & Company

SMOCK·STERLING
Strategic Management Consultants

Meet the Firm

Smock-Sterling Strategic Management Consultants is made up of highly experienced, results-oriented professionals with a wide array of backgrounds and skills. The firm's principals are John Smock and John Sterling.

John Smock is the leader of the law and professional services firm management consulting practice. He has more than thirty years of experience as a consultant with functional specialties in strategic management and planning and overall professional service firm management.

Prior to opening Smock-Sterling SMC, John Smock spent more than sixteen years with Arthur Young (ten as a partner), and three years with Cresap, McCormick & Paget. John speaks widely on a law and professional service firm management and conducted numerous retreats and management planning sessions.

John Sterling specializes in marketing and strategic management. He has more than ten years experience in strategic management, marketing and market research.

Earlier in his career, John Sterling was a Senior Consultant with Ernst & Young's Great Lakes Strategic Management and Marketing Group and worked at the University of Illinois at Chicago as a Senior Policy Analyst. He is a frequent speaker and has published several articles on topics related to strategic planning and management, as well as the application of technology in the strategy development process.

For more information on Smock-Sterling SMC or to speak with one of their principals, please call 847-615-8833 or log onto www.smocksterling.com.

Please direct interview requests to Chris Janson at 312-923-1010.

#

Smock-Sterling SMC choose to view each client separately and work to create unique, valid solutions, rather than recycle commonly held instruction.

For more information on Smock-Sterling SMC or to speak with one of their principals, please call 847-615-8833 or log onto www.smocksterling.com.

Please direct interview requests to Chris Janson at 312-923-1010.

Branding

What Works, What Doesn't*

John Sterling, *Legal Times*, 05-26-2003

As law firm strategists, we have watched the rising interest in and discussion of "branding" in law firm marketing and management circles. Though we do not provide marketing program implementation services, we are troubled by the noise and misinformation that has emerged around the term *branding* in law firm management circles.

If the misunderstandings surrounding branding were limited to consultant speeches, advertising agency bromides, and self-serving Internet listserv discussions, we would not give the topic a second thought. However, we have seen some stark examples of branding efforts leading to outright destructive and wasteful allocations of resources in law firm marketing budgets.

Undoubtedly the most egregious example of this was Brobeck, Phleger & Harrison's $10 million television image advertising campaign. Certainly, many other factors led to the demise of Brobeck—partner defections, massive overhead growth, aggressive and irrational use of debt, an excessive focus on IPOs at the expense of traditional commercial practices—but the unconscionable spending on a branding campaign spotlighted how wasteful such efforts can be.

Make no mistake, Brobeck's branding campaign followed the rules of good branding by reflecting the firm's direction and the

* Information courtesy of DiMeo & Company

"promise" it was making to the marketplace, by actively seeking to differentiate Brobeck from its competition, and by being reasonably consistent with what the firm was "known for." But it was a tremendous waste of resources precisely at the moment that the firm's core market was crashing.

Over the past four or five years, the meaning of branding has been hijacked by marketing professionals and consultants—some well-meaning and earnest, others self-interested, still others willfully ignorant—who are attempting to make a renewed case for the importance of marketing and business development in a law firm environment.

We applaud the broader intent: to underscore the value of marketing. But the definition and. application of branding have been contorted.

First, and most obviously, branding is a concept best-suited to business-to-consumer applications.

Ultimately, a brand is a combination *of* image, reputation, and performance. It is the gestalt *of* the rational, emotional, and psychological reactions that individual consumers have when they are exposed not only to the product, but also to the cues associated with the brand (e.g., the golden arches, the Nike swoosh, the Intel "chimes," and countless other examples).

Successfully marrying cues, advertising, and other communications with consumer experiences that are consistently in line with those cues and communications is extraordinarily difficult, despite the fact that manufacturing lends itself to measured, controlled processes.

Controlling a service experience is even more difficult.

No Pain, No Gain

Many attorneys continually search for silver bullets to make marketing easy and painless. As professionals, we would all like to rely purely on the excellent work we have done in the past and the brilliant articles we have published to get new business. Unfortunately, it does not usually happen that way.

Getting work from new and existing clients often requires hard work on the part *of* attorneys. Furthermore, the business development process puts lawyers in a position where a client or prospective client might say no—and no one, least of all successful professionals, enjoys rejection.

We have long believed that marketing and business development activities can be charted on a "pain/effectiveness scale." While activities should be undertaken across the full range *of* the scale—from writing thoughtful articles to meeting with prospects—it is the-'more painful activities (i.e., those with the greatest chance for rejection) that are the most effective in bringing in new legal work.

Branding initiatives tend to put an emphasis on the less painful side of the scale—brochures, advertisements, public relations, and the like. That is enormously appealing to the psyche of attorneys: It promises results without pain. And firms and attorneys are, and have been, willing to pay for pain-free results. Unfortunately, putting those less painful activities under the branding umbrella does not make them any more effective.

Yet it is not enough to commit yourself to doing painful things. The branding advocates are right when they say that marketing initiatives must be closely aligned with strategy. That means allocating market resources to the practices and activities that are expected to drive the growth of the firm (rather than to service practices). It means planning and budgeting for marketing and business development at the firm, practice group, and client service group levels.

Managing Partners Agree

Among the topics *of* discussion at a recent roundtable for managing partners was: What's *really working in marketing and business development?*

Managing partners agreed that campaigns that highlight genuine practice strengths, extraordinary individuals, and/or uniquely positive client relationships have the greatest chance of success.

Ads that highlight genuine practice strengths are considered more productive than firm image ads, but they do have a political cost ("Why wasn't my practice featured in those ads?").

Ads that break from the mainstream—whether they focus on individual attorneys, unique client relationships, or other novel insights about the firm—are also considered more valuable than general image advertising.

Branding efforts that lead to consistent design standards across all firm marketing materials (e.g., brochures, letterhead, Web site, invitations, etc.) help to ensure a high level of marketing professionalism and quality, said the managing partners at the roundtable.

They went on to identify some performance criteria for in-house marketing departments:

- Having high-energy professionals, positive thinkers, and self-starters—people who generate ideas, but do not become too attached to any single one. A firm is better served, it was agreed, by spending more on fewer, really effective marketing professionals.
- Realizing that a firm's first marketing director (and often the second or third) is likely to fail which is more a reflection on the firm's inability to understand what it needs or wants than on its marketing director.
- Recognizing that professional marketing people can only help lawyers who want and can effectively use the help. Some simply do not or cannot use marketing assistance.
- Having a "concierge for marketing"—someone to organize parties, seminars, and social events (a junior-level function)
- Understanding that experience in classical product marketing organizations is often a barrier to success for a law firm marketing director.

Investments in Clients

There was widespread enthusiasm among the managing partners for client visits (by the managing partner and/or others not handling the relationship day-to-day) and for client service planning. Clients generally appreciate the investment of time and effort in improving the relationship, and the long-term outcome is almost always growth of quality work for good clients.

Managing partners agreed that involvement in industry trade groups and industry meetings and shows are highly valuable investments *of* marketing resources and efforts. All of these activities yield positive results for practice groups that have genuine expertise and experience.

Targeting specific companies for direct marketing is an effective tactic, particularly at the practice group level. Cold calling prospective clients generally has a low success rate. Waiting for an RFP opportunity is too passive. It's not that difficult to find a path that is "two degrees of separation" (or less) from the decision-makers at most target companies. "Warm" contacts give lawyers an opportunity to present their qualifications to targets.

This approach requires taking the most "painful" steps along the continuum discussed above. And the sales cycle is long—rarely will you meet someone with an immediate need and desire to hire you. But a face-to-face meeting with the target eventually leads to good things.

Surveys of CEOs and general counsel demonstrate over and over that decision-makers like getting newsletters and other information from their professional services vendors, provided that the information is timely and useful. And these executives will attend seminars and even host in-house workshops if a firm or practice group demonstrates that it can deliver valuable content.

Effective marketing and business development is critical to the profitable growth of a law firm. But focusing time, effort, and scarce resources on a "branding" campaign—relying on image advertising at the firm level—is both ineffective and wasteful. Instead, the focus must be on a mix of activities that result in qualified attorneys getting in front of true decision-makers and referral sources.

John Sterling is a partner at Smock-Sterling Strategic Marketing Consultants, a management consulting firm based in Lake Forest, Ill. He can be reached at (847) 615-8833 or jsterling@smocksterling.com.

Sample Newsletters

UNIVERSITY VILLAGE VOICE

FALL 2003   VOLUME 5

PHASES I AND II NEAR CLOSEOUT WITH OVER 90% SOLD

More than 600 homes have been purchased at University Village, making Phases I and II of this successful development over 90 percent sold. Homes are selling quickly still, but nevertheless, interested buyers have an excellent array of available townhomes and condominiums to choose from.

Kathy Ryan, director of sales, says she is not surprised by the continual vigorous sales University Village has seen. "This exciting new community has so much to offer," Ryan explains, "with such an incredible location, a large mixture of innovative floor plans and the high-tech, energy-efficient advantages of new construction. And with such a wide range of pricing available, we are able to meet the needs of almost any buyer."

Among the residences still available are spacious townhomes featuring two and three bedrooms and floor plans ranging from 2,508 to 3,395 square feet of living space.

A fully furnished Plan C townhouse is included among those offered. Buyers can purchase this three-story, 3,395-square-foot plan completely decorated by Lynn Rosenberg Design. The three-bedroom, 3.5-bath display model features numerous windows and overlooks a recreational field across the street.

The first section of Phase II includes two mid-rise condominium buildings featuring one to three-bedroom units. Available plans range from 854 to 1,969 square feet of living area and are priced from $207,900 to $588,900. Also being offered in Phase II is a loft building that includes a mix of one-bedroom, one-bedroom plus den and two-bedroom plans, in addition to eight penthouses, ranging from 792 to 1,710 square feet. Lofts are priced from $295,900 to $312,900. Three-bedroom plans are available in the penthouse units, and prices range from $396,900 to $461,900.

For more information on University Village homes, please visit the sales center at 1440 S. Halsted, open daily from 11 a.m. to 6 p.m. and from noon to 5 p.m. on Saturday and Sunday. Call us at (312) 421-4330 or visit the web site at www.universityvil.com. ⓤ

Kathy Ryan, director of sales

UNIVERSITY VILLAGE
VOICE

WINTER 2001 VOLUME 1

MEET YOUR NEIGHBORS—RAFI & JENNIFER ARBEL

The new residents of University Village will be as diverse as the distinctive housing and quaint neighborhoods in which they will be residing!

The allure of a brand new community being developed from the ground up next to the university is what initially drew Rafi and Jennifer Arbel to the project where they have purchased one of the townhomes. The Arbels love the different elements that make up University Village. With a unique mix of residential, retail and university facilities, this family agrees they have found the perfect home.

The Arbels, who currently reside in the Fulton River District, selected a 2,800 square-foot townhome that Rafi says,

"offers the couple a lot of space at a great price in a fantastic location."

Rafi is an attorney with West Group, a legal research firm, and has recently completed some courses at Second City Improv. Jennifer is a programmer at CCH and recently designed and built an Asian-inspired ottoman for their home. Their neighbors will see the Arbels walking through University Village with Gabi, a red Doberman with floppy ears. However, Gabi will soon have a playmate in her new home as the Arbels are expecting their first child. The couple shares a love for hiking, often visiting the lakefront trails in Wisconsin and Indiana. Both are members of the East Bank Club where they enjoy working out.

Jennifer and Rafi Arbel—new University Village residents

PHASE II SALES BRISK

Following the recent official opening of Phase II, sales have soared at University Village, a $600-million mixed-use community being developed near the University of Illinois at Chicago Campus.

University Village's housing stock is complemented by the first student residence hall, which is located at 811 W. Maxwell.

"Although sales have been brisk in all of the development's housing stock, there are still a variety of homes in a wide range of prices available for homebuyers to choose from," reports Terrie Whittaker of New West Realty, exclusive sales and marketing agents for University Village. She also believes by offering this wide range of pricing, the project is able to meet the various budget needs of perspective buyers thereby

factoring into the community's success. "Prices range from the affordable to luxury, so there is something for everyone," says Larry D. Justice, Project Executive for the South Campus Development Team.

Since the 'sneak-preview' opening of Phase II in late February, the development has seen phenomenal sales success in the townhomes, mid-rise condominium residences and loft condominiums. Whittaker attributes the brisk sales of this phase, and the overall sales success of the community, to innovative floor plans, great location and the demand for the high-tech, energy-efficient advantages of new construction.

Homes available in Phase II range in price from $165,900 to $676,900. Condominiums in the Phase II mid-rise are planned with 1 to 3 bedrooms and 1 to 2½ baths with 671 to 2,399 square feet of living space. Prices range from $165,900 to $397,900. The Phase II loft building will consist of a mix of 1-bedroom, 1-bedroom plus den and 2-bedroom residences and eight penthouses, featuring 798 to 1,710 square feet of living space. Lofts are priced from $178,900 to $312,900. The Penthouse units, some of which include 3 bedrooms, are priced from $329,900 to $552,900. Townhomes are priced from $415,900 to $676,900 and feature 3 bedrooms, 2½ to 3½ baths and 2,154 to 3,000 square feet of living space. When completed the entire community will consist of 930 units.

University Village, under the guidance of the South Campus Development Team, is made possible by the joint venture of Mesirow Stein Real Estate Inc., The Harlem Irving Companies and New Frontier Companies. Mesirow Stein Real Estate Inc. is one of the Midwest's largest and best-known development firms and has been responsible for many of the area's most significant public and private sector projects. New Frontiers Companies is a group of 11 firms with expertise in new construction, real estate development and retail/residential management, while The Harlem Irving Companies brings more than 40 years experience in retail development, leasing and management to the project.

MILLENNIUM PARK UPDATE

MILLENNIUM PARK'S ICE RINK IN ACTION

The McCormick Tribune Ice Rink at Millennium Park has become a major attraction this winter. Just steps from The Heritage, the rink offers free skating lessons throughout the season.

Skaters at the Park's Ice Rink

GEHRY TO GRACE CHICAGO'S MILLENNIUM PARK

Regarded as today's premier modern architect, Frank Gehry has redefined modern architecture with renowned works of art that attract tourists from all over the world. Born in Toronto but long considered a Los Angeles native, Gehry has been honored with numerous architectural awards like the

The Gehry Bandshell in Millennium Park

National Metal of Art in 1998 and the Pritzker Architecture prize in 1989. In the last 40 years, Frank O. Gehry and Associates has designed everything from concert halls and museums to hospitals and schools, all appreciated as much for their distinguishable style of design as for addressing the cultural and contextual aspects of the sites. The firm's ambitious plan for Millennium Park's Music Pavilion and Great Lawn features 35-foot tall sheets of stainless steel in Gehry's trademark swooping style above and around the sides of the stage that blossom like a flower. The Great Lawn will feature an advanced sound system that will engulf the audience with sounds from overhead. Gehry is also designing the Walt Disney Concert Hall in Los Angeles, MIT's new computer science building in Cambridge, Mass. and the Center for Human Dignity in Jerusalem.

CONSTRUCTION UPDATE

The Heritage at Millennium Park has completed a major step in the construction process with the drilling of 122 caissons that will serve as the foundations for the building columns. Seventy-five percent of the sheeting around the perimeter of the site is complete. In April the ground retention and site excavation will be complete and pouring of the ground floor will begin. Work on the structural frame will immediately follow with the building topping off scheduled for August 2004.

Live Construction Coverage:
Tune into www.heritagecondo.com/webcam.htm for up-to-the-minute updates of The Heritage construction site. Watch day-by-day as the building rises!

Breaking down the numbers at The Heritage:
* 235,000,000 pounds of concrete (equal to 58,000 cubic yards or 6,500 truck loads of concrete)
* 6,500 tons of rebar
* 2,800,000 square feet of drywall
* 180,000 square feet of glass
* More than 3,000 doors, 8,000 light fixtures and 23,000 receptacles
* More than 544 miles of electrical wire

Progress at The Heritage at Millennium Park

HERITAGE HERALD

SPRING • 2002

TRANSFORMING GARLAND COURT

As envisioned by the development team, Garland Court, one-half block west of Michigan Avenue at Randolph Street, will be transformed into an inviting courtyard and a stately private entrance for Heritage homeowners and their guests. Plans call for extensive landscaping including trees, bushes, seasonal flowers and park benches as well as a handsome porte cochere. A prominent sculpture by noted Chicago artist Richard Hunt has been commissioned for the corner of Randolph and Garland Court.

Construction Begins at The Heritage

On site construction has begun. Following the groundbreaking in December, construction forces built pedestrian walk ways, completed demolition preparations inside the existing buildings and erected construction barricades within the Pedway area. With necessary permits in hand, exterior demolition-related activities began earlier this month. An elaborate steel frame will soon be erected along Wabash to protect building facades during demolition. Next steps include excavation and foundation work.

Grant Park
HAPPENINGS
Volume 3, October 2003

News Flashes
at
Grant Park

Grant Park Named "Best of the Twin Cities" New Developments

Grant Park was chosen as the best new real estate development in the Twin Cities by The Twin Cities Business Journal. Judges voted Grant Park as "Best Overall" new development for 2002, from among a crowded field of 48 different entries.

MPLS-ST. PAUL Admires Grant Park (from the July issue of MPLS-ST. PAUL Magazine):

Grant Park, the fastest selling large urban development in the country, is a prestigious 27-story residential condominium high rise and multi-story City Home community featuring 9- and 10- foot ceilings, a lobby with granite and marble architecture and a lovely outdoor fountain and courtyard. Residents will enjoy the experience of living in downtown Minneapolis – including spectacular city views – and a wealth of on-site amenities such as a health club and spa, indoor swimming pool, whirlpool and steam room, hospitality room with a complete kitchen, guest suites and guest parking.

Great Time to Lock in Rates

Good news for Grant Park Purchasers! After steady increases since late June 2003, mortgage rates have dipped again for the third consecutive week. Average rates for the benchmark 30-year fixed-rate mortgage are at levels that have not been seen since late in July. Because of the dip in rates, there has been an increased demand from new construction homebuyers for extended rate locks that go beyond the traditional 60-day lock. Some of our preferred lenders provide an interest rate lock up to 18 months in advance of closing! The sales staff at Grant Park can help direct you to a qualified preferred lender who offers an extended rate lock program. Please let us know if we can assist you in any way by calling us at 612-359-0555.

First Grant Park Homes Readied for Fall Occupancy
Condominium Tower Growing by One Floor Every 7 Work Days

Warm, dry summer weather produced ideal "growing conditions" for Grant Park construction.

Homeowner occupancy of Grant Park City Homes is set to begin this Fall, with the completion of the first of these handsomely designed, brick residences along the East Grant Street side of the development. Parking will be no problem for new City Home residents either, as the 510-stall Grant Park parking structure will be available for use as homeowners move-in.

Meanwhile work on the 27-story Grant Park condominium tower has surpassed the halfway mark. As of late-September, construction had reached the 16th floor of the tower, with a new floor being added every seven working days on average. The construction schedule may slow down slightly with the arrival of colder – and snowier – weather later this year. But the overall pace of construction is proceeding very well, according to David Hunt, Senior Project Manager, OPUS Northwest, L.L.C.

"Some of the architectural details of the tower are beginning to be seen, giving people a flavor for what it will ultimately look like," Hunt says. Pre-cast architectural panels are being put in place around the lower floors of the tower, he notes. Window glass is also scheduled to be put in beginning this Fall, he adds.

Design details of the common areas of the development, such as the tower lobby, are now complete as well. "Finishing work on the common areas will likely begin by the end of the year," says Hunt. For those who cannot make it to the Sales Center, there is a virtual tour of the common spaces on the Grant Park website: (www.grantparkhomes.com).

85% SOLD!

WINNER "BEST OVERALL" WINNER "BEST NEW MULTI-FAMILY RESIDENTIAL" 2002 BEST IN REAL ESTATE AWARDS MINNEAPOLIS-ST. PAUL BUSINESS JOURNAL

Development Update
- Grant Park will welcome its first new City Home occupants in late October.
- Grant Park is 85% sold out.
- Tower construction is on floor 16 and proceeding at a brisk pace, with a new floor being added every seven working days.

Vol. 47, No. 6, June 2003

YLDNews

YOUNG LAWYERS DIVISION NEWSLETTER • ILLINOIS STATE BAR ASSOCIATION

YOUNG LAWYERS DIVISION UPCOMING EVENTS

Upcoming CLE events and seminars for young lawyers.
To register, call 217/525-1760.

As a YLD member, please consider this a special invitation to join your colleagues June 19-22, 2003 at the ISBA Annual Meeting at the Abbey Resort on Lake Geneva.

The Annual Meeting is a great way to mix business and pleasure. And don't miss the Young Lawyers Division boat cruise on Lake Geneva on Friday, June 20th.

Get details and registration information at www.isba.org.

Our youngest jurors—the Internet Generation

——— By LaDonna Carlton, M.S., Vice President, Bowne DecisionQuest, Chicago

Introduction

As attorneys enter the courtroom today they are beginning to see more and more young people in the venire. They represent yet another generation of individuals with attitudes and experiences different from generations ahead of them. These individuals were born between 1978 and 2000.

What do we know about our youngest group of potential jurors? Do you want them on your jury or not? What do they expect from lawyers in the courtroom? What is important to them? Do they assert themselves and try to influence other jurors? What type of impact do they make in the jury room? What makes them respond to courtroom procedures? How do they view injured parties in a lawsuit and the large corporations being sued? And what do they need from attorneys seeking their support? These are just a few of the questions lawyers are beginning to ask about the growing numbers of our youngest members of the jury pool.

Insights into a new generation

This new generation of young adults is identified as "Generation Y," "Nexters," "Millennials," "Echo Boomers," and the "Internet Generation." One book that covers this generation is *Generations at Work* by Ron Zemke, Claire Raines and Bob Filipczak. These authors provide a wealth of information about all groups including the Gen Ys.

Generation Y jurors are experiencing a lifestyle that is quite different from any other generation before them. They have been trekking their way into adulthood during a very affluent time in American society, at least up until 2001. The majority of their life experiences have tended to be one of a secure sense of having. Unlike the Gen-Xers who grew up during a time when their parents were experiencing changes from a single-career family to a dual-

career family, or lived in a single-parent family where they had more freedom and independence, Generation Y has been raised by very involved parents. Generation Y feels loved, wanted and they fully expect to achieve their goals—even in light of the most recent economic downturn.

Case study demonstrating Generation Y's compassion

One might think that the events of September 11, 2001 would have a major impact on how Generation Y views plaintiffs and defendants in lawsuits. That perhaps this single event would tarnish their sense of caring and being cared for. This does not appear to be the case. Generation Ys have not changed their minds about whether or not lawsuits should be filed or defended. They state in a survey conducted by Bowne DecisionQuest that if a plaintiff has a legitimate lawsuit, they would have no hesitation in awarding money damages. They feel that what has happened in our country since September 11th has nothing to do with lawsuits that have merit. They listen to both sides of a case and courteously join in the group discussion.

This is illustrated in one mock trial deliberation group involving an accident that seriously injured a 14-year-old passenger. Sarah, 21, is one of the surrogate jurors. She is Caucasian, single, has no children, has some college and is employed as an administrative assistant. She expressed herself, but took a more timid approach when expressing her feelings. She tended to talk with others in the group that were close by rather than project her ideas to the entire group. She also asked questions that demonstrated her attentiveness to details of the accident scene. She took her job seriously and was more responsive to her fellow mock jurors rather than taking on a leadership role. When it came time to awarding money,

Continued on page 7

Postscript

The oil company responsible for the largest environmental disaster on record continues to post record profits. A lot of people are angry about that.

Juries award huge amounts of money to people who contract fatal diseases from smoking while major concerts and sports events promote cigarette brands on tickets, shirts and souvenir programs. A lot of people are angry about that too.

So if all that anger can result in sold-out concerts and windfall profits, how much does the public's opinion matter?

Despite these and other examples, quite a lot actually.

The July/August 2003 issue of *The Atlantic Monthly*, a magazine with an upscale, literate demographic, carried a full color ad that spread across its inside front cover and first page. The ad's headline read, "The Longest Road in the world is the road to redemption." In the subhead, the advertiser said 30 years ago the quality of its products was the best in the world; but 20 years ago, it wasn't. The ad promised to tell the story of the company's long journey back. It used the phrases "breaking out of our bureaucratic gridlock" and "learning some humbling lessons from our competitors." It concluded with the expression, "The road to redemption has no finish line. But it does have a corner. And it's fair to say we've turned it."

The advertiser was General Motors.

Not so long ago there was no way such a sentiment dared be whispered in the halls of GM, much less be articulated in a glossy ad in a magazine read by major decision-makers. General Motors was once the "world's largest automaker" and the publicly traded company with more stockholders than any other company in America.

The line, "As GM goes, so goes the nation," was accepted as truth.

In a corporate advertising campaign, General Motors was asking the public—decision-makers included—to give it another chance.

Earlier that same year (May 5, to be exact), an ad in the *Chicago Tribune* began with the words, " . . . pants on fire! Telecom trickster MCI/WorldCom is at it again, as if it thinks Illinois consumers don't know a big lie when they hear one." And that was just the headline.

In the body copy, the ad accused MCI/WorldCom of "spreading a bunch of misinformation about pending legislation" and reminding readers of the paper, "Then again, this hardly comes as a surprise, considering that MCI/WorldCom is the same company that improperly accounted for nearly $9 billion and cost Illinois $107 million in state pension funds when they declared bankruptcy. Not to mention employed four executives who pleaded guilty to the largest accounting fraud in American history."

Not to mention *indeed*.

Ouch!

Who would create such an ad and pay the thousands of dollars it cost to run it—its several grammatical errors notwithstanding? A muckraker consumer group, perhaps?

No, actually, it was MCI/WorldCom's competitor, the giant phone company SBC.

Again, not so very long ago, it would have been highly undignified, inappropriate, and risky business for a company to even hint such things about a competitor, much less create a bold-type newspaper ad that would be read by customers, investors, legislators and regulators.

Times have changed. The game has changed. The gloves are off. All's fair. Go for it. (Insert a favorite cliché here.)

The public wants to know about the love lives of CEOs, the net worth of celebrities, who's using drugs, drinking, and renovating their property. The weekend grosses for a new film and advertising rates for the Super Bowl are now more interesting to people than the film or the game.

And public relations is at the center of it in business, entertainment, fundraising, sports, science, medicine, campaigning—telling the story, creating believers, changing people's minds.

Ads are effective, but they're expensive and limiting (despite the examples noted above). There's just so much time and space to tell the story and the odds are, without a big budget and a heavy media rotation, much of the audience will miss the ads most times they're run. High cost and clutter mean ads have to be better and work harder—and most of them aren't and don't. Ads are a powerful component in the marketing mix, but marketers are looking elsewhere and public relations is finding more ways to make a dollar go farther.

PR has options—articles, events, profiles, interviews, white papers, surveys, studies, newsletters, online chat rooms, talk radio, videos, seminars, speeches, panel discussions, annual reports, advisory councils, bylined stories, countdown clocks, in-store appearances, readings, town hall meetings, video conferences, costumes, contests, gallery exhibits, support programs, cause-related programs, taste tests, awards, brochures, project partnerships, photo opportunities, editorials and op-eds, word-of-mouth recommendations and endorsements . . . opportunities around the clock.

The public wants to know about and hear from the individuals, companies and organizations it does business with—and their alternatives.

Competition is intense in every industry, profession and subject area from space exploration, healthcare and hair care to real estate, auto sales, fast food, social issues and gourmet popcorn. With so many resources and options at every budget's price point, the ability and opportunities to present a quiet message or a big idea exist as never before. Make it happen.

Bibliography

Dave Barry. "The Year of Living Warily." *Chicago Tribune Magazine*, January 5, 2003.

Greg Burns. "Stewart Merely Reflects Lower Standards." *Chicago Tribune*, June 15, 2003

Joe Cappo. *The Future of Advertising.* Chicago: McGraw-Hill, 2003.

Robert L. Dilenschneider. *Power and Influence.* New York: Prentice-Hall, 1990.

Robert L. Dilenschneider, Editor. *Public Relations Handbook.* Fourth Edition. Chicago: The Dartnell Corporation, 1996.

Dorothy I. Doty. *Publicity and Public Relations.* Hauppauge, NY: Barron's Educational Services, 1990.

David Greising. "The Rug Pulled out from beneath Our Feet" *Chicago Tribune*, June 15, 2003.

Thomas L. Harris. *Marketer's Guide to Public Relations.* New York: John Wiley & Son, 1991.

Philip Lesly, Editor. *Lesly's Handbook of Public Relations and Communications.* Fifth Edition. Chicago: McGraw-Hill/Contemporary, 1998.

Steven Levy. "Flogging a Blog." *Newsweek*, March 10, 2003.

Steve Lohr. "New Media: Ready for the Dustbin of History." *New York Times*, May 11, 2003.

Dan McGrath. "Throwing the Fans an Ethical Curve." *Chicago Tribune*, June 15, 2003.

Joe Marconi. "Cause Marketing," in *Sales and Marketing Excellence*. Executive Excellence Publishing, December 2002.

Joe Marconi. *Cause Marketing*. Chicago: Dearborn Trade Publishing, 2002.

Joe Marconi. *The Complete Guide to Publicity*. Chicago: McGraw-Hill/Contemporary, 1999.

Floyd Norris. "Business Ethics and Other Oxymorons." *New York Times Book Review*. April 20, 2003.

People Mailbag: Letters to the Editor, July 14, 2003.

Adam Sternbergh. "Publicists, Once Again in the Cross Hairs." *New York Times Book Review*. April 27, 2003.

Michael Tackett. "Reasons Are Myriad to Doubt Politicians." *Chicago Tribune*, June 15, 2003

Sue Vering. "You Really Are What You Eat." *Chicago Tribune*, June 22, 2003.

Index